LAW LIBRARIANSHIP in the AGE of AI

ALA Editions purchases fund advocacy, awareness, and accreditation programs for library professionals worldwide.

LAW LIBRARIANSHIP in the AGE of AI

EDITED BY
Ellyssa Kroski

ALA Editions
CHICAGO 2020

ELLYSSA KROSKI is the Director of Information Technology at the New York Law Institute, as well as an award-winning editor and author. She is a librarian, an adjunct faculty member at Drexel and San Jose State University, and an international conference speaker. She was named the winner of the 2017 Library Hi Tech Award from the ALA/LITA for her long-term contributions in the area of Library and Information Science technology and its application. She can be found at: http://amazon.com/author/ellyssa.

ISBNs
978-0-8389-4627-5 (paper)
978-0-8389-4634-3 (PDF)
978-0-8389-4632-9 (ePub)
978-0-8389-4633-6 (Kindle)

Library of Congress Cataloging-in-Publication Data
Names: Kroski, Ellyssa, editor.
Title: Law librarianship in the age of AI / edited by Ellyssa Kroski.
Description: Chicago : ALA Editions, 2020. | Includes bibliographical references and index. | Summary: "This book will help law librarians prepare their firms and scholars for the dramatic changes promised by AI"—Provided by publisher.
Identifiers: LCCN 2019027009 (print) | LCCN 2019027010 (ebook) | ISBN 9780838946275 (paperback) | ISBN 9780838946329 (epub) | ISBN 9780838946336 (kindle edition) | ISBN 9780838946343 (pdf)
Subjects: LCSH: Law libraries—Information technology. | Artificial intelligence—Library applications. | Law librarians—Effect of technological innovations on. | Law librarians—Effect of technological innovations on—Case studies.
Classification: LCC Z675.L2 L38374 2019 (print) | LCC Z675.L2 (ebook) | DDC 026/.34—dc23
LC record available at https://lccn.loc.gov/2019027009
LC ebook record available at https://lccn.loc.gov/2019027010

Cover design by Kimberly Thornton.

Text design in the Charis SIL and Gotham HTF typefaces.

♾ This paper meets the requirements of ANSI/NISO Z39.48-1992 (Permanence of Paper).

Printed in the United States of America

24 23 22 21 20 5 4 3 2 1

Contents

Acknowledgments

I would like to heartily thank all the knowledgeable librarians and thought leaders who generously donated their time and expertise to make this book an outstanding resource for the library and information science field.

ELLYSSA KROSKI

Preface

Artificial intelligence (AI) has erupted on the legal technology scene of late with the promise to disrupt the legal industry. Machine-learning and augmented intelligence technology (such as IBM's question-answering computer system, "Watson"), as well as legal analytics tools, search enhancements, predictive coding, and e-discovery technology can be found amidst legal headlines, tweets, and blog posts on a daily basis. But what exactly is AI, what does it really mean for the legal field, and how does it affect law libraries and law librarians in particular?

Law Librarianship in the Age of AI provides answers to these questions and serves practicing law librarians who want to be at the forefront of information technology and law libraries. This resource discusses all aspects of how cutting-edge artificial intelligence tools and applications impact the law library field and the role that law librarians can play in their implementation, evaluation, and ongoing maintenance.

The opening chapters will give you a foundation in understanding what AI is and its impact on the law library field. Subsequent chapters will provide you with the essentials about what types of artificial intelligence technologies and applications are currently available and being adopted in the legal field, as well as inspirational case studies of how law libraries and librarians in particular are actively using these technologies. You will discover potential opportunities for new roles that librarians can play in AI adoption, the importance of AI tools in the areas of legal education, research, and access to justice, as well as the ethics, benefits, drawbacks, and risks of AI tools. Finally, you will be presented with a discussion of the future direction of AI technology in law libraries and an essential list of resources, such as books, blogs, podcasts, articles, and newsletters that you will want to subscribe to and/or read going forward to keep up with ongoing developments in the area of AI in law libraries.

Written by the field's top innovators from all areas of legal librarianship and legal technology, including academic and private law firm libraries along with industry experts, this book strives to provide inspiration and guidance to librarians of all backgrounds about artificial intelligence tools as they pertain to the LIS field.

JEAN O'GRADY

Introduction

The first rule of any technology used in a business is that automation applied to an efficient operation will magnify the efficiency. The second is that automation applied to an inefficient operation will magnify the inefficiency.—*Bill Gates*

AI is everywhere but not visible anywhere.—Anonymous

The 2018 Altman Weil *Law Firms in Transition Survey* reported that only 38 percent of law firms are actively engaged in experiments to test innovative ideas or methods. This indicates that the vast majority of law firms have a vacuum in innovation leadership waiting to be filled. While all innovation does not require AI, algorithms and analytics will play an important role in the transformation of the business and practice of law over the coming decades. Hopefully, this book will inspire reluctant librarians to grab a seat at the innovation table or even set out the innovation agenda at their organizations.

Over the past 10 years, many research products have morphed into workflow products. Algorithms are so ubiquitous they are often invisible. Startups such as CARA, Ravel (now Context), and Fastcase have used data associated with primary law to create new types of visualizations, deeper insights, and custom reporting.

All of the large legal information vendors, including Thomson Reuters LexisNexis®, Bloomberg Law, and Wolters Kluwer, have developed

JEAN O'GRADY, JD, MLS, is the senior director of research and knowledge at DLA Piper; and the author of the blog *Dewey B Strategic.*

or acquired tools using algorithms and analytics to streamline workflow and deliver custom insights. Librarians hold a unique position in their law firms in vetting the glut of sometimes fantastic claims of vendors offering "robot lawyer" solutions. Just because there is an element of AI in a product doesn't mean it is wise to assume that the product will deliver efficiency or a return on investment. It might give the firm a great press release—but that is not enough. Today's market requires law firms to be skeptical and invest their innovation dollars judiciously. Law librarians are well positioned to be skeptical advisors when their firm is assessing AI products.

Law librarians are faced with a dazzling array of new legal research tools and enhanced features in mature products. Legal research tools now include drafting tools, redlining tools, "what's market" reports, and customizable analytics insights.

Fastcase has developed a sandbox and a toolbox specifically designed to enable consumers to develop their own tools and insights. Lexis and Westlaw offer natural language "answers" to a subset of research queries. Lexis includes a predictive legislation tool that forecasts the likelihood that individual bills will be acted. Intelligize, Bloomberg Law, and Wolters Kluwer tools extract market data from deal terms in SEC filings. Context (formerly Ravel) provides insights into a judge's precedential history of rulings on specific issues. Lawyers can drop and drag a brief into CARA to get a report on any missing precedent. Lex Machina, Bloomberg, and Westlaw now offer a host of analytical insights for assessing litigation strategy and likely outcomes. News curation platforms have become commonplace. Predictive business tools, such as the Manzama Insights dashboard, are already in the legal market.

Who is best positioned in a law firm to put each of the options into market context and test the quality and need for each innovation? Who can best envision how commercial data can be aligned with internal data to generate custom insights that can "move the competitive needle?" None of these assessments can be optimal without consideration by the firm's content and market experts: law librarians.

In an increasingly competitive marketplace, law firms will have to select the right portfolio of tools in order to optimize the firm's efficiency and competitiveness.

It is not enough to purchase and deploy a technology. The technology must be used. Librarians are uniquely qualified to help spearhead innovation into practice. Law librarians have been tasked with driving lawyers' technology adoption since the early 1980s—long before PCs, the World Wide Web, and email became ubiquitous tools. Not only are they skilled at driving adoption, but more importantly, they understand where new technology solutions fit in lawyers' workflow. Lawyers will not adopt products that: 1) they have to "hunt down," 2) require burdensome installations or complicated protocols, or 3) are not embedded into their workflow.

In *The Future of the Professions,* Richard and Daniel Susskind predict that by 2025 lawyers will face re-branding as legal process analysts, legal project managers, and legal knowledge engineers. These same job titles could easily be opportunities for law librarians as well.

Librarians who are willing to utilize their existing skill set, which includes analyzing information quality issues, assessing user experience optimization, developing taxonomies, and defining user needs, will find unlimited opportunities to enhance all areas of the business and practice of law.

While I still love books and large research libraries, I embrace the transition of legal research from print to digital. Print libraries consume enormous budgets, occupy expensive real estate, and require low-value clerical work to be maintained. Worst of all, they are an analog, one-book-to-one-lawyer solution. Digital libraries, on the other hand, offer 24/7, "one-to-many" access for a mobile workforce. Most importantly, in a digital library, the budget and staff can be directed to delivering higher value solutions, including analytics, AI, custom portals, bots, widgets, and customizable dashboards. Digitization has enabled law library directors to focus on delivery problems with higher value information. Instead of delivering a book, they can now deliver a custom insight. Librarians who have chosen to make the transition have already climbed the value ladder.

The future is all about asking the right questions: What problems are we solving? How good is the data? "The reference interview" is a key skill set of the future.

Law Librarianship in the Age of AI assembled a cast of thought leaders from across the law library and technology spectrum. Their ideas should inspire and guide law librarians at all stages of their careers. This book also serves as a tool for executive directors and law school deans to understand the critical role that law librarians can and should play in driving innovation and insights into their institutions.

CASANDRA M. LASKOWSKI

1

AI Defined

Core Concepts Necessary for the Savvy Law Librarian

AI Fundamentals

Artificial intelligence (AI) systems can identify speech, recognize faces, transcribe language, and react to stimuli. With all that AI systems can do, it is difficult to pinpoint at all times what we mean by "AI." This effort becomes more muddled if we try to craft a definition that unifies the variable ways AI is used in legal-tech marketing, research, and science fiction. This chapter does not have such a lofty goal.

Law librarians might need additional knowledge to ask the right questions but already have the skills necessary to critically examine these technologies. This chapter will provide a general definition to use in evaluating legal technologies and a foundational overview of AI technologies to build on as needed or desired. It will provide an abridged history of AI, define commonly used terms, and provide a brief overview of common ethical issues in explaining the sources of these issues.

CASANDRA M. LASKOWSKI, JD, is a reference librarian and lecturing fellow at Duke Law.

A Brief History of AI Research

The origin of the term artificial intelligence is thought to have originated with a Dartmouth research project. The project held that "the artificial intelligence problem is taken to be that of making a machine behave in ways that would be called intelligent if a human were so behaving."[1] They believed every feature of human intelligence could be simulated by a machine. AI research looks to develop computer systems that mirror human intelligence, but it is not limited only to that subset of the "biologically observable."[2]

In 1956, the Dartmouth Research Project participants believed that if a group of researchers worked on the project together for a summer, significant progress in the field would be made in the field of AI. While a foundation for future research was set that summer, they overestimated what they could accomplish. Computers were not yet advanced enough to handle the necessary complex calculations, nor did they have the large datasets needed to train AI computer systems. They underestimated the time it would take to develop machine intelligence. While research started in this area more than 60 years ago, the power of computers today combined with the availability of massive sets of data (termed "big data") have led to some calling this era we live in the "Age of AI."[3]

A Definition for the Legal Tech Market

The field of AI research is in many ways aspirational, and the definition of AI has changed as the work has evolved. What once seemed impressive is now mundane. This is known as the AI effect.[4] The often-misquoted Tesler's Theorem echoes that perception: "Intelligence is whatever machines haven't done yet."[5] However, defining AI in this way creates an ever-moving target, which does not align with how it is used in practice. Defining AI depends, to some degree, on the context in which one tries to define it.

Law librarians in this age require a base level of knowledge to see through the marketing haze and navigate through the evolving legal technology landscape. Our definition of AI must be relevant to this context. To be an informed consumer of AI technology, we need a foundational definition that allows us to engage with the myriad technologies we see each day, while empowering us to be critical of how that term is used.

A legal contract review software claims to use AI that "understands legal language and its business implications regardless of form or phrasing, and compares them to your company's policies."[6] Some light digging will uncover that the program uses machine learning to review the contracts. Compare this with other systems that tout being AI powered, but mainly rely on decision trees for process automation. Acknowledging that the term AI is used to describe vastly different technologies highlights the need for specificity and encourages users to inquire more deeply about methods and structure.

In line with the Dartmouth Research Project, this chapter defines an *artificial intelligence system* as a machine behaving in ways thought to be intelligent if a human were so behaving. Intuitively it seems too broad, but that is why it serves our purpose so well. It is the definition that most reflects the ways legal technology users will encounter the term. It covers following a logical train to a conclusion (decision trees), evaluating complex data to identify patterns (machine learning), and producing unique content (generative adversarial networks). It takes some of the shine off of the term "AI" as a marketing filler and hopefully prevents some of the intimidation that surrounds the term.

Structures of Artificial Intelligence

Much of what we envision when we initially hear the term "artificial intelligence" comes from science fiction stories about AI systems, whether housed in a robot or a server: from the Machines in Isaac Asimov's *The Evitable Conflict* to the Cylons in *Battlestar Galactica* to Data in *Star Trek: The Next Generation*. A system that reasons and reacts to their environment as a human would is an *artificial general intelligence* or *strong artificial intelligence*. However, current AI applications have only narrow artificial intelligence.

Narrow AI or *weak AI* is focused on one particular problem. For example, AlphaGo (the system that beat the world master at the game "Go") would not be able to accurately perform a contract review.[7] That does not make these technologies any less impressive. A legal contract review software was pit against humans and reviewed the contracts more quickly and with a lower error rate than its human competitors.[8] Yet, how much we want to trust software will require us to review the process, to the best of our ability, and see how it aligns with our goals.

What ever the AI, they can all be boiled down to three components: input, system, and output (figure 1.1). Each of these labels can be more complex than the simplified image on this page indicates, but understanding this generalization is essential to understanding how problems might be rooted in any one of these stages. It is also important to understand the role humans play in the AI's development.

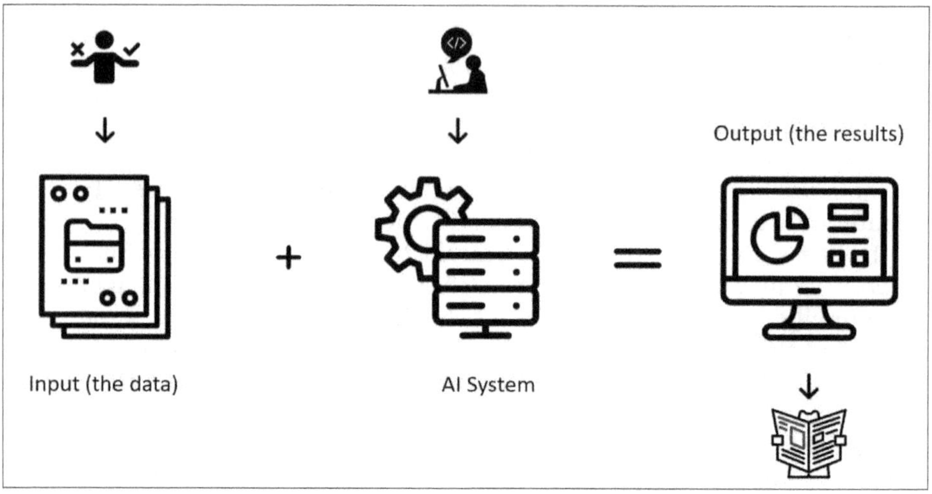

FIGURE 1.1
Three components of AI

AI Components

Input

Input consists of the information entered into a system. All input is created or curated by humans and carry with it the bias and intentions of the human doing the inputting. Bias can be introduced in the choice of dataset, how that set is partitioned into training and testing data, and how it is labeled, to name a few examples. [9] A recent study showed that several predictive policing systems are being trained on dirty data, that is, data embedded with "inaccuracies, skews, and forms of systemic bias."[10]

Input is not restricted to the initial training process; user input can also be problematic. Microsoft's Twitter chatbot, "Tay," had been trained to mimic conversational speech but was designed to continue learning and adapting its code through "conversations" with other users on Twitter.[11] Tay began tweeting racist content in less than 24 hours, because a malicious group of Twitter users conspired to "teach" the chatbot racist sentiments and inflammatory political commentary.

Output

Output refers to the computer-generated information that results from the system interpreting input according to its programming. When searching an integrated library system (ILS) by title, the title entered is your input, and the list of bib records would be your output. Not all output is so mundane. In fact, most AI headlines focus on the problematic output of AI systems. In its high-profile article "Machine Bias," ProPublica discovered that COMPAS, a risk-assessment software, provided racially biased scores. While the algorithm did not consider race directly, it likely identified correlative attributes from the training set that proxy for race as a factor in its decisions. The output made the news, but the issue is rooted in a combination of data curation and system construction.

AI Systems

AI Systems analyze input according to its algorithm and supply outputs based on that analysis.[12] Systems, too, are human generated, and humans can introduce bias at several stages in the system design process. For this reason, a well-informed consumer should attempt to learn about the data used and any information about the process that the developer is willing to share.

Before you write the code, you need to determine your goals. What do you want the system to look for? Karen Hao explains that in determining creditworthiness, if we set the goal as maximizing profits might lead to a predatory behavior, then "the algorithm [might discover] that giving out subprime loans was an effective way to maximize profit."[13]

All AI systems are computers running programs. The differences are in the configurations of these computers and the programs that are being run. Grouping AI is an exercise in priorities. Are they grouped by the sort of information they process (e.g., visual interpretation), the outputs they create (e.g., process automation), or the methods by which they arrive at their results? This chapter will take the latter approach. AI generally falls into one of two camps: rules-based systems or data-driven systems.

Rules vs Data Driven AI Systems

Rules-Based Systems

In *rules-based systems,* programmers write code instructing the computer exactly what to do when it encounters a piece of data or an error in process. This is evident when engaging with simple chatbots. When you ask particular questions, you received a scripted response, but when the program cannot quite understand what it is you are asking it, they ask for more information. These systems never learn from these experiences and all changes require updates to their code.

Rules-based systems include basic macros, decision trees, and other forms of automation. *Macros* make repetitive tasks easier by linking a string of actions together under simpler actions or code. In Microsoft Word, you can record macros of common tasks and tie them to shortcut keys. So updating cross-references can be done in one keystroke, instead of the two-step process it currently requires.[14] Macros can simplify much more complex processes than this.

A *decision tree* is a hierarchical series of questions that lead to a conclusion based on the information provided. The aforementioned chatbot would be powered by a decision tree, though there are increasing efforts to build more powerful chatbots through machine learning. You can build your own simple chatbot for your library's Facebook page to get a sense of the work it takes to build a useful decision tree.

Rules-based systems are tedious to create, as the developer has to consider every possible iteration of input in order to create a product that avoids frustrating its user. Because of this limitation, the world of acceptable input might be more limited than those that actually exist in the world. Consider body scan devices at airports. They were developed with only two options for the TSA agent to select before someone entered a machine—male or female. When transgendered individuals are scanned at checkpoints, the system flags their body as anomalous, since it did not conform to the binary options programmed into it.[15] This is problematic for obvious reasons.

Data-Driven Systems

To facilitate the creation of more powerful and complex systems, programmers are turning to data-driven systems. *Data-driven systems* analyze datasets to discern patterns according to the algorithm in its code, identify classification criteria, and apply that model to classify new inputs. This automated process of interpretting datasets to identify correlations is called *machine learning*.[16] Machine learning systems are what most people think of when they think of AI.

Machine Learning Systems and Legal Tech

Machine learning systems handle more complex tasks by having the computer discern the rules to follow instead of having the rules scripted entirely by the programmer. Imagine having to write a code for a program that could correctly recognize all the various images used for reCAPTCHA tests. The code would be complex and likely flawed, as programmers attempt to replicate how they *think* people make those distinctions. *Computer vision* is the field of research attempting to teach computers to distinguish between objects as a human might through machine learning.[17]

Because of the effort to train these systems, developers will protect their process as proprietary. This further exacerbates the phenomenon known as the *AI black box*, that is, the inability to discern what factors and "reasoning" led to a system's final output. Conversations around AI transparency reflect a desire for developers and companies to be more open with the processes they use. However, transparency is not necessarily a simple process depending on the complexity of a system (more on that shortly).

Machine learning systems are often labeled as either supervised or unsupervised, although many current systems fall somewhere along a gradient between the two. *Supervised learning* is the approach of training a system with a labeled set of data, where the inputs are tagged with the answers the system should find. The system is tasked with inferring the connection and building a model to apply in a future situation with new data.[18] Social media has been a great source of pre-tagged data for developers, but several debates have surface around privacy, diversity, bias, and ownership.[19]

Unsupervised learning trains the pretraining algorithm on unlabeled data so that the system can attempt to discern patterns in the data and extract useful features. The system can group the data by similar features, called "clustering," and it can flag outliers in the data, called "anomaly detection." While humans are not tagging this information, it is not without bias. Using arrest records to train a system will imbed in that system the historic inequities in police procedure and therefore disadvantage historically targeted minorities.

Semi-supervised learning trains the system on a mixed dataset, a small portion of which is labeled data while the majority is unlabeled.[20] Currently, training datasets need to be quite large to find reliable patterns, but some researchers theorize that next-generation systems will be able to do more with much smaller datasets.[21]

Machine learning system outputs are improved through reinforcement learning. Reinforcement learning provides the system positive feedback for output that align with the desired results, goals, and negative feedback for incorrect output. When a legal research database provides an answer to your search and asks, "Is this information useful?" your answer is that reinforcement learning feedback. Reinforcement learning is used with both supervised and unsupervised systems to help fine-tune the system's accuracy.[22]

Artificial neural networks are a popular machine-learning method, but they are not the only one nor are they new. The first neural networks were created in the 1950s and were inspired by the idea of neurons firing in the brain. Artificial neural networks are several algorithms linked together to process complex data. There are different structures, but, at its simplest, such as in figure 1.2, input is broken up and distributed to

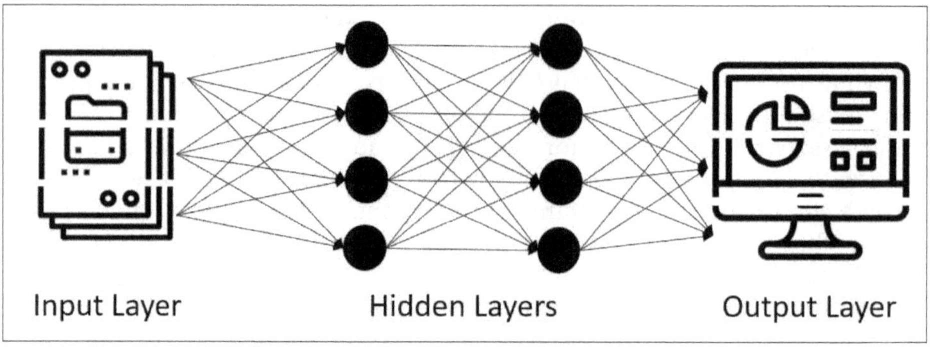

FIGURE 1.2
Simplified diagram of a neural network

different algorithms in a set, each of which analyzes a part of the whole and sends its results on to the next algorithm in the chain.[23]

Neural networks are organized in at least three layers: an input layer, a hidden layer, and an output layer. Each layer is only connected to the layers before and after it in the process. The hidden layer has the model that analyzes the input information, applies weights to its analysis, and sends its determination to the next layer. Each node in a hidden layer (the circles in figure 1.2) is called a perceptron.

Imagine a system that is designed to help with weeding decisions. Your training set might be a database of every item the library ever owned with various descriptions. One perceptron might be to consider if the book is a treatise, if it less than five years old, and if it is the only copy. Depending on how the system has interpreted the training information, it will apply a certain weight to each of these variables. The perceptron will provide a one or a zero to the next layer, depending on the sum of the weights.

Let's assume the weights are three for a treatise, two for a newer, and two if it is the only copy. If the threshold for keeping an item is set to three, none of the other information matters. The perceptron will send a one for every treatise, regardless of how old it is or how many copies are in the collection. If the threshold is set higher, say four, two of the measures will need to be true.

A more complex system, which would be needed if we were having it make weeding decisions, would consider vastly more variables and build on the threshold outputs in additional hidden layers to make more nuanced decisions. In addition to the perceptron described above, another might review the input variables to determine value and another might look at variables to discern depth of subject coverage. The output layer would take all these measures into account to provide a final weeding decision.

When neural networks employ many layers, this is referred to as *deep machine learning.* An image might be broken down by pixels when it is sent into a neural network. The first layer of algorithms might analyze each pixel for brightness. The next layer might take the first layer's determination and discern outlines of shapes from lines of similarly colored pixels. This continues through each layer until it moves through the entire system to the output layer where all the determinations are recompiled. At this final layer, the system might be able to identify facial features.[24]

Because of the complexity of these systems, it is difficult to peer into the black box and understand what factors weighed into the ultimate decision and to what degree.[25] While there are some efforts to build methods to alleviate the secrecy, some scholars are arguing for better design so that the systems are created to be interpretable.[26]

An increasingly popular AI system called *generative adversarial networks (GANs)* has two neural networks competing and learning from each other. GANs are comprised of a generator and a discriminator. Both are fed a dataset, but each system has different goals. The generator is tasked with developing a model that can produce synthetic results similar to the original, while the discriminator must create a model that can discern real from fake. Each item the generator makes is sent to the discriminator to determine if it is a genuine article or a phony.[27]

GANs are facilitating the creation of ever more convincing deepfakes. *Deepfakes* are images or videos that have been manipulated or fabricated but appear realistic enough to seem to be authentic representations of real events.[28] In one recent example, Barak Obama is seen to be warning against the threat of deepfake. At the end of the video, it is revealed that the video itself is a fake with Obama's fictional face manipulated to match the words being spoken by comedian and creator Jordan Peele.[29] Being able to evaluate sources in this post-truth environment requires key information literacy skills, and librarians are best suited to empower our communities with these skills.

Regardless of the system, the attempt to have computers interpret language is called *natural language processing.* Many legal technologies, especially the legal-research services, employ natural language processing in some form. Each holds their particular process close to the vest.

Recent efforts in natural language processing attempt to teach computers to understand language by having it review the words around it to, for example, better understand the different meanings of the word "herself" in the following two sentences: 1) She bought the book herself. 2) She bought herself the book. An algorithm analyzes all the words it is fed and translates this into a number, which it then plots in three dimensions. This is called "word to vector," which shortened is *word2vec.*

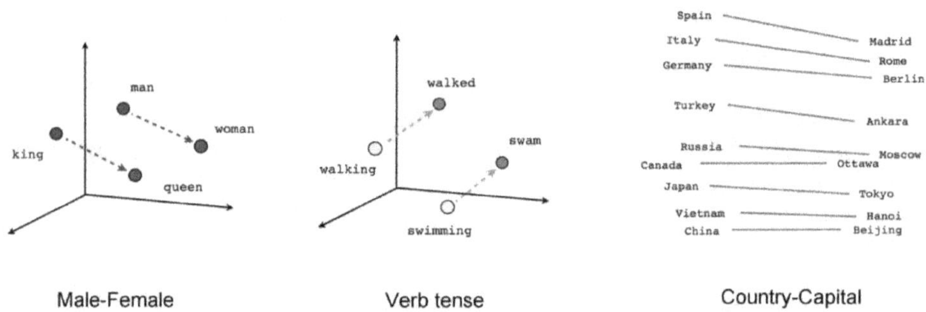

SOURCE: TensorFlow, "Vector Representations of Words," https://www.tensorflow.org/tutorials/representation/word2vec. Licensed under CC BY 4.0 (https://creativecommons.org/licenses/by/4.0/).

FIGURE 1.3

Examples of linear relationships between words in word2vec

Word2vec shows great promise, as the process has been shown to encode semantic information. Similar words are mapped near each other in space, and there are patterns in the distance between related words (figure 1.3). If the values of certain words are subtracted and the value of others are added, the resulting location would match a new word that would be related to the others by some abstract concept.

Simplifying the process, Paris – France + Poland = Warsaw. The algorithms had discerned, in a way, the concept of a capital city. You can see to the right in figure 1.3 the similarity in the relationships between various capital cities and their nations. Relationships are also mapped for verb tense and gender relationships. King – man + woman = queen. However, they are trained, as all algorithms are, on historic data, so bias was coded into certain relationships. Subtract man from doctor and add woman, you get nurse. Word2Viz is an interactive visual that allows you to map words and see the resulting relationships.[30]

Common Ethical Issues

AI systems are challenging our base principles. How is our current law to handle computer-generated resources? When machines produce problematic outcomes, whom do we hold accountable? As the systems get more complex and begin to create output that more closely resembles human creation, who holds the copyright?

As just covered, these issues find genesis in various stages of the system development process. Even framing the problem that the system is tasked with solving can lead to undesirable results. How might a law firm decide whether it should take on a new client? Is the decision algorithm to consider the success rate of the client's type of case? Or should it review the client's characteristics? What makes a "good" client? What determines a "good" case?

These are real concerns for the business of the practice of law, but it is easy to fathom how choosing particular answers to these questions can have inequitable affects and can affect individual's access to justice. Additionally, our justice system might value Blackstone's ratio, but that does not mean that the systems we adopt are programmed with that failure rate in mind.[31] With that information hidden inside of code, it makes it easier to inadvertently violate our foundational principles like Blackstone's ratio in the name of accuracy or efficiency.

Ada Lovelace once said, "The Analytical Engine has no pretensions to originate anything. It can do whatever we know how to order it to perform."[32] She spoke of the computer as it existed then, but computers are already able to do things beyond what we would be able to program it to do. As systems get more complex, it becomes ever more difficult to discern between human-generated materials and machine-generated material. Is a work less worthy of protection because it was not made by human hands?

Emerging systems have potential implications for our democracy. GANs are creating realistic synthetic photographs and, reportedly, extremely convincing fake news.[33] Overburdened courts and agencies are increasingly looking to automated systems to lighten some of the workload, which has resulted in proxies for race being used in criminal sentencing and the incorrect denial of government benefits.[34] The opacity of these systems and their implementation makes appealing those decisions difficult. Only through the cautious development of adoption and implementation procedures can we protect our democratic principles.

Where to from Here?

You needn't be a fully versed computer scientist to engage with frontier legal technologies. By understanding the differences between systems, you can intelligently deploy them in your workflows with their respective weaknesses in mind. This overview should provide a foundation on which you can build.

With this basic foundation, you can better investigate whether AI systems are the solution you need, or if you would be equally—and possibly more cheaply—suited with a simpler technology. You can be critical of claims and better versed to communicate with legal technology companies about their products. And should you be curious, you can read the recommended resources to begin developing a deeper knowledge of these technologies.

RECOMMENDED READING LIST

Hao, Karen. "What is machine learning? We drew you another flowchart." *MIT Technology Review,* November 17, 2018. https://www.technologyreview.com/s/612437/what-is-machine-learning-we-drew-you-another-flowchart/.

Hao's flowchart identifies the type of machine-learning system used.

Kaplan, Jerry. *Artificial Intelligence: What Everyone Needs to Know.* New York, NY: Oxford University Press, 2016.

Kaplan provides an accessible introduction to AI systems, related ethical issues, and frontier technology.

Lehr, David and Paul Ohm. "Playing with the Data: What Legal Scholars Should Learn about Machine Learning." *UC Davis Law Review* 51 (2017): 653–717.

Lehr and Ohm provide a great primer on the different stages involved in supervised learning to better inform future scholarship on best practices. This resource provides much more depth on the different stages than covered in this chapter and makes a great introduction for those looking to learn more.

Nielsen, Michael. *Neural Networks and Deep Learning* (2018). http://neuralnetworksanddeeplearning.com/.

This interactive book not only explains neural networks and deep learning, but also provides simple examples to make the concepts relatable.

Shoham, Yoav, Raymond Perrault, Erik Brynjolfsson, Jack Clark, James Manyika, Juan Carlos Niebles, Terah Lyons, et al. *The AI Index 2018 Annual Report.* Stanford, CA: Stanford, 2018.

This report provides a great summary of AI research and serves as a useful tool in forecasting what is on the horizon.

NOTES

1. J. McCarthy et al., "A Proposal for the Dartmouth Summer Research Project on Artificial Intelligence," http://www-formal.stanford.edu/jmc/history/dartmouth/dartmouth.html.
2. J. McCarthy, "Basic Questions," What Is Artificial Intelligence, http://www-formal.stanford.edu/jmc/whatisai/node1.html. Professor Emeritus McCarthy attempts to provide some clarity on what AI is, but he admits that his answers do not represent a consensus in the field.

3. Max Tegmark, *Life 3.0: Being Human in the Age of Artificial Intelligence,* New York, NY: Random House, 2017.
4. Peter Stone et al., "Artificial Intelligence and Life in 2030," in *One Hundred Year Study on Artificial Intelligence: Report of the 2015-2016 Study Panel* (Stanford, CA: Stanford, September 2016), http://ai100.stanford.edu/2016-report.
5. Larry Tesler, "Adage and Coinages," *Curriculum Vitae,* http://www.nomodes.com/Larry_Tesler_Consulting/Adages_and_Coinages.html.
6. LawGeex, Platform, https://www.lawgeex.com/platform/.
7. DeepMind, *AlphaGo,* https://deepmind.com/research/alphago/.
8. Artificial Lawyer, "LawGeex Hits 94% Accuracy in NDA Review vs 85% for Human Lawyers," *Artificial Lawyer,* February 26, 2018, https://www.artificiallawyer.com/2018/02/26/lawgeex-hits-94-accuracy-in-nda-review-vs-85-for-human-lawyers/.
9. For a great overview of the various stages of machine learning development where human decisions are involved, read David Lehr and Paul Ohm, "Playing with the Data: What Legal Scholars Should Learn about Machine Learning," *UC Davis Law Review* 51 (2017): 653-717.
10. Rashida Richardson, Jason Schultz, Kate Crawford, "Dirty Data, Bad Predictions: How Civil Rights Violations Impact Police Data, Predictive Policing Systems, and Justice," New York University Law Review Online (forthcoming).
11. Peter Lee, "Learning from Tay's introduction," *Official Microsoft Blog,* Mar 25, 2016, https://blogs.microsoft.com/blog/2016/03/25/learning-tays-introduction. Elle Hunt, "Tay, Microsoft's AI chatbot, gets a crash course in racism from Twitter," *The Guardian,* March 24, 2016, https://www.theguardian.com/technology/2016/mar/24/tay-microsofts-ai-chatbot-gets-a-crash-course-in-racism-from-twitter.
12. The terms *algorithm* and *model* are often used interchangeably to describe both the system before and after it is trained. For specificity, "pre-training algorithm" will refer to the system before and during training and "running model" will be used for the system after it is deployed. See, David Lehr and Paul Ohm, "Playing with the Data."
13. Karen Hao, "This is how AI bias really happens—and why it's so hard to fix," *MIT Technology Review,* February 4, 2019, https://www.technologyreview.com/s/612876/this-is-how-ai-bias-really-happensand-why-its-so-hard-to-fix/.
14. Updating cross-references requires the user to select all text (Ctrl + A) and then update the field codes (F9). Once recorded this can be simplified to just Ctrl+9.
15. Katie Rogers, "T.S.A. Defends Treatments of Transgender Air Traveler," *New York Times,* September 22, 2015, https://www.nytimes.com/2015/09/23/us/shadi-petosky-tsa-transgender.html.

16. Lehr and Ohm, "Playing with the Data," 671.
17. Jerry Kaplan, *Artificial Intelligence: What Everyone Needs to Know,* New York, NY: Oxford University Press, 2016, 30.
18. Jerry Kaplan, *Artificial Intelligence,* 30.
19. The IBM Flickr controversy is a recent example, though there have been many more. Stephen Shankland, "IBM stirs controversy by using Flickr photos for AI facial recognition," CNET, March 13, 2019, https://www.cnet.com/news/ibm-stirs-controversy-by-sharing-photos-for-ai-facial-recognition/.
20. Isha Salian, "SuperVize Me: What's the Difference between Supervised, Unsupervised, Semi-Supervised and Reinforcement Learning?" *Nvidia Blog,* August 2, 2018, https://blogs.nvidia.com/blog/2018/08/02/supervised-unsupervised-learning/.
21. Ying Zhang and Chen Ling, "A strategy to apply machine learning to small datasets in materials science," *npj Computational Materials* 4:25 (2018), https://www.nature.com/articles/s41524-018-0081-z.
22. Zhang and Ling, https://www.nature.com/articles/s41524-018-0081-z.
23. Kaplan, 28.
24. Kaplan, 28.
25. Kaplan, 28.
26. Cynthia Rudin, "Please Stop Explaining Black Box Models for High Stakes Decisions," NeurIPS 2018 Workshop on Critiquing and Correcting Trends in Machine Learning, 2018.
27. Martin Giles, "The GANfather: The Man Who's Given Machines the Gift of Imagination," *MIT Technology Review,* February 21, 2018, https://www.technologyreview.com/s/610253/the-ganfather-the-man-whos-given-machines-the-gift-of-imagination/. "Is Artificial Intelligence Set to Become Art's Next Medium?," Christie's, December 12, 2018, https://www.christies.com/features/A-collaboration-between-two-artists-one-human-one-a-machine -9332-1.aspx.
28. Robert Chesney and Danielle Citron, "Deepfakes and the New Disinformation War: The Coming Age of Post-Truth Geopolitics," *Foreign Affairs* 99:1 (2019).
29. "You Won't Believe What Obama Says in This Video! 😉," BuzzFeedVideo, Apr 17, 2018, https://www.youtube.com/watch?v=cQ54GDm1eL0.
30. Julia Bazińska and Piotr Migdał, "Explore Word Analogies," *Github,* https://lamyiowce.github.io/word2viz/.
31. "[I]t is better that ten guilty persons escape than that one innocent suffer." Blackstone, William. *Commentaries on the Laws of England in Four Books* (1753): Volume 2, 358.
32. Alan Turing, "Computing Machinery and Intelligence," *Mind: A Quarterly Review of Psychology and Philosophy* 59 (1950): 450.

33. This Person Does Not Exist, https://thispersondoesnotexist.com/. Tom Simonite, "The AI Text Generator That's Too Dangerous to Make Public," *Wired,* February 14, 2019, https://www.wired.com/story/ai-text-generator-too-dangerous-to-make-public/.
34. Julia Angwin et al., "Machine Bias," ProPublica, https://www.pro publica.org/article/machine-bias-risk-assessments-in-criminal-sentencing. Brant Fries, "What Happens When an Algorithm Cuts Your Health Care?," *IHPI News,* March 21, 2018, https://ihpi.umich.edu/news/what-happens-when-algorithm-cuts-your-health-care.

ERIK Y. ADAMS

2
What Machine Learning Can Tell Us about Shakespeare

One of the earliest complete collections of Shakespeare's plays, now known as the First Folio, divides the plays into three groups: comedies (which are funny), tragedies (which are sad), and histories (which feature real historical figures). The groups are inconsistent and arbitrary in places. For example, *Macbeth* is categorized as a tragedy, even though it is about English kings; and *Julius Caesar* is also considered to be a tragedy, even though Julius Caesar was a historical figure who happened to have the misfortune to not be born English.

But machine learning doesn't start with historical knowledge. When a machine analyzes text, all it sees are letters strung together. In the process of machine learning, we seek out order from the chaos, by doing a lot of counting, generating statistics, and then trying to infer insight from those statistics. Artificial intelligence (AI) then acts on those insights, forming new inferences from data already observed. Would we arrive at the same grouping of Shakespeare's plays if we were

ERIK Y. ADAMS, MLIS, is a research analyst at Sidley Austin LLP.

just counting words and looking at other statistics? Let's find out.

Before we get counting, we have to talk a little bit about natural language processing (NLP). There are several clever things computers do to manage the vagaries of natural language. There are entire books devoted to the techniques and methods of natural language processing and several online classes that provide a hands-on approach. For our purposes, however, only a few things need to be mentioned.

Before we do any kind of analysis of the text of the plays, we have to break them into smaller units. It isn't useful to just look at letters: Saying that the letter "e" is the most frequently used letter in Shakespeare's plays tells us nothing useful (table 2.1).

TABLE 2.1
Most frequently used letters in Shakespeare's plays

Letter	*Number of Times Letter Appears*
e	335,456
t	237,987
o	235,308
a	202,046
h	182,258
s	170,890
n	175,557
r	171,951
i	165,119
l	122,392

Breaking text into smaller units is called "tokenizing," and generally means extracting the words from a text. Tokenization takes a sentence, for example, "We few, we happy few, we band of brothers" and breaks it into individual words: "we," "few," "we" (again), "happy," "few" (again), "we" (a third time!), "band," "of," "brothers."

Another part of NLP is stemming: whittling words down to their roots using rules that are easy for a computer apply. For example, stemming might automatically remove "ing," "es," and "en" from the ends of words, leaving only the root: "Taking," "takes," and "taken" all become "tak" and are treated as the same word. Stemming is a crude process, and might not result in a real word, but it is fast and good enough, and often used in machine learning.

Lemmatizing is similar to stemming, but with some intelligence. It adds knowledge of grammar and irregular verbs to the crude process of stemming— it isn't just removing letters from the ends of words. A lemmatizer knows that "taking" and "takes" are two forms of the same word, and as such will change them to "take." A stemmed "geese" would be "gees," but a lemmatized "geese" would be "goose." Since lemmatization is much slower than stemming, it's not used as frequently.

TABLE 2.2
Top ten most frequently used words

Stop word	*Number of Times Word Appears*	*Word*	*Number of Times Word Appears*
the	22,257	good	2,526
and	20,920	lord	2,387
I	20,059	come	2,166
to	16,615	well	2,022
of	13,735	love	1,784
you	12,502	man	1,711
a	12,299	like	1,600
my	10,722	know	1,588
that	9,703	one	1,540
in	9,123	upon	1,521

In machine learning, before doing any analysis, words are generally removed that have no significant meaning. These are called "stop words," and they often are the most frequently used words used in a body of text. For example, the most popular word in all of Shakespeare's plays is the word "the." If we remove common stop words like "the," the most popular word then becomes "good" (table 2.2).

The problem with stop words is that you have to decide which words don't have cognitive meaning. And, as anyone who has tried to research English post-punk band "The The" knows, sometimes even stop words are significant. An additional wrinkle when looking at Shakespeare is that a modern lists of stop words generally does not include words that were in common use in 1600, such as "thou," "thy," and "thee."

To generate the numbers in this paper, I wrote a program in Python, a popular programming language, using the NLTK and pandas software libraries. (I strongly recommend anyone interested in learning programming and experimenting with machine learning start with Python.) The text of the plays was downloaded from Project Gutenberg and manually edited into a form that could be easily loaded and manipulated. (The Gutenberg text does not include *Edward III*. All numbers in this chapter should be considered approximate.)

There are 90,000 lines of dialog in Shakespeare's plays and 23,000 different words. If we stemmed or lemmatized the words, it would be less, but I did not because the software I used does not work particularly well with Shakespeare's English—which means that Helena's "promise" is a separate word from Mariana's "promises." Lastly, I supplemented the standard list of stop words with several extra words, including the previously mentioned "thou," "thy," and "thee."

Simple counting gives us some interesting facts. The character with the most lines in any one play is Hamlet, with 1,200 lines. Anyone who has sat through the tragedy in Elsinore should have no trouble believing that. This suggests, logically, that *Hamlet* is all about him. Romeo (510) and Juliet (490) have roughly the same number of lines as each other, and the most in their play of the same name, so it makes sense that they get top billing. But that pattern doesn't always play out: In *The Tragedy of Julius Caesar*, the ancient Roman with the biggest mouth is Brutus, with 600 lines to the Caesar's 140. Based on the number of lines per character, we might group Shakespeare's plays into three alternate groups: those where the title character does the most talking (e.g., *Hamlet, King Lear, and Macbeth*); those where the character with the most lines does not get top billing (e.g., *Julius Caesar, Othello, and Cymbaline*); and those where the top character isn't in the title at all (e.g., *All's Well That Ends Well, As You Like It,* and *The Comedy of Errors*). This breakdown doesn't line up at all with the three-part organization of the First Folio.

We can also look at the frequency of words used, rather than who is saying them. We count the number of times each word is used and then group the plays according to word popularity (table 2.3). The word "king" is one of the ten most commonly used words within 13 plays (including *The Tempest*, *Henry V*, and *Hamlet*), and "love" is in the top ten for 12 plays (including *All's Well That Ends Well*, *Othello*, and *Troilus and Cressida*) with one play overlapping for each word, that being *King Lear.* The remaining plays have neither "love" nor "king" in the top ten. These divisions don't line up with the First Folio, either: All of the histories are about kings, but so are *The Tempest* and *Hamlet.* Most of the comedies are about love, but not *The Comedy of Errors*, and some of the tragedies have a lot to do about love as well. And the "everything else" category brings together plays that don't seem to have much in common at all, like *Macbeth* and *The Comedy of Errors.*

We could have looked at the least popular words used in the plays, but frankly, that would not be useful. *Antony and Cleopatra* mentions tambourines once; *Comedy of Errors* has "imprisonment" once. All of the plays have many words that are only used once and don't really provide any insight into the plays. And that is part of the challenge of machine learning: deciding which terms will provide insight and which will not.

TABLE 2.3
The Shakespearean popularity contest

Play	Tragedy, Comedy, or History	Character with the Most Lines	10 Most Frequently Used Words
All's Well That Ends Well	Comedy	Helena	lord, know, good, well, love, say, make, yet, one, mine
Antony and Cleopatra	Tragedy	Antony	Caesar, Antony, good, come, well, make, us, upon, say, like
As You Like It	Comedy	Rosalind	love, good, man, well, Rosalind, come, Orlando, like, go, yet
Coriolanus	Tragedy	Coriolanus	Rome, good, Marcius, come, well, people, one, us, like, upon
Cymbeline	Tragedy	Posthumus	good, us, one, make, must, yet, upon, come, lord, made, know
First Part of Henry IV	History	Hotspur	lord, good, well, king, come, upon, man, us, art, like
First Part of Henry VI	History	Talbot	lord, Talbot, king, France, like, us, Henry, may, death, come
Hamlet, Prince of Denmark	Tragedy	Hamlet	lord, good, come, Hamlet, like, king, know, well, father, go
Henry V	History	Cantebury	king, good, France, us, majesty, may, like, upon, well, day
Henry VIII	History	King	king, lord, good, man, one, may, must, know, grace, yet
Julius Caesar	Tragedy	Brutus	Caesar, Brutus, know, Cassius, men,come, us, good, man, Antony
King John	History	Bastard	upon, king, well, hand, heaven, may, must, like, day, come
King Lear	Tragedy	Lear	lord, know, good, come, man, father, well, king, take, love
Love's Labor's Lost	Comedy	King	love, one, sweet, well, three, man, good, like, fair, may
Macbeth	Tragedy	Macbeth	upon, yet, us, good, like, time, come, know, say, well
Measure for Measure	Comedy	Duke	good, lord, come, well, Angelo, brother, know, duke,, may must
Merchant of Venice	Comedy	Shylock	well, jew, good, man, love, come, go, lord, upon, Antonio
Merry Wives of Windsor	Comedy	Falstaff	page, Ford, master, good, come, well, go, mistress, man, John
Midsummer Night's Dream	Comedy	Helena	love, come, man, night, sweet, Hermia, Pyramus, must, good, Lysander

(cont.)

TABLE 2.3 The Shakespearean popularity contest *(cont.)*

Play	Tragedy, Comedy, or History	Character with the Most Lines	10 Most Frequently Used Words
Much Ado About Nothing	Comedy	Leonato	man, good, love, lord, God, well, come, prince, hero, Claudio
Othello	Tragedy	Iago	Cassio, good, lord, well, come, love, know, say, Iago, yet
Pericles	Comedy	Pericles	like, come, well, lord, yet, upon, gods, good, make, may
Richard II	History	Bolingbroke	king, lord, god, good, come, may, say, Bolingbroke, death, upon
Richard III	History	Gloucester	lord, good, god, king, grace, well, come, go, death, upon
Romeo and Juliet	Tragedy	Romeo (Juliet is a close second)	love, Romeo, good, come, night, man, go, well, say, death
Second Part of Henry IV	History	Falstaff	good, lord, come, well, John, master, man, like, king, god,
Second Part of Henry VI	History	Queen	lord, king, duke, York, like, Suffolk, come, make, well, say
Taming of the Shrew	Comedy	Petruchio	well, come, good, go, father, love, Kate, say, master, know
Tempest	Comedy	Prospero	monster, like, good, upon, make, us, mine, king, come, man
The Comedy of Errors	Comedy	Adriana	us, come, chain, husband, man, go, Dromio, Antipholus, see, home
Third Part of Henry VI	History	Warwick	king, Warwick, father, brother, Henry, lord, Edward, Clifford, like, queen
Timon of Athens	Tragedy	Timon	lord, Timon, good, man, men, servant, art, one, know, well
Titus Adronicus	Tragedy	Titus	Rome, come, lord, emperor, sons, see, us, Andronicus, know, make
Troilus and Cressida	Tragedy	Troilus	Hector, lord, come, Troilus, man, good, Achilles, go, love, great
Twelfth Night	Comedy	Proteus	love, good, well, lady, one, know, say, madam, come, yet
Two Noble Kinsmen	Comedy	Palamon	doe, love, one, must, yet, Palamon, good, us, may, like
Winter's Tale	Comedy	Leontes	good, come, say, one, lord, see, may, know, upon, father

Generally speaking, machine learning does much more than simply count words. The words will be grouped into phrases, compared to similar phrases in other contexts, and a variety of very complicated statistical analyses will be done. Machine learning does more than count, but it always starts with counting, and this is the foundation on which machine learning is built.

Machine Learning Defined

> And Crispin Crispian shall ne'er go by,
> From this day to the ending of the world,
> But we in it shall be remembered—
> We few, we happy few, we band of brothers;
> For he to-day that sheds his blood with me
> Shall be my brother; be he ne'er so vile,
> This day shall gentle his condition;
> And gentlemen in England now-a-bed
> Shall think themselves accurs'd they were not here,
> And hold their manhoods cheap whiles any speaks
> That fought with us upon Saint Crispin's day.
>
> — (Henry V, Act IV, Scene III)

I have long had a fondness for the "Saint Crispin's Day" speech in *Henry V*. Partially this is because it is a really good speech, and partially because my birthday is Saint Crispin's Day. My enjoyment of the speech arises from the fact that I understand the words that are used, I can assemble the words into clauses and sentences, and I derive meaning of the sentences. I can see that Henry is trying to rally his troops and put their fears to rest, I understand the importance of the upcoming battle, and what it means for England, and I know how the speech has been used in other contexts to similar effect.

I also understand the relative importance of words. I know that words like "this," "that," and "of" are not as important as "Crispin," "band," "brothers," and "gentle." I know, from years of being forced to read Shakespeare in high school, how to group the words into meaningful units: "ending of the world," "Saint Crispin's day," "gentlemen in England."

A computer does not have my background information, and whether or not it was assembled on St. Crispin's Day probably has no effect on how it behaves. The challenge of machine learning is to find a way to simulate the understanding and background that a human brings to a body of text, but with the tools available to a computer. Or, as *A People's*

Guide to AI puts it, “In machine learning, we give computer programs lots of information and those programs use specific algorithms to see patterns in the information.”[1]

Different methods of machine learning will be discussed next in detail. But all of them have the same basic goal of generating statistics and finding patterns that can be used to make inferences. When we speak about “building a model,” we are talking about the process of gathering data and generating statistics. Sometimes, those statistics and those patterns are very easy to understand: If the play is about Henry IV, he should have the most lines. Sometimes, however, the statistics won’t make much sense at all, as is the case with deep learning.

Types of Machine Learning

Decision Trees

In many ways, decision trees are the easiest form of machine learning to understand, because people use them every day. A *decision tree* is a series of tests that lead to specific answers, as shown in figure 2.1. Going back to the original grouping of comedies, tragedies, and histories, we can put together a series of questions that lead eventually to one of those three categories.

The interesting thing about decision trees is that they can be generated automatically, assuming you have the data. If we labeled each play

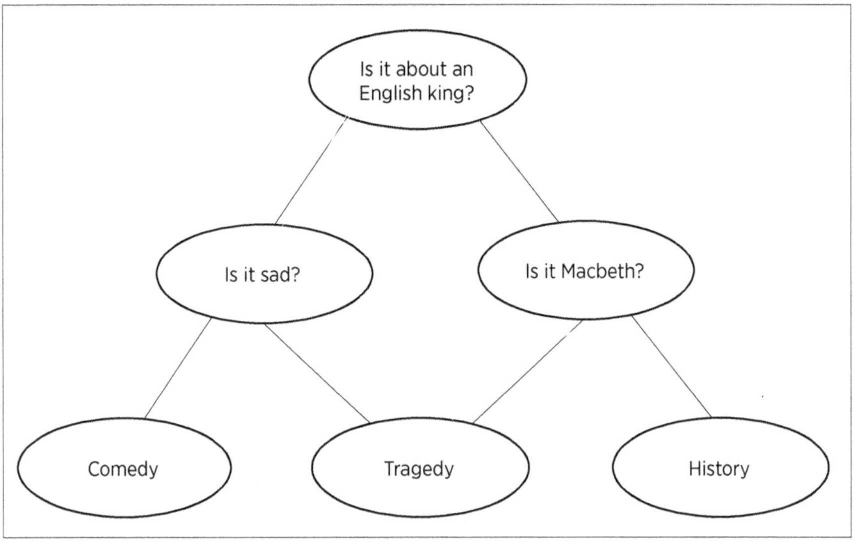

FIGURE 2.1
Simple decision tree

to indicate whether it was about a historic person, was happy, or was sad and gave the system the goal of sorting the plays into three groups accordingly, it could produce the decision tree shown in figure 2.1.

Vector Machines

Vector machines, like decision trees, are also fairly easy to understand. Imagine for a moment that we could measure how humorous a play is and could assign that humor level a number between one and ten. Comedies like *Twelfth Night* and *As You Like It* would rank very high on the humor scale, while tragedies like *Timon of Athens* would score very low. Further imagine that we could measure how sad a play was, with *Timon of Athens* and *Coriolanus* scoring very high, and *Comedy of Errors* scoring very low. And, somewhere in the middle of these extremes, would be plays like *Richard III,* which is both funny and sad in nearly equal measure. Now suppose we create a graph of those scores, where funny is the x axis and sad is the y axis (figure 2.2).

As you can see in figure 2.2, most of the tragedies are grouped in the upper-left corner of the graph (plays that are sad and not funny), the comedies are grouped in the bottom right corner (plays that are funny and not sad), and the histories form a clump in the middle. Vector machines see these clumps and can extrapolate from them. So, if a new play was discovered (for example, *Love's Labour's Won*), and it turned out to have a high funny score and a very low sad score, a vector machine would see that it was close to the comedies and group it with them.

Vector machines get complicated when there are more than two attributes being measured. If you have three attributes (e.g., funny, sad, and about an English king), you could still graph them, but you would need three dimensions. If you had 15 different attributes, you would need a 15-dimensional graph, which is well beyond my ability to picture—but I have read that this is something that can be done.

Bayesian Classification

In August 2002, Paul Graham, then a computer programmer at Yahoo, laid out a strategy for separating unwanted email messages (which he called "spam") from messages he actually wanted to read (which he called "ham"). The article, "A Plan for Spam," lays out in simple terms how to train a system to recognize spam. The method employed is Bayesian Classification, and the essay is one of the most readable treatments I have ever seen on how to implement this kind of machine learning.

Thomas Bayes was an English statistician, and the machine learning method that bears his name relies on the idea that the probability of

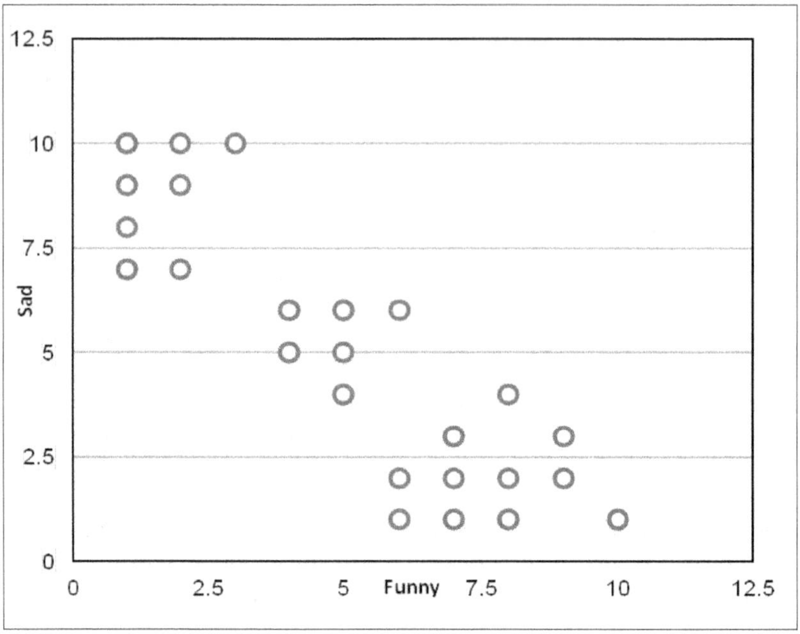

Play	Funny	Sad
Antony and Cleopatra	1	9
Coriolanus	1	7
Hamlet, Prince of Denmark	1	10
King Lear	1	10
Macbeth	1	9
Timon of Athens	1	7
Troilus and Cressida	1	8
Cymbeline	2	7
Julius Caesar	2	9
Othello	2	9
Titus Adronicus	2	10
Romeo and Juliet	3	10
First Part of Henry IV	4	5
Richard II	4	5
Third Part of Henry VI	4	6
First Part of Henry VI	5	6
Henry VIII	5	5
King John	5	4

Play	Funny	Sad
Richard III	5	4
Second Part of Henry VI	5	6
Henry V	4	6
Pericles	6	1
Second Part of Henry IV	6	6
Two Noble Kinsmen	6	2
Measure for Measure	7	3
Merchant of Venice	7	3
Merry Wives of Windsor	7	2
Winter's Tale	7	1
As You Like It	8	1
Love's Labor's Lost	8	2
Taming of the Shrew	8	4
The Comedy of Errors	8	1
All's Well That Ends Well	9	2
Tempest	9	3
Midsummer Night's Dream	10	1
Twelfth Night	10	1

FIGURE 2.2

Hypothetical funny / sad ratings

something can be inferred from related conditions. If 90 percent of all spam messages seen to date contain the name of a popular medicine, while none of the ham messages have that word, then if a new message has the name of that popular medicine, the message is probably spam. On the other hand, if every message from your best friend is ham, when a new message that is from your friend arrives with the name of that popular medicine, it is still likely to be ham.

Neural Networks, a.k.a. Deep Learning

Neural networks, also known as deep learning, are currently getting the most attention in machine learning. They are also, in my opinion, the least easy to understand method of machine learning and feel a lot like magic.

Neural networks are inspired by the structure of the human brain and nervous system: Multiple input leads to multiple processors, which are connected in turn to multiple processors, and so on in a chain that eventually leads to a single conclusion. They are currently popular for two reasons: They are very, very fast, and they can be surprisingly accurate.

Neural networks are a little like a single elimination basketball tournament. At one end of the network, we input basketball teams, and those are processed through multiple layers. Each layer produces slightly different output—instead of a basketball team, you have quarterfinalists, and then semifinalists, and finally, a champion.

However, unlike a single elimination basketball tournament, the internal workings of a neural network are the least easy to pick apart and understand. Each input might affect each of the initial nodes. Perhaps a team from one game attends another and chooses a side for which to cheer. They aren't the primary factor, but they are a factor. Those influences will affect some or all of the nodes further in. Another complication of neural networks is that training them will adjust how each node responds to different inputs. Maybe the input from the left-hand node is more important than the data from the right-hand node. When researchers talk about how hard it is to explain how a neural network came to a certain solution, it is their many layers of analysis that have undergone a lot of adjusting. It simply is not possible to point to any one part of a neural network and explain that this was the part that resulted in a positive test or negative test. It is no more practical than pointing at a neuron in a person's brain and saying that this neuron—and it alone—was responsible for some specific action. Figure 2.3 depicts the many interactions.

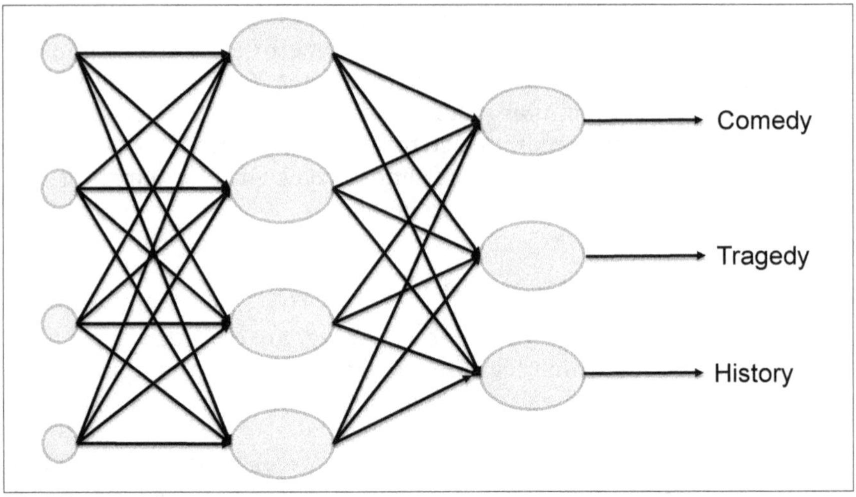

FIGURE 2.3
Neural network

Training Your Machine
Extras and Featured Characters

Suppose you have a list of all the characters in *All's Well That Ends Well*—or, more specifically, all the headings in front of spoken lines, which is a little different. On that list, you'd have: All, Bertram, Both, Clown, Countess, Diana, Duke of Florence, First Gentleman, First Lord, First Soldier, Fourth Lord, Gentleman, Helena, King of France, Lafeu, Mariana, Page, Parolles, Second Gentleman, Second Lord, Second Soldier, Servant, Steward, Third Lord, Violenta, and Widow.

Some of these are important characters and have names (like Bertram); some are extras and are only listed by description (like the First, Second, Third, and Fourth Lords); some are important but are still listed only by description (like the Countess and King of France); and a few are treated as groups of characters, rather than individuals (like "Both" and "All").

Telling the difference between the three is fairly straightforward for a person, because we as human beings know what words are used for names and what words are used for titles, and we know which titles are important and which ones are not. But a computer does not know these fine distinctions, and for a machine to learn the differences, it will need some data to count in order to find patterns. This is called training: the process of giving a machine data from which it will learn. There are, generally speaking, three kinds of training: supervised, unsupervised, and reinforcement.

Supervised Learning

Supervised learning starts with a set of data that has been labeled; the system works out patterns that correspond to the labels. We might take the cast of characters just listed and assign an importance to each one: Bertram is a featured character, First Gentlemen is an extra, the Clown is a featured character, First Soldier is an extra, and so on. Once the assigning is complete, we load the labeled data into the system as training data. The system could then infer from that data the importance of roles in another play. For example, since First Lord is an extra in *All's Well That Ends Well*, the system could assume that the First Lord in *As You Like It* is also an extra, and the system would be correct.

Supervised learning really is the easiest form of training to understand, because it is how parents teach their children. Point to a blue thing and say, "This is blue," point to another thing that is blue and repeat, and so on, until eventually the child figures out the common element and is able to identify blue things all on his or her own.

Unsupervised Learning

Unsupervised learning is the opposite of supervised learning: Let the machine find the patterns without any help. Going back to the character example, there probably isn't enough data in a single play to determine who is a featured player and who is an extra, but if we look at the casts of all the plays, patterns begin to emerge. For example, there are several characters called "First": First Lord, First Outlaw, First Lady, First Page, etc. Many of these appear in more than one play. An unsupervised system could notice these patterns and discern that characters with the word "First" are always extras, no matter the play. An unsupervised system could also look at data and extrapolate from it that characters who are unique to a play (like Romeo and Juliet) are featured players, while characters that appear in more than one play are extras. That division would not be perfect, as there are three plays about Henry VI, and the character of Falstaff also appears in three different plays. But a good system could combine the names with the frequency to get to the same results.

Reinforcement Learning

Reinforcement learning is not used very much with natural language processing and will not be discussed in detail. However, it is worth mentioning because it is used for recommendation systems. If you make a purchase on a website, you will see advertisements for other, related products. If you follow an ad and purchase another product, that is counted as a positive reinforcement; if you ignore the ad or click but don't make a purchase, that is a negative reinforcement. Positive reinforcement will lead to other ads for similar products, while negative reinforcement will lead to ads for different products. Annoyingly, no action you can take will reduce the number of ads overall.

Reinforcement learning is also used to refine music and video recommendations. If I listen to a popular song, other similar popular songs will be recommended, and each choice I make refines the model of recommendations.

The Mechanical Turk
Separating Hype from Actual Technology

In the eighteenth century, a wonderful mechanical device called the "Mechanical Turk" toured Europe. It appeared to be able to play a strong game of chess against a human opponent, powered by springs and clockwork. In fact, the Turk was an elaborate hoax—hidden underneath the playing surface, in the substantial cabinet the Turk rested upon, was a regular human operator.

When reading about a new product or new feature of a product, it seems like machine learning and artificial intelligence are the new acai berry or macha powder: something that has been added to an existing product that might make it better, but exactly how is unclear. Machine learning and artificial intelligence are amazing technologies, but like any new feature, they need to be viewed with a healthy level of skepticism: Just because the drink is green, doesn't mean that it is actually better than the old version. It is worth remembering that at root, all machine learning is counting and statistics.

REFERENCES AND RECOMMENDED READING

Bird, Steven, Ewan Klein, and Edward Loper. *Natural Language Processing with Python*. O'Reilly Media, 2009.

Graham, Paul. *A Plan for Spam*, http://www.paulgraham.com/spam.html.

Natural Language Processing with Python, http://www.nltk.org/book/ch00.html.

Natural Language Toolkit, http://www.nltk.org.

Onuoha, Mimi, and Diana Nucrea. *A People's Guide to AI*, https://www.allied media.org/peoples-ai.

Pandas: Python Data Analysis Library, https://pandas.pydata.org.

Project Gutenberg. *The Complete Works of William Shakespeare*, http://www .gutenberg.org/ebooks/100.

NOTE

1. Mimi Onuoha and Diana Nucera, *A People's Guide to AI* (Allied Media Projects, 2018), 46, https://www.alliedmedia.org/peoples-ai.

HEIDI W. HELLER

3
Types of AI Tools in Law

Artificial intelligence (AI) tools in law use machine learning, natural language processing, analytics, and visualization to enhance our work experience or work product. Most types of AI tools in law still require a significant amount of human input; hence, the use of the term "enhanced" throughout this chapter. Some products are already fully evolved, meaning that they have been broadly adopted across legal sectors. Others are still being developed or have not yet been broadly adopted. Impediments to full development or adoption in the legal industry include the costs of development and implementation, lack of trust in or ability to verify the results, and ethical considerations and professional regulations, such as privacy and security concerns. One reason law has evolved as an industry targeted by AI developers is that it has abundant, high-quality data in the form of publicly available information, including cases, dockets, statutes, regulations, and regulatory filings.

HEIDI W. HELLER, JD, MLIS, is the director of research and information resources at Schnader Harrison Segal & Lewis LLP.

There are multiple categories of and uses for AI in the legal industry, and these have an impact on different groups of legal industry employees, including lawyers, librarians, other legal staff, clients and the public, and law students and faculty.[1] Rather than explaining types of AI in the legal industry based on their technical features or the results they provide, this chapter explains the types of AI based on whom they affect in the legal marketplace, using these five categories:

1. Enhanced Lawyering
2. Enhanced Marketing
3. Enhanced Legal Administration
4. Enhanced Access to Justice
5. What law schools should teach now

Enhanced lawyering

These are AI tools that enhance attorneys work product, including legal research, document review, drafting, litigation strategy, and pricing.

Legal Research Tools

Some AI tools primarily enhance the reach and quality of our legal research, whether the research is for litigation or transactional work, and whether it is conducted by librarians or attorneys.[2] These research-specific AI tools include the following:

Knowledge management tools, which incorporate internal documents into searches of external material

Document management systems or other data stored in a company can be used for internal analytics, but it can also be combined with external content to enhance research capabilities. This type of combination of external and internal content is created by knowledge-management tools and can provide greatly enhanced access and use of a lawyer's data, both generally and when specifically related to a particular subset of content (e.g., contracts or documents pertaining to a particular matter).

Verifying that cases or other authority are good law

While legal research tools have always provided products that allow users to verify that a legal document being cited is still good law or to determine whether it has been cited in other legal sources, recent product advances enhance the ability of researchers to make this determination either more easily or more reliably. For example, Westlaw Edge includes an enhanced citator, which uses machine learning and natural language processing to identify cases that might have been implicitly overruled and might therefore no longer be good law. This tool provides information on the validity of cases a person is "KeyCiting." "Ravel View on Lexis Advance" is a visual citator that shows relationships between cases and enhances researchers' ability to find the most-cited cases on points of law in the highest relevant jurisdictions quickly.

Finding better cases faster

Other new products change the searching paradigm completely by using a full text document as a search string. One example of this kind of tool is CARA A.I. on Casetext. CARA asks a user to drag and drop a complaint, brief, or other document into a box, enter a few search terms, and hit search. Because using an entire document as the search string results in a more fact-based dataset than a typical Boolean or natural language search, and because the tool uses AI and machine-learning technologies, Casetext claims that CARA A.I. is be able to rank the most relevant cases first and find cases a searcher might otherwise miss. This is a paradigm shift.

Previous paradigm shifts in legal searching included the shift from terms and connectors—or "Boolean" searching—in preselected subsets of legal databases (e.g., Pennsylvania cases or federal statutes only), to natural language searching in preselected subsets of legal databases. After natural language searching evolved, another paradigm shift in legal search engines was the shift to federated searching across all content, with post-filtering rather than pre-filtering (although it is still possible to pre-filter using these tools). The newest paradigm shift just described uses an entire document as the search string, with either pre-filtering or post-filtering. Other recent AI-enhanced case law search products include WestSearch Plus on Westlaw Edge, which is trained to recognize responsive text and ignore text that is not responsive.

All search engine algorithms are different, and the results from product to product vary. A researcher with access to multiple search tools would do well to search using multiple legal research products to find the best law for their issue, but this is not always feasible.

"Answer" or summary tools

These tools create shortcuts to understanding the legal document or body of law being researched. "Answer" tools and other AI search enhancements in major vendors' products also use AI to make suggestions to users about secondary sources or other primary law, and they purport to give quick answers to legal questions, such as the elements of causes of action, statutes of limitations, and judicial definitions. They can increase the ability of users to find the most relevant authority more quickly.

Judge-specific information

Many other tools create litigation analytics, which can help attorneys understand litigation trends or tendencies of a particular judge by mining the judge's body of work, such as a judge's motions and cases. At least one tool on the market analyzes judicial language to determine the language most likely to influence a judge.[3] This information could enhance an attorney's decision-making process regarding which precedent to cite or how to phrase an argument. This type of tool also enhances the ability to create a sensible litigation strategy.

Mapping of multiple state or country legislation

In addition to mapping of hot news topics (covered in the section, Enhanced Marketing), some products provide visual heat maps for legislation. On Bloomberg Law, for example, state and local law activity heat maps provide a researcher with at-a-glance displays of where new laws are being introduced and where existing laws are changing.

Document Review

These tools use machine learning, natural language processing, analytics, and visualization to enhance a user's ability to perform tasks historically associated with the work lawyers do in the course of business for transactional or litigation purposes. They enhance users' ability to find the most relevant documents, facts or evidence in a case, deal, investigation, or decision.[4]

Contracts and due diligence

Many tools assist with the creation of contracts. Some of these tools use an attorney's or law firm's own documents to analyze contract provisions, and some use a data set gathered by the product developer to suggest clauses or language. Many of these products learn from the user(s) and adapt with experience to become "better" over time based on continued usage. However, some are pretrained by the developers with a closed set of documents, which subsequently may be updated. For due diligence in trademark clearance searches, there are now tools that enhance the speed and reach of trademark searches. For deals and agreements (for example, mergers and acquisitions), tools that highlight where a document's language differs from the market standard enhance an attorneys' ability to determine "what's market."[5]

Regulatory compliance

Public disclosure analytics, for example, might enhance users' ability to research, prepare and draft SEC filings, corporate transactions and various agreements. Some tools access regulations and recent regulatory changes and compare them to attorney work product to search for compliance issues. These products enhance the ability of users to plan for and make adjustments to contracts, etc., to reflect these regulatory changes.

Electronic discovery (e-discovery)

Examining documents during discovery is one of the primary applications of pattern recognition in AI in law and is a fully evolved area. First generation "technology assisted review" (TAR), also called "predictive coding," included software tools that required input by a subject-matter expert to train the algorithm on a random sample of documents to determine responsiveness. Once the tool is stabilized, the algorithm is used to make automatic classifications of responsiveness on the entire document set. Second generation TAR tools, also called "continuous active learning" tools, function a bit differently. These tools continuously score and assess responsiveness as the reviewer codes documents and floats the documents with the highest responsiveness score to the top of the pile for review, thus expediting the organization and prioritization of the documents in review. Other AI or analytic tools used in e-discovery include tools that visualize data, do sentiment analysis, thread emails, provide duplication analysis, and expand on keywords by learning to use the relationships between concepts to reveal "code words" that can assist in linking documents otherwise thought to be unrelated to a word or phrase.[6]

Drafting Memos or Pleadings

Some tools enhance the pleading drafting process on specific topics or in specific jurisdictions by exploring a body of content for similar fact patterns and legal issues. At least one product has a legal memo-drafting feature, which drafts a memo based on a legal issue presented by a user. However, human input might still be required for production of this memo or brief, and could add time and cost to the project.[7] These products are not necessarily available for all practice areas or jurisdictions. There are also products that help non-attorneys draft pleadings, and these are discussed later in this chapter, regarding access to justice products.[8]

Litigation Strategy and Pricing

At the time of this writing, many law firms, companies, and organizations use legal analytics to supplement traditional legal research and reasoning with previously unavailable strategic insights. These products work primarily by using analytics to find patterns in data and assist attorneys in making predictions about future cost or behavior, based on those past patterns. These products include motion analytics, decisions analytics, and even language analytics, and enhance attorneys' ability to predict the behavior of courts, judges, lawyers, or law firms and determine which jurisdiction, court, judge, strategy, or argument is most likely to result in a favorable outcome. They also demonstrate what a firm, opposing counsel, client, or judge has done in similar circumstances in the past, how long the litigation might take, and how much it might cost. However, not all products include all jurisdictions, and many products include analytics for specific subject areas only.[9]

Like e-discovery, judicial analytics is a well-developed field, with more products coming on the market to fill in coverage or capability gaps in other products. Analyzing the content of analytics tools to determine the best product to buy or teach is a complex endeavor and requires taking many factors into account, including the projected users, the sources of data, the scope of coverage, the level of granularity (for example, whether it has dockets only or also contains the full text of pleadings), the way in which the data is processed, and the frequency with which the tool is updated.

Currently, analytics are available for all federal courts, because the dockets and filings are publicly accessible and have uniform coding. Administrative law analytics and state and local judicial analytics tools are fully evolved in some forums, but are still evolving in others. These products can be expensive to develop, can require multiple rounds of research and funding, and can require time-consuming negotiations with courts and agencies for their work product. They might also require large staffs and extensive time to train the AI system underlying the tool. Moreover, they might be limited to particular practice areas or natures of suit.

Enhanced Marketing

Some legal AI products include analytics that enhance lawyers' and law librarians' competitive intelligence (CI) and business development (BD) efforts by providing information about the litigation trends of a company, entity, individual, or institution. Information frequently sought by lawyers or provided by librarians about a company, for example, includes common natures of suit and jurisdictions for its litigation, recent attorneys or law firms used for deals or litigation, and trends in dealmaking or litigation over time.

BD and CI analytics can be used to enhance attorneys' abilities to be well-informed in order to better market themselves to companies, other lawyers, or individuals at pitches, meetings, or client reviews. Authors can also use news aggregation products or other products with visualizations or mapping of trending or "hot" topics to help market themselves because these tools enhance the ability of attorneys to write smarter, more relevant articles.[10]

Similarly, for a law firm or legal entity trying to determine areas of focus or competition, law firm and attorney data analytics help attorneys know who their competitors are and how much work they are doing in the area. This can assist in strategic decisions about the future direction of resources.

Enhanced Legal Administration

These types of AI tools enhance lawyer efficiency or financial decision-making, including document production, records management, calendaring and business intelligence tools, or library functions. These tools include litigation calendaring products that link to relevant and updated court rules, word processing products that point out discrepancies, proofread, embed hyperlinks, correct errors in citations, or organize documents, and tools that help librarians to enhance their services by analyzing research workflow.

Tools Enhancing Financial Decision-Making or Business Intelligence

Some AI products or tools enhance users' ability to create actionable "business intelligence" with their own financial data. These tools may provide business intelligence in the form of charts or other visualizations of financial systems data. They allow users to create dashboards containing personalized or persona-based billing information or key performance indicators. These tools add what is referred to as a "semantic layer" to the data so that it is more accessible to lawyers. A semantic layer is a business representation of corporate data that helps end users access data autonomously. It maps complex data into familiar business terms such as product, customer, or revenue to offer a unified, consolidated view of data across the organization.[11]

Enhanced Access to Justice

The phrase "access to justice" (A2J) refers to tools that remove systemic barriers to law or legal advice. These include free internet products containing law, secondary materials, or products that assist non-attorneys in gaining access to justice for themselves or others. Tools enhancing public access to legal knowledge or assistance, including chatbots and drafting products created by law students, are proliferating. Some of these tools are created by private companies, some by educational institutions, some by nonprofits, and some by a combination of all of these. Many of these tools are created with small budgets to perform limited or specific tasks. For example, students at a law school might create an application that assists people who are being evicted from their homes in a particular state or county. Because these applications can be very limited in scope, great opportunity exists for the creation of new ones to serve needs of discrete communities.[12]

Chatbots/Legal Q & A

Chatbots are artificial intelligence systems that use natural language processing capabilities to carry on a conversation with a user. Traditional chatbots are script-based, new "virtual assistants" that operate using machine learning; as such, they continually improve their ability to understand questions and respond appropriately to natural language queries.

Litigation or Contract Assistants

Like the tools just described that enhance memo, pleading, or contract drafting for lawyers, these products assist nonlawyers in the drafting of simple pleadings or contracts, which are often created by students and can then be reviewed by a legal professional.

What Law Schools Should Teach Now[13]

As of this writing, legal practice includes robust adoption of certain types of AI products, and students should be exposed to these products in law school. These products include e-discovery and AI contract tools, judicial and docket analytics, enhanced citation tools that provide useful information that goes beyond traditional KeyCite and Shepard's on Westlaw and Lexis, tools that use the full text of a document as a search, legal research tools that assist users with finding "what's market" or appropriate clauses or terms for contracts, and analytics or legal research tools that enhance a lawyer's ability to understand a judge's perspective on a legal issue. Law schools should also expose students to ways in which these tools are used for marketing and business development, to strategize about litigation or pricing, and to better understand attorney financial information. Finally, in support of the legal profession's pro bono responsibilities, law schools would do well to provide opportunities for students to design or develop software or applications that enhance access to justice.

RECOMMENDED READING LIST

Atchison, Amy and June H. Liebert, "Data-Driven Decision-Making: Getting Started with Reference Tracking Systems & Data Analytics," *AALL Spectrum* 23, no.1 (2018): 20–22.

Baker, Jamie J., "2018: A Legal Research Odyssey: Artificial Intelligence as Disruptor," *Law Library Journal* 110, no. 1 (2018): 5–10.

Chen, Sherry Xin and Mary Ann Neary, "Artificial Intelligence, Legal Research and Law Librarians," *AALL Spectrum* 21, no. 5 (2017): 17–20.

Etzioni, Amitai, and Oren Etzioni. "Should Artificial Intelligence Be Regulated?" *Issues in Science and Technology* 33, no. 4 (2017): 32.

"Forty-Ninth Selected Bibliography on Computers, Technology, and the Law," *Rutgers Computer and Technology Law Journal* 44, no. 2 (2018): 334–470.

Hildebrandt, Mireille, "Law as Computation in the Era of Artificial Legal Intelligence: Speaking Law to the Power of Statistics," *University of Toronto Law Journal* 68, no.1 supp., (2018): 12–35.

Remus, Dana, and Frank Levy (American medical professor). "Can Robots Be Lawyers? Computers, Lawyers, and the Practice of Law." *Georgetown Journal of Legal Ethics* 30, no. 3 (2017): 501–558.

Telly, Nancy B., "Imagining the Use of Intelligent Agents and Artificial Intelligence in Academic Law Libraries," *Law Library Journal* 108, no. 3 (2016): 383–401.

Walters, Ed and Morgan Wright, "Putting Artificial Intelligence to Work in Law Firms," *AALL Spectrum* 23, no. 1 (2018): 17–19.

NOTES

1. While this chapter occasionally refers to specific products in the current marketplace, reference to any specific product is not an endorsement, nor is the lack of reference to any specific product a lack of endorsement. This chapter's scope does not include the discussion or categorization of specific products. For a fuller discussion of specific products for many of the tools discussed in chapter 3, see chapter 4, "AI Tools and Applications," by Chris Laut.
2. For a fuller discussion of AI tools for legal research, see chapter 8, by Jamie Baker.
3. Lexis Context is a new tool that analyzes phrases judges frequently use.
4. These tools are more fully described in chapter 4.
5. "What's market" is a term of art used in negotiating transactions (for example, mergers and acquisition transactions) and includes finding precedents of deal terms and applying internal experience gained in past transactions to determine whether a particular term is "market." Current products for finding "what's market" include Bloomberg Law and Practical Law.
6. Because e-discovery is fully evolved, readers are advised to consult books and articles specifically about e-discovery for further information on this topic.
7. Steve Lohr, "I, Robot, Esq.? Not Just Yet," *New York Times,* March 20, 2017, page B1 of the New York edition.
8. "Access to justice," or "A2J," refers to tools that remove systemic barriers to law or legal advice, such as free internet products containing law, secondary materials, or products that help non-attorneys gain access to justice for themselves or others.
9. Examples of analytics products include Lex Machina, Courtlink, Docket Alarm, Gavelytics, Bloomberg Law docket analytics, Lexis Context (formerly Ravel Law), and West's Monitor Suite.
10. Content aggregation tools include BNA Convergence and Manzama.
11. Current products include Thomson Reuters 3E and Qliq.
12. "Access to justice" is more fully addressed in chapter 9, by Tawnya Plumb.
13. A full discussion of AI in legal education is contained in chapter 8, by Theresa Tarves.

CHRIS LAUT

4

AI Tools and Applications

The disruptive rate of change of the legal marketplace for artificial intelligence (AI) solutions means that much of what you will read in this chapter will have been altered in some form or fashion in two years' time. Zion Market Research recently published a market research report estimating the global legal AI market will grow at a rate of 36 percent per year in terms of revenue between 2019 and 2026.[1] In 2017, there were few true AI solutions in the legal ecosystem, and not many law firms and law departments had implemented them. In ILTA's 2017 Technology Survey, the use of AI was reserved for only the largest legal institutions, and the survey only listed five tools: Kira, RAVN, Lex Machina, Watson, and eBrevia.[2] These solutions focused on document and contract review/classification/extraction, workflow efficiencies, and answering basic legal questions in a narrowly defined area of law. ILTA placed AI under the moniker "machine learning" in 2017, and although lawyers registered a growing awareness of use cases and

CHRIS LAUT is the director of law libraries and knowledge services at Liberty Mutual Insurance.

solutions to it that year,[3] the ILTA survey a year earlier in 2016 failed to include any questions on the subject.

In 2018, Erin Hichman of ALM Intelligence authored the excellent study *Law Firms Need Artificial Intelligence to Stay in the Game,* in which she defined AI as a branch of computer science that "enables machines to execute humanlike tasks. Moreover, just like humans, machines using AI learn from past experiences and adjust behavior."[4] This is a standard definition, which means that expertise automation systems (such as Neota Logic and Onit, which cannot be trained) will not be included in this chapter since they exhibit no learning functionality. Legal AI solutions are cropping up with greater frequency, so this chapter will limit the discussion to only market leaders and strong niche players.

AI benefits the practice of law and the business of law by synthesizing text, finding relationships in data, applying understanding for predictive and potentially proscriptive analytics, and optimizing information to forecast outcomes and augment decision making. Capgemini charted the use cases by benefits and complexity through a study of companies implementing AI.[5]

More specifically for the legal ecosystem, AI offers solutions in five broad areas:

1. Contract/Document Management Review, Extraction, and Automation
2. e-Discovery
3. Legal Research and Litigation Analytics
4. Compliance and Regulatory Review/Monitoring
5. Administrative Analytics and Automation.

Contract/Document Management Review, Extraction, and Automation

Solutions in this category typically automate the drafting and review of contracts and documents by analyzing and extracting metadata, recognizing patterns, and indexing and classifying them. For attorneys, there are multiple benefits. By training the AI, attorneys automate repetitive tasks, saving time and allowing them to focus on higher-end work. These solutions provide insight by extracting valuable intelligence and offering risk assessment, along with a high degree of accuracy scaled to volumes of content. Some products offer workflow solutions, delivering the capability to disaggregate work so professionals with varying levels of expertise can collectively manage different components of the work.

Solutions

Beagle

Beagle offers machine learning (ML) and natural language processing (NLP) contract analysis. The program reviews contract language to highlight key clauses for acceptance or rejection, from which it learns user preferences based on accepted/rejected clauses. Beagle counts among its clients Volkswagen, LexisNexis, Law Made, Dentons, and Thomson Reuters.

ContractPodAi

ContractPodAi is a contract creation and lifecycle management solution that allows users to assemble, automate, approve, sign, and manage all their contracts and documents. Utilizing ML and NLP, ContractPodAi also acts as a document management repository and has teamed up with Ernst & Young and Bosch Siemens, among others.

ContraxSuite

ContraxSuite is a contract analytics and legal document platform owned by LexPredict, which was acquired by Elevate in November 2018. ContraxSuite helps organizations build document and contract analytics solutions that they can audit and customize through various AI technology, including NLP, ML, network science, gamification, and deep learning. Baker McKenzie is a client.

Diligen

Diligen is a contract assistant that helps lawyers review contracts quickly by automatically identifying key provisions, thus producing contract summaries and helping teams manage the contract review process. Through ML and NLP, Diligen specializes in mergers and acquisitions (M&A) due diligence and lease review.

Diligen has partnered with Lex Mundi, making the AI contract review tool available to its 160-member firms.

eBrevia

eBrevia extracts and classifies data from contracts, bringing accuracy and speed to contract review and analysis through ML and NLP. Donnelly Financial acquired eBrevia in December 2018. Legal organizations such as Goldman Sachs, ING, Linklaters, Baker McKenzie, and Evercore use the tool to analyze documents for risk assessment, due diligence, data analytics, and data reconciliation.

Ironclad

Ironclad combines contract management and workflow automation into a single platform to create a true system of record for contracts. Ironclad integrates with customer relations management (CRM), storage, and e-signature providers while extracting the metadata. The solution utilizes ML and NLP and has been adopted by Reddit, DropBox, GoFundMe, and Glassdoor.

Kira

Kira searches and analyzes contract text and can be deployed for contract metadata extraction, due diligence, lease abstraction, and other projects where visibility into contract provisions is critical. Using ML, Kira has been implemented at Freshfields Bruckhaus Deringer, Clifford Chance, Allen & Overy, Fenwick & West, Davis Polk & Wardwell, Deloitte, DLA Piper, Integreon, McCann FitzGerald, Allens Linklaters, and Perkins Coie.

KM Standards

KM Standards is a drafting and assembly tool that uses ML and NLP to analyze securities and exchange commission (SEC) documents in order to provide a library of standardized contracts and clauses. The service also offers a contract analysis platform to automate contract portfolio review through extraction analysis, and reporting. Originally called KIACC and available to all ACC members, KM Standards includes as its customers Allen & Overy, ACC, the Bank of Montreal, Cassels Brock, Reed Smith, Seyfarth Shaw, and Littler Mendelsohn.

LawGeex

LawGeex helps in-house legal teams automate the review and approval of everyday contracts by learning from their documents and crowd-sourced contracts using ML. LawGeex has been adopted by Deloitte, NetApp, McDonald's, Google, Microsoft, AIG, Travelocity, Vodafone, Del Monte, L'Oréal, and Novartis.

Legalmation

Legalmation leverages IBM Watson to produce high-quality, automated responses to complaints drafts in two minutes. Although their solution is currently limited to California, they expect to expand to New York,

Florida, and Texas in the near future. Legalmation uses NLP and ML for their clients, who include Oglatree Deakins and Walmart.

LegalSifter

LegalSifter is trained to read text, look for specific concepts, and learn over time to review documents and identify important concepts that demand attention or are missing entirely. TLT, Horty Springer, and Estrella use this ML and NLP AI solution to review documents for negotiation purposes.

LEVERTON

LEVERTON provides insights from unstructured data found in corporate and legal documents in more than 30 languages for transactional due diligence. Mainly used outside of the U.S., Linde, Clifford Chance, and JLL have adopted its NLP and Deep Learning AI solution.

LinkSquares

LinkSquares is a contract analytics tool for in-house legal and finance teams. The tool automatically detects and retrieves key contract terms and provides full-text search to find key keywords and phrases. Clients such as Carbonite, CloudHealth Technologies, and DraftKings use the solution for due diligence, M&A, and finance projects.

LISA

LISA is a product that enables the creation of legally binding non-disclosure agreements. Using NLP and ML, LISA empowers two parties to negotiate and create together through an impartial "attorney robot." Clients include IDR Law, Monsanto, Allstate, Beyond Sales, InfaBode, and D/Sruption.

Litera Microsystems

Litera Microsystems offers a portfolio of products across the document drafting lifecycle for precedents and clauses, document styling, proofreading, comparing documents, and file sharing. Litera uses ML and NLP for their clients, which include Clifford Chance, Baker McKenzie, Dentons, Seyfarth Shaw, Linklaters, DLA Piper, Herbert Smith Freehills, Norton Rose Fulbright, Latham Watkins, and Freshfields Bruckhaus Deringer.

Luminance

Luminance is a contracts analytics service that provides a global overview of any body of legal documents, finding significant information and anomalies without instruction. Luminance employs ML, Pattern Recognition Algorithms, and Advanced Statistical Probability for due diligence and contract management. The service includes among its list of clients Cravath, Swaine & Moore, Ice Milk, Holland & Knight, Slaughter and May, Bird & Bird, and Allens Linklaters.

PrivacyPolicyCheck

PrivacyPolicyCheck offers a suite of contract management drafting and review tools. PrivacyPolicyCheck supports automated contract review and summarization to assess risk, gain insight, and manage deals. The suite of solutions uses NLP and ML for clients, which include Clifford Chance, Simmons & Simmons, National Grid, and Eversheds.

RAVN

RAVN is a contract management solution in the iManage platform that classifies, extracts, and understands documents to automate routine cognitive tasks, provides insights, and streamlines how professionals work. RAVN uses Bayesian algorithms, NLP, and ML for due diligence for their clients, which include Johnson Winter & Slattery, Keoghs, Reed Smith, and Linklaters.

e-Discovery

Products in this segment were some of the earliest adopters of AI. There is some crossover between contract and document review tools and e-discovery tools since they exhibit many of the same characteristics, namely analysis of vast amounts of unstructured data to find patterns, anomalies, and connections between seemingly unrelated content. Traditionally, e-discovery processes encompassed harvesting electronically stored information (ESI), electronically duplicating the data, then posting it for attorney review in a document review platform.[6] By using technology-assisted review (TAR), lawyers initially generated relevant documents by keyword searching, as well as content from participants related to the litigation. AI has expanded the capabilities of e-discovery by deducing links between parties and issues and even extending AI into areas of litigation analytics to make strategic and tactical decisions on how to pursue options for a given case.[7] AI helps attorneys through all phases of e-discovery, including identification, collection, processing, and production of evidence.

e-Discovery AI adoption rates are much higher than the general adoption rates of all AI legal solutions. Respondents to ILTA's 2018 Technology Survey had at least one AI tool in production at a rate of 8 percent. In contrast, Exterro's 2018 Law Firm Benchmarking Report showed that respondents use AI for e-discovery "often" at a rate of 12 percent and "sometimes" at a rate of 28 percent.[8]

Solutions

ABBY

ABBY utilizes NLP technology for processing unstructured data contained in scanned documents used for data culling and knowledge discovery. They count Deloitte and Cricket Legal Technologies among their clients.

Brainspace

Brainspace ingests documents in multiple forms to provide analysis such as how many times a certain clause is found, jurisdictions of documents, and the offices in which the documents were produced. Brainspace mines the text of documents and presents multidimensional results through a visualization tool. Clients such as KPMG, Ropes & Gray, Ernst & Young, PWC, and Deloitte benefit from semantic search, ML, and NLP AI.

Casepoint

Casepoint is an end-to-end e-discovery platform that supports sophisticated workflows across millions of documents and hundreds of users, with custom reporting and data management tools built in. Casepoint's product Case Assist leverages AI for litigation predictive data analytics to determine tactics and strategy. Casepoint uses ML and NLP for their clients, which include the DOJ, U.S. Congress, Briggs & Morgan, Barnes & Thornburg, Cohen Milstein, and Beveridge & Diamond.

DISCO

DISCO is an end-to-end e-discovery solution that provides next-generation software as a service (SaaS) review technology to give clients complete control over their data, workflows, and costs. DISCO uses ML and counts among its clients Wilson Elser, Kennedys, Greenberg Traurig, Mayer Brown, K&L Gates, Quinn Emanuel, Southwest, and WeWork.

Everlaw

Everlaw's e-discovery software saves attorneys and review teams valuable time in discovering key documents, collaborating internally and with third-party firms, and litigation preparation through an intuitive interface, blink-speed document search, and ML-powered analytics. Clients include Zenefits, Benesch, Friedlander, Coplan & Aronoff, Hanson Bridgett, Macfarlanes, Hagens Berman, McDonald Carano, and all 50 U.S. state attorneys general offices.

OpenText

OpenText e-discovery solutions provide digital forensics and unstructured data analytics for searching, collecting, and investigating enterprise data to manage legal obligations and risk. OpenText has enhanced its suite of discovery tools through the acquisition of Catalyst in January 2019 and Recommind and Guidance Software in recent years. The company's ML and NLP help clients such as TransCanada Pipelines, Drinker Biddle, Sun Chemical, Pillsbury Winthrop, and Prime Healthcare quickly find critical discovery information.

Relativity

Relativity brings the complete process of e-discovery onto one platform to manage high volumes of electronic evidence using ML and NLP. Relativity integrates with many partner solutions through their App Hub. The company's clients include Littler, Steptoe, Herbert Smith Freehills, Reed Smith, Ballard Spahr, U.S. DOJ, Prudential, Oracle, Mattel, Ingersoll Rand, Purdue Pharma, and Deloitte.

Text IQ

Text IQ looks through documents using ML and NLP to flag what's privileged or irrelevant by deducing links between parties that aren't spelled out in the text. The company counts among its customers Twitter and Walmart.

Legal Research and Litigation Analytics

AI helps attorneys identify relevant cases, statutes, and regulations, and generates newsfeeds for business development and competitive intelligence purposes. By training AI in narrow areas of law, attorneys can develop customer self-help tools to answer high-volume, low-risk questions legal professional previously fielded. Attorneys train the AI to identify research to proactively send alerts on cases and briefs and automatically tag results to tracked matters. There are some similarities between legal research, compliance, and regulatory review since each area relies on reviewing and analyzing legal authority to track material changes and discover materials for risk mitigation and legal strategy purposes.

Solutions

Bloomberg Law's Points of Law

Bloomberg Law's Points of Law finds and connects legal language in federal and state court opinions by highlighting and finding critical language to a court's reasoning and linking it to governing statements of law and other relevant on-point case law. Smart Code combines ML with human experts to assign ratings of a court's discussion of law to find relevant and high impact arguments in court opinions. All Bloomberg Law clients get Points of Law and Smart Code as part of their subscription to the research platform.

Casemine

Casemine is litigation information retrieval system that derives context from entire passages and briefs to retrieve other documents with similar legal concepts. Casemine incorporates NLP and ML for data visualization, collaboration, archiving, and drafting. Casemine's analysis system is available in the USA and UK and has several hundred paying customers, according to the company.

Casetext

Casetext's search engine CARA finds similar cases on the same facts, legal issues, and jurisdiction as your matter by reviewing and analyzing briefs or complaints to find on-point cases. Casetext provides free access to state and federal cases, as well as other users' annotations to which attorneys may add their own annotations. Furthermore, CARA follows dockets and sends attorneys pertinent research when an opposing counsel files a motion. Clients such as Fenwick & West, Blank Rome, Quinn Emanuel, DLA Piper, White & Case, Cozen O'Connor, Baker Donelson, Ogletree Deakins, and O'Melveny & Myers benefit from the use of NLP.[9]

Fastcase

Fastcase is a full-service legal research platform that provides AI tools within the Fastcase AI Sandbox, its secure platform in which attorneys load their own unstructured or structured data to gain deep insights. Fastcase users can analyze their own data independently or compare it to Fastcase's collection of primary law, docket information from Docket Alarm, a data bank of contracts from Contract Standards, or expert witness data from Courtroom Insight. Clients such as Baker Donelson, DLA Piper, and Baker Hostetler use Fastcase's ML and NLP to develop litigation strategies and develop best practice contracts.

Gavelytics

Gavelytics is a predictive analytics solution that studies what judges do in the courtroom so litigators can garner behavioral insight that leads to more successful outcomes for clients. Gavelytics currently covers California courts and harnesses NLP to score judges against county averages.[10] They count among their clients Shepard Mullin, Reed Smith, Davis Wright Tremaine, and Glaser Weil.

InfoNgen

InfoNgen is a news aggregator that delivers customized content using sophisticated analysis. The addition of ML neural networks allows attorneys to find hidden patterns, trends, and anomalies. InfoNgen counts Littler Mendelson among its clients.

Judicata

Judicata breaks down the law into core constituent pieces to unearth underlying facts (such as cause of action) and grades the strength of arguments against precedent to predict the odds of winning. Attorneys load briefs into the solution to discern case vulnerability, find supporting cases as well as identifying missing cases, and balance arguments. Clients are currently limited to California and the company expects to expand to other jurisdictions soon.

Lexis

Lexis has either acquired or developed a number of AI-driven research solutions such as Context (formerly Ravel Law), Lex Machina, and Lexis Answers. Context and Lex Machina act as a litigation predictive analytics package, with Context providing visualization context for judges and expert witnesses, and Lex Machina producing deep dives in analyzing judicial behavior, evaluating outside counsel, and reviewing other litigation parties. Lexis Answers uses NLP, ML, and cognitive computing to understand attorney's natural language questions in order to deliver concise and authoritative answers across state and federal topics.[11] Lexis Answers is available to all LexisAdvance clients for free.

Manzama Insights

Manzama Insights identifies indicators and themes to highlight opportunities and risks around individual companies and industry sectors. Manzama Insights sifts through content and categorizes into areas of interest through ML to help identify content as positive or negative. Clients include Allens Linklaters, Kennedys, White & Case, Perkins Coie, DLA Piper, Akin Gump, Kirkland & Ellis, and Mayer Brown.

Picture It Settled

Picture It Settled predicts settlement negotiation amounts through behavioral analytics. Picture It Settled gives attorneys an edge during negotiations by predicting what an opponent does through ML neural networks. Clients include Rackspace, Debevoise & Plimpton, and Cadwalader, Wickersham & Taft.

Premonition

Premonition is a deep-dive, predictive analytics platform for Connecticut case law as well as federal jurisdictions. The tool helps attorneys determine who wins specific case types for particular litigation. Premonition uses NLP and ML for their clients, which include Orchard Global Asset Management, Spring Creek Development Group, Waterstone Capital, Oxbow Partners.

ROSS

ROSS is a tool developed by IBM and has a number of legal AI solutions centered on deciphering meaning in text. ROSS retrieves cases and passages that answer legal questions through NLP and then organizes them into a collection of answers that fit case strategies. Baker Hostetler and Dentons developed ROSS tools to research and answer bankruptcy questions; other clients include Jackson Lewis, Pierce Bainbridge, and Chavez.

Westlaw

Westlaw created a new platform, Westlaw Edge, which integrates AI to identify cases that are no longer good law and to provide quick answers for legal doctrine questions. Westlaw's WestSearch Plus uses ML and NLP to answer thousands of questions and provide relevant documents. The platform further offers litigation analytics into search results with visualization tools to drill down to underlying documents.[12]

Compliance and Regulatory Review/Monitoring

Tools in this area review and analyze unstructured data and flag results to help attorneys mitigate risk and remain vigilant on regulatory affairs. Solutions help lawyers assess their policies and procedures, log and screen incidents and issues, and keep in compliance with changes to federal and state laws.

Solutions

FTI Technology

FTI Technology roots out fraud, maintains regulatory compliance, protects sensitive materials, and quickly finds facts to harness organizational data through document and data analysis. FTI Technology uses NLP and ML on behalf of their clients, which include Baker McKenzie, Lovells, and JMBM.

ComplianceHR

ComplianceHR offers a suite of compliance applications to address changes in federal and state employment law requirements for minimum wage, overtime, independent contracting, FMLA leave, and more. ComplianceHR is the brainchild of attorneys at Littler Mendelson, who partnered with Neota Logic to simplify the employment compliance process using NLP. The AI compliance solution counts among its customers AsureConsulting, ADP, nextSource, Innovative Employee Solutions, and bambooHR.

FiscalNote

FiscalNote is a legislative tracking service that monitors stakeholders and public policy in order to assess positions and discern impacts.

FiscalNote uses ML to identify influencers and stakeholders as well as the probability of passage. Customers include Foley, Nestle, Intel, Johnson & Johnson, and AstraZeneca.

Intraspexion

Intraspexion finds risk by investigating employee communications for signals or "True Positives" in order to avoid disputes. Intraspexion's use of neural networks and NLP surfaces patterns and alerts investigators to potential risks.

NextLP's Story Engine

NextLP's Story Engine turns disparate, unstructured data such as email communications, business chat messages, contracts, and legal documents into meaningful insights that can be used as a monitoring tool for compliance. The tool creates a comprehensive view of the entire regulatory, conflicts of interest, data security, and HR issues to feed into one narrative. NextLP leverages ML, NLP, and Cognitive Analytics to identify patterns of behavior and intent that is unusual in nature for their clients. The company counts Dentons and McDermott Will & Emery among its clients.

PenaltyAI Search

PenaltyAI Search identifies compliance clauses in legislation on a global scale, extracting the actual penalty amount. This tool is intended for risk and compliance professionals to search and identify risk levels and compliance requirements across jurisdictions on a specific topic using NLP and ML.

ServiceNow

ServiceNow delivers a host of governance, risk, and compliance integrated risk management solutions. ServiceNow's NLP solution offers virtual desk agents to provide customers with compliance recommendations. Clients include Unum, Prudential, Campbell Soup, and Blackbaud.

Seal Software

Seal Software launched a suite of tools to adhere to various financial services compliance requirements. Seal's NLP packages identify risks for procurement, Brexit, GDPR, M&As, and LIBOR to help financial services companies to adhere to regulatory and reporting requirements in the industry. Clients include PayPal, United Technologies, Salesforce, Bosch, DocuSign, Experian, Dell, Aetna, Humana, and Kaiser Permanente.

Administrative Analytics and Automation

This area is somewhat of a catchall for solutions that are geared more for the business of law than the practice of law. Tools in this arena tackle tasks that help with setting fees, marketing, managing finances, and timekeeping insights. Solutions may also handle intake and workflow efficiencies, while providing visualization of data analysis to aid in helping legal organizations make data-driven decisions.

Solutions

Brightflag

Brightflag offers complete legal spend management solutions to legal departments, including e-billing, matter management, invoice review, and accruals management. Using NLP, Brightflag categorizes narratives for bill time entry to aid with invoice review and legal pricing. Clients such as Yahoo, Uber, Telstra, and Rimini Street use the product for legal operations.

Bodhala

Bodhala provides insights into legal procurement trends for law firms and legal departments by analyzing legal bills and finding trends in public legal data.[13] Clients such as United and Amalgamated Bank use the ML to index legal spend against the market to accurately forecast legal spend and evaluate legal representation.

iManage RAVN Insight and iManage TimeCard Narrative

iManage RAVN Insight and iManage TimeCard Narrative are legal efficiency tools that use ML and NLP. RAVN Insight leverages AI to find, analyze, and identify organizational information buried in disparate systems, surfacing connections between people, expertise, and knowledge. Customers such as Keoghs, Howard Kennedy, Withers, and Bech-Bruun use the solution to build internal communities of experts and expertise. iManage TimeCard Narrative automates and classifies the time taken to complete matters and projects to improve resource allocation and task management. The automation robot uses what it learns from reading and analyzing timecard records to accurately forecast future costs.

Intapp

Intapp supports law firms' efforts in business development, onboarding engagements, and client service efficiency initiatives by reengineering legal services delivery processes, allocating talent through process automation, and integrating applications, legacy systems, and data silos. Intapp leverages NLP and ML to help law firms such as Baker McKenzie, Ballard Spahr, McMillan, O'Melveny, Orrick, Seyfarth Shaw, Alston & Bird, and BakerHostetler become more data driven.

LegalVIEW BillAnalyzer

A Wolters Kluwer solution, LegalVIEW BillAnalyzer is another bill analyzer like Brightflag and Bodhala, which uses ML to analyze and find hidden patterns in legal spend. LegalVIEW clients such as Microsoft take advantage of BillAnalyzer's expansive database of invoices for benchmarking purposes.

RubyLaw

RubyLaw is an enterprise content management system designed for legal marketers to leverage internal experience for business development activities such as proposal generation. The platform's MLP and NLP-generated recommendation engine delivers relevant and personalized content to target audiences. RubyLaw counts among its clients Akin Gump, Kramer Levin, Winston & Strawn, Bryan Cave, Latham & Watkins, Paul Hastings, and Morrison Foerster.

Tali

Tali allows attorneys to capture time through a voice assistant, such as Alexa, by connecting to billing software, populating client and matter fields, and sending full-formed time entries. Clients such as PK Law, St. Augustine Law Group, and Integrated FPS use the NLP to capture time by audio.

Time by Ping

Time by Ping tracks every activity a lawyer undertakes by being integrated into the native environment of such everyday tools as MS Word, Excel, Outlook, and telephones, and it automates the timekeeping function. The application captures, categorizes, and describes time entries automatically to specific clients, eliminating the need to write down the task, time, and client's name.[14] Ping leverages ML for clients such as Mishcon de Reya.

NOTES

1. Artificial Lawyer, "Legal AI Market to Grow 36% Per Year, Says Market Research Report," March 28, 2019, https://www.artificiallawyer.com/ 2019/03/28/legal-ai-market-to-grow-36-per-year-says-market-research-report/.
2. International Legal Technology Association, *ILTA's 2017 Technology Survey analysis and results*, 136. On file with author.
3. International Legal Technology Association, 7.
4. Erin Hichman, *Law Firms Need Artificial Intelligence to Stay in the Game,* (New York, NY: ALM Intelligence, 2018), 5.
5. Capgemini Digital Transformation Institute, "Turning AI into concrete value: The successful implementers' toolkit," 12, https://www.capgemini.com/us-en/wp-content/uploads/sites/4/2018/01/turning-ai-into-concrete-value-the-successful-implementers-toolkit-2.pdf.
6. Kyle Cambelle, "E-Discovery's Evolution: Critical Implications for Law Firms, Providers," *The Legal Intelligencer,* February 1, 2019, https://www.law.com/thelegalintelligencer/2019/02/01/e-discoverys-evolution-critical-implications-for-law-firms-providers/.
7. David Lat, "How Artificial Intelligence Will Revolutionize eDiscovery," Above the Law, January 25, 2017, https://abovethelaw.com/2017/01/how-artificial-intelligence-will-revolutionize-ediscovery/.
8. International Legal Technology Association, "ILTA's 2018 Technology Survey: Analysis and Results," 187; Exterro, "2018 Law Firm Benchmarking Report," 22.
9. Artificial Lawyer, "US Law Firms Line Up for AI-Driven Legal Research," May 16, 2018, https://www.artificiallawyer.com/2018/05/16/us-law-firms-line-up-for-ai-driven-legal-research/.
10. Artificial Lawyer, "California Legal AI Co. Gavelytics Aims to Be Case Prediction Local Hero," November 14, 2017, https://www.artificiallawyer.com/2017/11/14/california-legal-ai-co-gavelytics-aims-to-be-case-prediction-local-hero/.
11. Jean O'Grady, "Lexis Answers: Artificial Intelligence without the Hyperbole; No Robot Lawyers in Sight–A Fastrack to Legal Answers," *Dewey B Strategic* (blog), June 26, 2017, https://www.deweybstrategic.com/2017/06/lexis-answers-artificial-intelligence.html.
12. Bob Amgrogi, "Move Over Westlaw – Meet the Next-Generation Westlaw Edge, With Advanced AI and Analytics," *LawSites* (blog), July 12, 2018,

https://www.lawsitesblog.com/2018/07/move-westlaw-meet-next-generation-westlaw-edge-advanced-ai-analytics.html.

13. Rhys Dipshan, "Bodhala Bets on Big Data with Legal Spend Analytics Platform," *Legal Technology,* September 5, 2017, https://www.law.com/legaltechnews/sites/legaltechnews/2017/09/05/bodhala-bets-on-big-data-with-legal-spend-analytics-platform/.
14. Artificial Lawyer, "Legal AI Market to Grow 36% Per Year, Says Market Research Report," March 28, 2019, https://www.artificiallawyer.com/2019/03/28/legal-ai-market-to-grow-36-per-year-says-market-research-report/.

VALERI CRAIGLE

5

Law Libraries Embracing AI

One need not possess a degree in computer science to appreciate the benefits of artificial intelligence (AI), nor should a background in data science be a prerequisite for developing AI tools. The thought of working with AI technology can be intimidating, but the reality is that AI is nothing more than a set of tools that perform specific functions—albeit functions that are highly intuitive. Today, AI is so deeply integrated in our research and analytics tools that many people do not even realize it's there. Natural language processing (NLP) and machine-based neural networks have been in existence for decades, but these technologies have only recently been adopted in law firms and law schools. Although the time between adoption and awareness has been slow, the current status of AI in the legal space looks promising going forward. A 2018 survey conducted by business analytics firm, RELX, found that among legal industry executives in the USA, only about a quarter of them said they do not use AI, and only 12 percent had never heard of AI.[1]

VALERI CRAIGLE is the associate librarian for digital and e-publishing services at the James E. Faust Law Library, University of Utah.

The utilization of AI provides insights for legal clients, future-proofs careers for attorneys and law librarians, and elevates the status of the information suite.[2] AI training in law schools makes students more practice-ready in an increasingly tech-centric legal environment; access to justice (A2J) initiatives are embracing AI's capabilities to provide guidance to educational resources and legal services for the under-represented. AI's presence in the legal community is becoming so common that it can no longer been seen as an anomaly—or even cutting edge. Some even argue that its absence in law firms will eventually be akin to malpractice.[3]

This chapter explores some practical uses of AI in legal education and law firms, with a focus on professionals who have gone beyond the role of AI consumers to that of AI developers, data curators, and system designers. In addition to these examples, the author recommends two excellent use case compilations that focus on the use of AI in law firms: Alex Davies' *AI in Application: An In-Depth Examination from the Legal Profession*, and Joanna Goodman's *Robots in Law: How Artificial Intelligence Is Transforming Legal Services*.

AI Already in Use

Virtual assistants like Alexa and Siri, self-driving cars, medical imaging devices, movie-streaming services, and even spell check, all use AI technology to deliver the services and experiences we have become accustomed to in modern society. Big data and complex algorithms turn information into actionable intelligence and power the smart technology that makes these services possible. When we use our computers or smartphones, each click or swipe creates a data point that AI systems use to build personalized profiles, which inform our individual online experiences. For example, the "More movies you might like" feature in Netflix is made possible by a smart machine that has committed online behaviors to memory and is able to recognize patterns in past behavior to predict future behavior.

The legal research and analytics tools used by law librarians every day leverage AI to produce results that are more intuitive and insightful than ever before. For example, Lexis Answers, an AI component of Lexis Advance, uses advanced NLP to "understand" a user's question and to even suggest questions that can anticipate a research path.

The New Westlaw Edge has a feature called "Statutes Compare" that displays changes in the language of state and federal statutes over time, providing new insights into the evolution of a piece of legislation and the authority behind it. Regulations Compare similarly compares changes to federal regulations going back to the early 2000s.

Points of Law, a new AI feature in Bloomberg Law, offers greatly improved case law research efficiency by "enabling litigators to quickly identify statements of law within a court opinion and then see the most cited, most relevant, and most recent cases related to those statements."[4]

Each of these tools leverages big data, sophisticated NLP, and machine learning (ML) to improve legal research. However, despite the growing sophistication of these tools, they are not yet autonomously intelligent. Machines still need to be trained by humans to automate tasks and produce insightful results. As such, our current utilization of AI could be more appropriately characterized as "artificial augmentation," as opposed to artificial intelligence.[5]

AI in Legal Practice

Before AI, law firms were resigned to the reality of having to allocate human resources to the time-consuming and repetitive tasks of due diligence work and document review. New associates and law librarians dutifully executed their roles as readers, writers, reviewers, and researchers on projects that could take weeks or months, depending on the complexity of the matter at hand.

RAVN ACE

When Berwin, Leighton, and Paisner deployed a "contract robot" (which they named LONald) in 2005, the true value of AI's ability to automate due diligence with high accuracy and little to no human intervention was revealed. LONald, a product of RAVN Ace's due diligence application, was developed to compare real estate information, from in-house contracts to public records databases. LONald was able to check the accuracy of these comparisons at a much faster rate—or according to one attorney at the firm, a rate that was "12 million times quicker" than a human doing the same work.[6]

Fastcase

Since LONald's appearance, attorneys and law librarians have come to rely on AI automation and insights and are even asserting themselves as AI developers. One resource growing in popularity among developers is the Fastcase AI Sandbox, which facilitates the testing and development of innovative AI products. DLA Piper, BakerHostetler, and Baker Donelson, are just a few of the law firms using the Fastcase AI Sandbox.[7]

In her AALL 2018 presentation, "Powered by AI, Built in the Law Library," Stacy Pangilinan of DLA Piper talked about her firm's experience using the Fastcase AI Sandbox.[8] DLA Piper is currently in the early stages of working with Sandbox, but they have developed an in-house test model that uses ML and NLP to generate analytics from legal documents. The tool allows them to more rapidly and precisely identify documents targeted for analysis. It then extracts metadata that can be used to produce certain insights. Stacy stressed the importance of beginning the development process with community conversations and training opportunities via think tanks and CLEs. Identifying the right documents for training the machine, metadata quality control, and a focus on quality metrics were also mentioned as important aspects of the development process. Critical to the process, she said, is ensuring librarian involvement and interaction with the data scientists involved in programming the system and librarian input in the design of the user interface.

In addition to their own in-house data, firms can also utilize Fastcase's public legal data repository of judicial opinions, statutes, regulations, and PACER data to run training models. To build the training models themselves, Fastcase has partnered with IBM Watson Developer Cloud, Neota Logic, and LexPredict for experimenting in the AI Sandbox environment.

Casetext

Casetext, an AI-powered legal research platform, now used by thousands of law firms across the country as a more cost-effective alternative to Lexis and Westlaw, uses an AI research assistant named CARA A.I. to find on-point legal resources based on the facts, legal issues, and jurisdictional information the machine extracts from a document. Quinn Emanuel, Fenwick & West, DLA Piper, Baker Donelson, Blank Rome, and Ogletree Deakins are just a few of the firms that have adopted the platform.

Business Law Firm Moye White brought Casetext onboard in May 2018 to assist attorneys in their research on transactions and disputes. With Casetext, the firm hopes to realize greater efficiency and improved outcomes for their clients through smart technology.[9] Attorneys researching complex matters can utilize CARA A.I's document drag-and-drop feature, in conjunction with keywords and Boolean operators, to produce a highly precise set of results instantaneously. The results are more precise because they are based on CARA's "understanding" of the language in the document. Boolean and keyword search alone lack the kind of pattern recognition and context that CARA provides. In addition to surfacing on-point cases, CARA can also harvest results from databases containing other materials such as briefs, holdings, black-letter law, and analyses.

SCOTUSblog is also partnering with Casetext to help their readers access court opinions, statutes, and other primary legal content cited in their posts. SCOTUSblog readers will now see references to court opinions in the blog to direct them to the full text of the opinion published on Casetext. CLE programs and other practical resources for litigators will also be published periodically through the partnership.[10]

SharePoint/Skype

Katherine Lowry of Baker & Hostetler LLP (who was also a presenter at AALL 2018 on the "Powered by AI" panel) discussed the company's Bankruptcy Q&A chatbot, which has been hand-curated with 2000 questions. The bot was developed with SharePoint and uses Skype as the interface. A simple question such as "Do you have the colliers e-book?" results in the chatbot providing a link to the resource in the firm's Lexis digital library. Lowry also described their development of a decision-tree type bot that is designed to help guide a user through a more complex bankruptcy problem.

Law firms often use AI for internal solutions, but AI products can also be built to scale for the global legal services market. Brexit, as a case in point, had the potential to set off a flurry of government and regulatory changes if Great Britain had chosen to leave the European Union on March 29, 2019. With the confusion surrounding Brexit's implementation, businesses whose operations will be impacted will look to future-proof contractual agreements, whatever the Brexit outcome may be.[11] Legal services with a focus on regulatory advice—Brexit's biggest legal challenge—will need technology solutions that can handle large-scale contract review and revision as a result of Brexit.[12]

Luminance

Luminance was the AI platform of choice when CAS, a managed legal service company, launched a review of contracts across their client base to identify obligations and risks associated with Brexit.[13] In its initial analysis of the contract types and pertinent clauses most likely to be affected, CAS found that Luminance was able to identify Brexit-affected contracts 70 percent of the time. Knowing which contracts were vulnerable allowed CAS to correct language in the contracts, then use the corrected contracts to train the system on how to automate detection and correction on a large scale. Luminance's clustering feature allowed for the batching of contracts with particular types of clauses for review by legal advisors, who were then able to flag risks within the system. Ultimately, Luminance reduced the work of reviewing, sorting, and identifying of problematic clauses to hours, as opposed to days.

AI in Libraries and Legal Education

Law librarians are well equipped to drive innovation in the age of AI. As experts in data curating and legal content, librarians should be collaborating with data scientists and computer programmers in the construction and management of these tools. As legal research instructors, law librarians are aware of the importance of preparing practice-ready law students to be equipped to navigate the complexities of tech-centric law firms. For law schools navigating the age of AI, doctrinal training and trial advocacy might soon give way to process engineering, predictive coding, and other technical skills that will be required of future lawyers.[14]

Academic law librarians have been experimenting with artificial intelligence to augment library services since the early 2000's. Roy Balleste, one of the first law librarians to develop a chatbot virtual assistant for Nova Southeastern University Law Library, was one of the first to realize AI's potential, while also recognizing its limitations at that time.[15]

AI in Library Reference

Face-to-face interactions at the reference desk remain a valuable service in libraries, but the demand for virtual reference services is on the rise.[16] This new reality is inspiring the design of a subset of AI tools that can offer quick and easy access to resources and virtual reference experiences. To better serve a new generation of tech-savvy patrons, libraries have turned to chatbots and virtual assistants to answer frequently asked questions and direct users to basic library information and research guides.

Xiaotu

One of the earliest implementations of a library chatbot with advanced natural language abilities was Xiaotu. Developed in 2010 at Tsinghua

University's Library in Beijing, China, Xiaotu can be accessed through China's internet via desktop computer and mobile device. She (Xiaotu is a female name) is also integrated with Renren.com, China's equivalent to Facebook.

Xiaotu can answer broad-based questions or questions tailored specifically for Tsinghua University faculty's areas of expertise. She can search the library's OPAC, as well as China's version of Wikipedia—Baidu Baike. Xiaotu learns from her interactions with patrons and can integrate with other systems.[17]

Xiaotu was developed using ALICE, a natural language chatterbot developed by Richard Wallace in 1995.[18] ALICE is an open-source program currently written in Java, using Artificial Intelligence Markup Language (AIML). Because Xiaotu learns from the people she communicates with, the librarians monitoring Xiaotu discovered that she is susceptible to acquiring bad language. As a result, the library occasionally removes Xiaotu from service to delete any inappropriate content she may have acquired from the public. Xiaotu's tech team calls this "brainwashing." Constant updates are made to her vocabulary to improve her ability to converse.

Statistics published in 2016 report that Xiaotu has approximately 2,000 interactions per month. She maintains a fairly positive reputation with students; however, librarians at Tsinghua report that about 90 percent of the interactions with Xiaotu are for play and do not constitute serious research.[19]

Law Library of Congress Chatbot

The Law Library of Congress has developed a chatbot that is available through its Facebook page via Facebook Messenger. The chatbot connects patrons to research guides, foreign law reports, and primary sources of law that are available on the Law Library of Congress blog, in Custodia Legis, and on its website, Law.gov.

According to Robert Brammer, Legal Information Specialist at the Law Library of Congress, the chatbot is still primarily geared toward handling frequently asked reference questions received at the reference desk and online through "Ask a Librarian." Its responses have been streamlined to make them more compatible with the Facebook Messenger window on a mobile device, and it is now more menu driven, with commands added to its vocabulary that are based on logs of previous user interactions. Brammer hopes to someday rebuild the chatbot in a framework that has better natural language recognition. The chatbot was built using Chatfuel, which offers a free basic plan for beginning developers.

AI in Legal Research

AI is making legal research tools more intuitive. The old methodological paradigm of relying solely on keywords and Boolean operators to return search results is reaching obsolescence. Context (formerly Ravel Law), Neota Logic, RAVN, ROSS, Lex Machina, and NextLaw Labs, among others, are leveraging advancements in AI to build the next generation of legal research platforms.

ROSS Intelligence

Law schools are beginning to incorporate AI tools training into the curriculum with varying degrees of success. In 2017, Northwestern Pritzker Law School entered into a partnership with ROSS Intelligence, a Watson-derived natural language processing legal research platform. Pritzker planned to integrate ROSS training into law courses and library research, with a special focus on access to justice issues. Students would also have an opportunity for hands-on experience with ROSS through a fellowship that involved partner institutions, Illinois Legal Aid Online, and Lawyers Trust Fund of Illinois.

Pritzker's partnership with ROSS began with momentum, but has since fizzled, according to Jesse Bowman, Associate Law Librarian for Technology Initiatives and Instruction at the Pritzker Legal Research Center. Bowman says he is uncertain of whether Pritzker's partnership with ROSS has officially ended, but he has not seen any movement on the project as of late.

Robot Lawyer LISA/DoNotPay

During the 2018 fall semester, Professor Andrew Torrence at the University of Kansas School of Law taught a Legal Analytics course using Robot Lawyer LISA, an AI platform that creates non-disclosure agreements and property contracts, and DoNotPay, a popular AI web-based program that handles traffic tickets and will soon provide tools for divorce disputes (DoNotPay is discussed later in this chapter).

"We were able to use an . . . AI [tool] to analyze an existing contract to find errors and suggest improvements across all major legal jurisdictions around the world," Torrance said. "Perhaps most fun was a free AI [tool] that drafts appeals to parking tickets in the United States or United Kingdom, even citing case law where appropriate." "It's not attorneys who demand these new approaches," Torrence added, "it's clients, who want better, faster, and less expensive legal advice, and will ruthlessly seek out attorneys who are most adept at providing it."[20]

LawX

LawX, a legal design lab created at the law school at Brigham Young University to address issues with access to legal services, debuted in the fall of 2017 for second- and third-year law students. The lab, developed by dean Gordon Smith and professor and practicing attorney Kimball D. Parker, aimed to close the gap in access to legal services for the underserved. The course was structured "as a design-thinking process, in which students will have fast-paced deadlines and responsibilities that are much like being in a startup. The course will be an immersive, hands-on experience by law students in collaboration with students and professors in other departments at BYU."[21]

The course has since produced a document automation tool for Utah debt collection cases. In 2018, the project began a partnership with the University of Arizona's Innovation for Justice program to teach parallel classes, which will develop AI tools to reduce evictions in Utah and Arizona.[22]

AI in Technical Services

As digital objects gain prominence in library collections, creating descriptive metadata for these materials will become increasingly time-intensive for technical services staff. As such, librarians are seeking ways to produce quality metadata for large digital collections in a more timely and efficient manner.

To address the need for more efficient metadata cataloging for their large collections, the J. Willard Marriott Library at the University of Utah recently received a Catalyst Fund Grant from Lyrasis to find a way to automate metadata creation for images using machine learning. The project, "Machine Learning Meets Library Archives," is currently developing a model for applying machine learning techniques to extract useful information from historical images to increase the efficiency of metadata creation for archives, libraries, and museums of all types.[23]

The project has four phases. The first phase, currently under way, involves setting up the hardware and selecting a ML program. Initially, Google's TensorFlow—an open-source, deep-learning software solution developed by engineers in Google's Deep Brain initiative—is being used, as is Weka, another open-source, ML solution. The AI software will then be loaded with pre-training data models.

Phase two will involve data preparation on approximately 450,000+ manually curated historical images in Marriott's digital library. These images have already been cataloged with high-quality metadata, so about 80 percent of the collection will be used as training data to enhance the model. Metadata will be extracted as XML or JSON, then converted to a format compatible with the machine-learning platform.

In phase three, the training data set will be loaded into the machine so that it can learn how to suggest useful metadata in the form of keywords and image captions.

As with most AI training models, this is an iterative process that includes loading training data into the system, running the machine-training model, comparing the results against a pre-determined threshold for accuracy, and tweaking the system to achieve the needed results. These steps are repeated until the threshold accuracy is achieved. The test will be considered a success when the machine-generated metadata is comparable to the human-created metadata.

Once they have perfected their model, the Marriott Library will make the source code available on github.com, a software development platform that hosts open access projects. Law libraries that wish to use the algorithm will be able to access it for free on github.com, hopefully in the near future.

AI in Access to Justice

Innovative AI tools are being developed to address gaps and inefficiencies in the provision of legal services for the underserved. These tools are designed to be easy to use, are freely available online, and can direct users to helpful resources and/or potential legal representation.

Basic legal advice on eviction, divorce, bankruptcy, or estate planning is currently out of reach for many Americans. The 2017 Justice Gap Report found that 86 percent of Americans with civil legal problems receive either inadequate or no legal help.[24] Machines currently cannot provide complex legal advice, but online legal services powered by AI are making basic legal help more accessible and cost-effective.

DoNotPay

Chatbots and virtual assistants democratize access to basic legal services for the underserved. Perhaps the most well-known legal chatbot at the moment is DoNotPay, an online tool that guides users through a series of questions designed to dispute parking tickets. In recent months, the DoNotPay chatbot has expanded considerably to address a variety of legal concerns including consumer rights, employment law, and landlord-tenant disputes. Soon, the creator of the site, Josh Browder, hopes to offer a chatbot that can handle divorces.[25]

Hate Crime Help

Hate Crime Help, a project of the American Bar Association's Center for Innovation and CuroLegal, helps people who have been victims of hate crimes involving violence, verbal attacks, property damage, and harassment. The app allows a user to identify whether a crime was motivated by discrimination based on race, ethnicity, religion, immigration status, gender, or sexual orientation. Resources localized to the user's zip code are made available after a series of questions are answered. Information resources on hate crime statutes are available as well.[26]

ProTechMe

ProTechMe, a chatbot originally designed for Harris County, Texas, and based on the Texas Attorney General's Protective Order kit, collects information needed for securing a protective order.[27] The information gathered via the chatbot auto-populates a PDF document that the user can then print out and submit to the district attorney or to a legal aid office. Victims of family violence are often closely monitored by their abusers, so using the internet to search for help may not be a safe option. The chatbot offers a secure environment, tailored to the specific needs of this population.

Learned Hands

Learned Hands, a project of Stanford Legal Design Lab and Suffolk's Legal Innovation and Technology Lab, is an online game that uses crowdsourcing to tag some 75,000 legal questions taken from Reddit's legal advice board, with lay legal terms found in common language. The legal terms used to tag the questions are derived from a taxonomy of lay legal terms being developed as part of the project. When completed, the tagged legal questions will serve as a training dataset for an algorithm that will be used to guide people to the appropriate legal resource, based on the question they asked. Court websites, online legal research tools, and web-based access to justice portals could all potentially benefit from the use of the algorithm.

Anyone can play the game, but the participation of legal content experts, including law librarians, would be particularly valuable. The game can be accessed at https://learnedhands.law.stanford.edu.

Conclusion

The use cases mentioned in this chapter illustrate the growing ubiquity of AI's presence in law firms and law libraries today. Though we might not always be aware of AI's presence in our everyday lives or fully appreciate its potential, law librarians can benefit from an awareness of the different types of AI products in use and the processes involved in developing them. Equally important is an awareness of the value that law librarians can bring to the evolution of AI technology going forward.

NOTES

1. "RELX Group Survey Reveals Gap between Awareness and Implementation for AI and Machine Learning in the US," RELX Group Press Release, November 15, 2018, https://www.relx.com/media/press-releases/year-2018/emerging-tech.
2. Ed Walters et al., "Powered by AI, Built in the Law Library" (presentation, 2018 AALL Annual Meeting & Conference, Baltimore, Maryland, July 15, 2018), https://www.aallnet.org/recording/aall2018-poweredbyai.
3. Gary E. Marchant, "Artificial Intelligence and the Future of Legal Practice," *SciTech Lawyer,* November 1, 2017, https://www.americanbar.org/groups/science_technology/publications/scitech_lawyer/2017/fall/artificial-intelligence-and-future-legal-practice/.
4. Bloomberg BNA, "Bloomberg Law Launches Artificial Intelligence Solution to Deliver Faster, Smarter Case Law Research," Bloomberg BNA Press Release, September 26, 2017, https://www.prnewswire.com/news-releases/bloomberg-law-launches-artificial-intelligence-solution-to-deliver-faster-smarter-case-law-research-300525512.html.
5. Nancy B. Talley, "Imagining the Use of Intelligent Agents and Artificial Intelligence in Academic Law Libraries," *Law Library Journal* 108, no. 3. (Summer 2016): 383–402.
6. Joanna Goodman, *Robots in Law: How Artificial Intelligence Is Transforming Legal Services* (Peoria, IL: ARK Group, 2016).
7. Sean Tate, "Fastcase, BakerHostetler, DLA Piper, Baker Donelson, and AmLaw 100 Law Firms Reveal Unique Insights with AI Sandbox," *fastcase* (blog), https://www.fastcase.com/blog/fastcase-bakerhostetler-dla-piper-baker-donelson-and-amlaw-100-law-firms-reveal-unique-insights-with-ai-sandbox/.
8. Walters et al., "Powered by AI, Built in the Law Library."
9. Erin Harrison, "Business Law Firm Moye White Launches Casetext," *castext* (blog), May 17, 2018, https://blog.casetext.com/business-law-firm-moye-white-launches-casetext-385f0e485eb.

10. Tom Goldstein, "SCOTUSblog Is Partnering with Casetext," *SCOTUSblog,* February 28, 2019, https://www.scotusblog.com/2019/02/scotusblog-is-partnering-with-casetext/.
11. David Silbert, "Using AI Contract Analysis to Achieve Deeper and Clearer Preparedness for Brexit," Artificial Lawyer, November 6, 2018, https://www.artificiallawyer.com/2018/11/06/using-ai-contract-analysis-to-prepare-for-brexit-seal-software/.
12. Joanna Morris and Jim Leason, "Catalyst or Catastrophe: How Brexit Will Impact Law Firms?" https://info.legal-solutions.thomsonreuters.co.uk/brexit-impact-law-firms.
13. Luminance, "Luminance Customer Case Study: Brexit Compliance Review," https://www.luminance.com/files/case-studies/CAS%20Brexit%20Compliance.pdf.
14. Marchant, "Artificial Intelligence and the Future of Legal Practice."
15. Talley, "Imagining the Use of Intelligent Agents and and Artificial Intelligence in Academic Law Libraries."
16. Stephen P. Buss, "Do We Still Need Reference Services in the Age of Google and Wikipedia?" *The Reference Librarian* 57, n. 4 (2016): 265-71.
17. Fei Yao, Chengyu Zhang, and Wu Chen, "Smart Talking Robot Xiaotu: Participatory Library Service Based on Artificial Intelligence," *Library Hi Tech,* June 15, 2015.
18. Wikipedia, "Artificial Linguistic Internet Computer Entity," https://en.wikipedia.org/wiki/Artificial_Linguistic_Internet_Computer_Entity.
19. IOP, "Xiao Tu the Talking Robot at Tsinghua University Library," January 9, 2016, https://ioppublishing.org/news/xiao-tu-the-talking-robot/.
20. Ed Silverstein, "University of Kansas School of Law Brings AI to the Classroom," December 26, 2018, https://www.law.comlegaltechnews/2018/12/26/university-of-kansas-school-of-law-brings-ai-to-the-classroom/.
21. Joe Hadfield, "BYU Law Launches LawX, an Idea Incubator within a Classroom," June 19, 2017, https://news.byu.edu/news/byu-law-launches-lawx-idea-incubator-within-classroom.
22. Zach Warren, "Year Two of BYU's LawX Initiative Has a New Focus and a New Partner: The University of Arizona," Law.com, August 14, 2018, https://www.law.com/legaltechnews/2018/08/14/year-two-of-byus-lawx-initiative-has-a-new-focus-and-a-new-partner-the-university-of-arizona/.
23. Gary Price, "Machine Learning Meets Library Archives: Lyrasis Catalyst Funded Project Form the University of Utah," (Video) https://www.infodocket.com/2018/12/06/new-video-machine-learning-meets-library-archives-lyrasis-catalyst-funded-project-from-the-university-of-utah/.
24. "The Justice Gap: Measuring the Unmet Civil Legal Needs of Low-Income Americans, 2017 Justice Report," Legal Services Corporation, https://www.lsc.gov/justicegap2017.

25. Elliott Krause, "This Robot Will Handle Your Divorce Free of Charge," *The Wall Street Journal* online, October 26, 2017, https://www.wsj.com/articles/this-robot-will-handle-your-divorce-free-of-charge-1522341583.
26. CuroLegal, "Curo Announces Launch of Hate Crime Help," September 21, 2017, https://www.curolegal.com/curo-announces-launch-hate-crime-help/.
27. Christy Leos and Ian Coldwater, "ProTechMe: A Chatbot That Collects Protective Order Info Quickly & Efficiently," https://github.com/TechForJustice/protechme.

GRACE BOIVIN

6
Opportunities for Law Librarians

Over the past century, law libraries have evolved along with shifting economies and technological developments to reflect changes in the legal industry. They have transitioned from large spaces serving as showpieces of firms' interior designs, to reduced physical spaces and primarily digital collections, to librarians not working in "libraries" at all, but instead embedded in the practice groups, technology groups, and knowledge management departments. The adaptability of the information profession has enabled law librarians to remain essential members of the organizations they serve. As the artificial intelligence (AI) revolution enters workplaces, it will fall on librarians to adapt to the new challenges and tremendous opportunities it will create for the legal industry and workplaces as a whole.

The majority of the current AI applications for the legal market utilize machine-learning (ML) technology, providing new ways to access large sets of data to answer questions and draw insights. As professionals

GRACE BOIVIN is a KM administrator at Fox Rothschild LLP.

focus on providing access to vast amounts of information, managing data, and providing meaningful answers to information needs, librarians are perfect partners in facilitating the adoption of AI across the legal profession. AI-enabled solutions offer librarians enhanced capabilities to meet business needs and solve problems by creating efficiencies and offering higher levels of service. Individuals willing to step outside their comfort zones and embrace the challenges of understanding and adopting new AI-enabled solutions will be poised to take on new responsibilities in their organizations and create novel career paths.

Trends in the Legal Market

Beyond the media hype that AI has received, surveys show that its integration into the legal market has begun. However, there is a large spectrum of adoption by firms, with some making no investment in innovation, while others are in advanced stages. In a 2017 survey by legal consulting firm Altman Weil, more than half (54.6 percent) of the largest firms surveyed with more than 1,000 lawyers were "already using tools involving AI" and none of them identified themselves as being "unaware of legal technology developments."[1] Outside the largest grouping, the survey found firms to be much more at the early stages of technology adoption. In the smallest-sized firms surveyed with between 50 and 99 lawyers, only 5.7 percent said they were "already using tools involved with AI," and 38.3 percent were "unaware of legal technology developments." In total, the survey found that across the 386 firms questioned, "only 7.5 percent of firms said they have begun to make use of legal AI tools, and another 29 percent are beginning to explore their options." The remaining approximately 64 percent of firms were either not making efforts toward AI solutions or not even aware of these technological trends.[2]

A 2018 survey by analytics company RELX Group compared AI adoption across industries and found that legal industry leaders were one of the least likely groups to take advantage of AI or other emerging technologies.[3] Only 44 percent of law firm leaders surveyed said they offer employee training on these technologies, 26 percent said they do not use AI or ML in their work, and 12 percent were not aware of the use of ML by others in their industry. In contrast, across all industries surveyed, 56 percent reported employing ML or AI in their businesses.[4]

It is important to consider what might be holding legal organizations back from embracing innovation. ALM Legal Intelligence identifies having clean, prepared, and reliable data, the right talent onboard, and the fostering of a flexible and open-minded culture as some of the key building blocks of AI in legal organizations.[5] However, they point out that these building blocks can also be major roadblocks for legal organizations. Other obstacles preventing firms from adopting AI-enabled solutions include the impact alternate services could have on typical attorney compensation and fee arrangement models. If attorneys are spending time testing and training solutions, how will that affect their billable hours requirements, how will fees be credited for on-demand AI solutions where clients will pay a flat fee, and how will fees billed shift from paying for hours worked to clients paying for expertise and results?[6] ALM asserts that firms tend to respond best to client demand, whereas some of these innovations would be unsolicited changes to procedures and require proactive work by firms to present these innovations to clients. Lastly, successful AI implementation requires patience and investment in time and effort from those at the top of the organization. To achieve the necessary culture changes, advocates for AI must communicate their vision for solutions over the long term and secure buy-in from key stakeholders.[7]

Law librarians are perfectly situated to capitalize on these trends and address the roadblocks that legal organizations face. While firm administration and leaders spearhead advancements and new innovation groups at some of the largest firms, the librarians on the ground using AI enhanced tools every day and seeing the potential application of these solutions are perfect partners in this transformation across all firm sizes, courts, public law libraries, and law schools. In a presentation at the AALL 2018 Annual Meeting, Ed Walters, CEO at Fastcase, described the skills required to create solutions using AI as the "literacies of information professionals for the rest of the twenty-first century."[8] As natural problem solvers and content owners of crucial information resources, adaptable law librarians leading efforts in the education and adoption of AI tools and solutions will establish themselves as key players in this new landscape and "future-proof" their careers in the process.[9]

Future-Ready Skills

As AI expands into more workplaces, there is no doubt that employers will recruit highly technical developers with advanced knowledge of new technologies. However, beyond the most technical positions, there are indispensable skills and approaches that will set professionals apart. Experts forecasting changes in the workforce over the next ten years predict the most important characteristic will be a mindset shift toward cultures of lifelong learning and educational growth.[10] They describe a focus on continuous educational opportunities, training in new resources, and advanced literacy skills, echoing philosophies that have long been inherent in the mission of libraries.

A recent report from Accenture and the Aspen Institute Business & Society Program on the skills required for successful human and AI collaboration refers to the "missing middle skills" or the "uniquely human" higher-level intelligence abilities that bridge the gap between intelligent technology and jobs exclusively performed by humans.[11] To grow these skills, employees must develop a "lifelong learning mindset," while employers must invest in skills development and "nourish the desire and capability of people."[12] In the new AI-based workplace, the skills required will not necessarily be expertise in ML or robot programming, but rather companies will "require thoughtful people who are better able to apply socio-emotional, creative, and complex reasoning skills to the specific needs of the business." Companies will rely on individuals who demonstrate the skills to visualize AI solutions, are willing to test multiple iterations, and possess the communication skills required to evangelize for solutions across the organization.[13]

Steps to Build Understanding of Legal AI

In addition to the intelligence skills already described, librarians can take practical steps to increase their own understanding of how others in the legal industry are utilizing technology, in order to leverage existing skills and develop a career working with AI.[14]

Become familiar with how leading players are using these tools

Explore new technologies and their capabilities and improve understanding of how leading players in the industry are changing their business models. Understand applications of AI for the practice of law and in improving the business of law. Attend online seminars and conferences to increase understanding of these trends. For law librarians, organizations including the American Association of Law Libraries (AALL) and the International Legal Technology Association (ILTA) offer frequent programming and publications providing educational content, case studies, and overviews of AI technologies in the legal industry. Set up email alerts to receive daily headlines of new articles and blog posts on legal technology. If you do not have someone in your organization that can serve as a mentor in acquiring these skills, consider connecting with others in your network or professional association that can provide guidance and feedback.

Find ways to use this knowledge in your current role

Focus on what brings value to your organization and clients. Start talking to people and understand their processes: What is not working? Where are the slow downs and problems? Ask people about their biggest pain points in their current work and processes. Then, build off your knowledge of the industry and products, and think about whether solutions exist in the market that might address these needs. Begin systematically mapping out the current processes your organization uses, and explore possible solutions for creating efficiencies.

Train yourself in the technologies

Through your organization or on your own, embrace the educational mindset just described, take classes, and test and build solutions. Keep in mind this growth will be part of adapting to the new workplace and will help you acquire essential literacies. Find employer-sponsored opportunities to gain these skills, or utilize online courses and tutorials in various technologies, such as MOOCs (massive open online courses) or those offered by Coursera. Practice utilizing tools like Microsoft Visio to map out current processes within the library and across your organization. Explore AI features in your current resources, such as smart search and analytics functions, and become your library's expert in them. Understand how they process information, and learn the limitations of their content sets and data. Investigate using raw data from the AI provider or an application programming interface (API) to create additional applications of the data.

Transition to an AI-based role at your organization or elsewhere

As you apply the knowledge you have acquired to your current role and connect with individuals within your organization with similar growth mindsets, you might find that your current role shifts to integrate these skills into your position and that you become an important member of the team driving innovation and creating real solutions for your organization. Being proactive with developing these skills will set you apart from others less willing to expand the responsibilities of their positions. As AI integrates into workplaces, organizations across many industries will be seeking individuals with future-ready skills who are willing to look for solutions to create efficiencies while deeply understanding business needs.

Opportunities from the Law Library

It is a misconception that in order to start innovation initiatives, you must be in a position of leadership or reside in a technology department. The building blocks of AI for legal organizations identified by ALM—data management, skilled staff, and adaptability—are already common emphases of law libraries.[15] Law librarians have a "unique institutional advantage" in overcoming the roadblocks already outlined.[16] Librarians are the members of their organizations better suited to take the time to learn and use new tools, and to educate the organization on those tools, than busy lawyers focused on billable work and law professors already stretched between teaching and publishing commitments. The first step for librarians in seizing the opportunities presented by AI will be embracing their role as change agents and becoming champions for AI from their current positions and organizations, building upon already well-established skills and experience.

Collection Development—Making Sense of the Ever-Expanding Legal Tech Market

Today's legal technology market is experiencing a flood of new products. Established publishers like LexisNexis, Bloomberg Law, and Westlaw are making frequent announcements about new AI-enhanced features, while startups and nonlegal software developers are focusing their attention on the legal market. "From 2017 to 2018, LawGeex found an increase of 65 percent in legal tech companies utilizing AI."[17] Crunchbase reported that in the first month of 2018 alone, legal technology startups raised over $49 million in funding, compared with $1.25 million in Q1 2017.[18] For organizations trying to keep track of new releases and players in this field, the pace can be overwhelming.

Librarians skilled in collection development can play a vital role in the evaluation and ongoing review of the deluge of new products. They possess established review techniques, trial and piloting procedures, and a deep understanding how potential products fit in with other resources, culture, and processes across the organization. They have the capacity and experience to manage the lifecycle of resources, continually review products, and keep up-to-date with constant changes in content and features. Firm and university administration, practice group chairpersons, and other key stakeholders need team members who can synthesize and compare tools, and succinctly summarize features and potential use cases throughout the organization.

Researchers—Expert Insights and Applications

Research librarians are experts in using legal resources and possess a firsthand understanding of resources' shortcomings. These librarians interact with users from across the organization and understand information needs from varied constituents. In utilizing AI-enhanced research tools, librarians can see what is going to have the greatest impact and application across all areas. As expert users of research tools, they can also identify gaps in products and work with vendors, lawyers, and clients directly to customize tools and clarify content sets and information.

Research librarians offer patrons the ability to take research out of lawyers' hands and have it performed more efficiently by experts aware of all available internal and external resources. By embracing AI-enhanced research tools and becoming experts in their benefits and limitations, librarians can reduce time spent per research question and increase precision. With tools like CARA A.I. from Casetext, users have the ability to go beyond the use of traditional Boolean and natural language search strings to using entire litigation documents and client emails as the search language. Just as librarians have shepherded their organizations to utilizing electronic resources and constantly evolving content from providers, they also must guide their firms through the integration of smart search functionality into existing research practices. As the technology around legal research continues to improve, librarians have a responsibility to educate themselves and their organizations on transitioning their search strategies appropriately.

Legal analytics present another area where research librarians can become experts and advocates. As of only a few years ago, an attorney looking for case statistics could only access court-supplied reports with basic information on caseloads and timing. The incredible insights now available from legal analytics providers can go beyond reports of total numbers of cases and show typical timing of cases, damages, outcomes, and rulings by motion type. A simple judicial profile can be enhanced with tremendous information that can inform an entire litigation strategy. However, it will fall on research librarians to educate their organizations on these tools and use simple research requests as opportunities to demonstrate the breadth of information available and start putting example insights in front of users.

Library Education and Training

As other industries adopt AI innovations and solutions become more mainstream across the legal field, attorneys will need to understand the market of tools available and how they can be best utilized in order to keep up with outside demands from clients, competitors, and judges. For librarians, information literacy instruction that helps users understand how to find, read, and interpret information as accurate and authoritative takes on increasing importance as the technologies supplying that information become increasingly sophisticated. Again, promotion of new tools and demonstration of how they can fit within attorneys' regular workflow will be crucial to help build awareness over time. Law schools and firms must find ways to build these tools into their existing resource training programs and consider offering additional educational opportunities, such as boot camps, workshops, and technology fairs, to aid in fostering a growth culture around technology.

In-House in the Library

These aforementioned examples describe possibilities for libraries to promote use of AI to their organizations. However, another large area of opportunity is to lead by example and focus on developing internal solutions to improve upon longstanding library processes. Librarians can use these tools directly for their own services and document collections, not just in a client service model. AI solutions can help libraries draw important insights from in-house data such as budget allocations, resource usage data, and reference requests statistics. Libraries can use these tools to

- convert large collections of documents into structured text to be searched and analyzed;
- automate cataloging and materials processing;
- build better search engines across firms' knowledge management systems; and
- build chatbots using natural language processing (NLP) to help answer common ready reference requests and provide basic library services during off hours.[19]

By creating successful internal solutions, libraries also have the ability to demonstrate the potential value and benefits of investing in these projects to other stakeholders in the firm. The key is that libraries must embrace the creativity required to become makers of solutions and become proactive to use technology to elevate services even if it requires additional training. By starting internally, libraries have the opportunity to build awareness and enthusiasm for bigger undertakings across the organization.

Opportunities for New Roles and Careers

Today, the skills of law librarians rarely fit in the confines of the terms "law" and "libraries." Librarians possessing the expertise just described are already finding positions inside other environments, such as technology departments, practice management groups, legal innovation labs, consulting firms, and technology companies. As the efficiencies offered by AI continue to change the structure of workplaces, opportunities for growth beyond library walls will exist for librarians that are willing to take the leap from traditional positions to embrace the potential applications of twenty-first century information skills.

Academic Innovation Labs

Over the past several years, academic law libraries have become a major breeding ground for experimentation and innovation in the legal tech field. Innovation labs are being created often as offshoots of or housed within traditional law school libraries, creating spaces where students, academics, organizations and vendors can come together to imagine, test, iterate, and launch new solutions. For many law schools, these labs have gone beyond technology and taken on a focus toward using innovation to improve existing systems and increase access to justice. Teaming up with local organizations such as legal aid groups and policy strategists, classes, "hackathons," research projects, and other initiatives focus on designing new tools, services, and policies.[20] Example projects include:

Harvard Law School Library Innovation Lab's Caselaw Access Project, which makes all U.S. case law freely available online with an API and bulk data service.[21] This is the first time in U.S. history where the public will have open and wide-ranging access to this information.

Suffolk University Law School's Legal Innovation and Technology Lab and Standard University Law School's Legal Design Lab have collaborated, along with funding and support from The Pew Charitable Trusts, to develop a dataset to support a natural language processor. The goal is to develop an AI application to interpret questions regarding legal issues searched by individuals with no legal training using plain English terminology and help guide them to relevant legal information.[22]

Law Firms

Many law firms are beginning to focus efforts toward alternative approaches to generate revenue, going beyond the billable hour service model already discussed. In some cases, this has led firms to change their organizational structure to include administrators and departments focused on integrating business strategy and technology that would provide internal and client-facing solutions, such as the support of practice groups, the leveraging of technology innovations, and the creation of novel ideas to address client issues. Leading firms in this area have designed subsidiaries built around providing alternative and fixed-fee legal services.[23] Individuals with library backgrounds are transitioning to positions within these new structures in firms, marrying their knowledge of data and information resources together with the understanding of the latest technology, knowledge management, and business process improvement.

Emerging roles for librarians in firms include the following examples of positions where individuals managing the library are also deeply involved with innovation leadership:

BakerHostetler's Director of Practice Services reports to the Chief Information Officer. The role infuses information and research services, knowledge management, and training together with the integration of business applications and business process improvement solutions. In addition, this position oversees the firm's legal innovation group focused on integrating blockchain technology, AI, and advanced analytics.[24]

Greenberg Traurig's Director of Knowledge Solutions oversees the firm's library teams, along with knowledge management, research and intelligence, licensing and contract negotiation, and outreach and education initiatives, while also serving as a member of a firmwide innovation team. This team includes attorneys, firm leadership, and administrative department directors focused on promoting an innovative culture and encouraging adoption of new solutions.[25]

Reed Smith's Chief Knowledge Officer oversees a team of legal engineers as part of the firms Practice Innovation Team. Many on this team have legal backgrounds, and others are technologists. Their role in the firm is to serve as a bridge connecting technology to attorneys looking to develop efficiencies in services and incorporate legal analytics into business and practice decisions.[26]

Technology and Consulting Companies

The legal market is exploding with new technology companies, startups, and consultants offering solutions to navigate the new legal landscape. Law librarians transitioning their careers outside of legal organizations are finding important roles in these organizations. Providers marketing their services to the legal industry seek individuals possessing the same important combination of understanding information resources and a deep ability to recognize firm culture and client needs. As the structure of organizations changes and the legal industry continues to shift, librarians can find many opportunities to apply their skills outside the context of traditional legal organizations. Text box 6.1 provides an

TEXT BOX 6.1

Case Study—A librarian working for an AI solutions provider[27]

Kira Systems is a contract analytics company based in Toronto, Canada. Their product uses ML to review large sets of documents related to due diligence projects. Kira works by categorizing large groups of documents uploaded by users; users then assign them to specific coworkers by document type, allowing the right people to review them in the most efficient manner. Kira provides many built-in fields within the documents to extract crucial information for each reviewer by content type. In early 2018, Kira began recruiting to fill the position of Machine Learning Knowledge Analyst, and as specifically described in the job announcement, they were seeking the unique skill set of a law librarian.[28] The position focuses on managing the taxonomy behind Kira's software—the structure used to "teach" the AI how to classify documents. The process requires a lot of research, time, and documentation, even before beginning to train the AI to learn the document types.

Kira hired Karen Anello for the position, who started her career as an academic business research librarian before transitioning eight years later to work in law firm libraries. She now works alongside a team of former lawyers on Kira's Legal Engineering Team. After Anello finds contracts to use to train the system, the lawyers work with the contracts to find specific provisions that fall within their areas of specialization, allowing users to access many insights about specific contracts with just a simple upload. For example, the system can be taught how to find specific financial terms that would signal a need for review in the event of a regulatory change.

In addition to requiring large amounts of research, Anello helps other teams in creating internal taxonomies and assists in database trials and negotiations. She states that one of the most valuable skills she has developed working in traditional libraries is the ability to take part in and lead various technology projects. She describes keen research skills: using technology to organize and locate information, as well as providing training to other users as key qualifications. She often uses reference interview skills to hone the information requests she receives from others in her organization.

overview of one librarian's experience transitioning to a role working for an AI technology company.

Conclusion

Pundits might speculate about a future robot age where machines will replace workers. However, the reality for the foreseeable future is that the skill sets of law librarians are undoubtedly relevant to the evolving legal industry. Individuals who are not afraid to ask the right questions of their current processes, seek out educational opportunities, and keep an open mind to changing organizational structures will be able to ride the AI wave and navigate the changes to come. As AI advances, library services might continue to evolve and certain tasks once performed by libraries might become increasingly automated. However, the adaptability and value of information professionals will continue to find enormous demand in innovative knowledge organizations.

RECOMMENDED READING LIST

Ambrogi, Robert. "Turning Challenges into Opportunities: New Directions for Legal Information Professionals." *LawSites* (blog), October 28, 2014. https://www.lawsitesblog.com/2014/10/turning-challenges-opportunities-new-directions-legal-information-profes sionals.html.

Bailey, Scott D. "Leveraging Research Analytics to Build Insight and Revenue." *JDSupra*, January 10, 2019. https://www.jdsupra.com/legalnews/leveraging-research-analytics-to-build-35697.

Duffer, Ellen. "Libraries Look to Serve as Leaders in Equitable AI Education." *Forbes*, January 28, 2019. https://www.forbes.com/sites/ellenduffer/2019/01/28/libraries-look-to-serve-as-leaders-in-equitable-ai-education.

Neary, Mary Ann and Sherry Xin Chen. "Artificial Intelligence: Legal Research and Law Librarians." *AALL Spectrum* 21, no. 5 (2017): 16–20.

Nobile, Jeremy. "Blind Justice No More: Law Firms Embrace AI, Other Emerging Tech." *Crain's Cleveland Business*, January 19, 2019. https://www.crainscleveland.com/legal/blind-justice-no-more-law-firms-embrace-ai-other-emerging-tech.

Talley, Nancy B. Talley. "Imagining the Use of Intelligent Agents and Artificial Intelligence in Academic Law Libraries." *Law Library Journal* 108, no. 3 (2016): 383–401.

NOTES

1. Thomas S. Clay and Eric A. Seeger, *2017 Law Firms in Transition: An Altman Weil Flash Survey* (Newtown Square, PA: Altman Weil, 2017), 122.
2. Clay and Seeger, 13.
3. Xiumei Dong, "Survey Finds Legal Industry in Last Place in AI, Machine Learning Adoption," *The Recorder*, November 19, 2018, https://www.law.com/therecorder/2018/11/19/survey-finds-legal-industry-in-last-place-in-ai-machine-learning-adoption.
4. Dong, *The Recorder*.
5. Erin Hichman, *Law Firms Need Artificial Intelligence to Stay in the Game* (New York, NY: ALM Intelligence, 2018), 16.
6. Hichman, 16.
7. Hichman, 16.
8. Ed Walters, "Powered by AI, Built in the Law Library" (presentation, 2018 AALL Annual Meeting & Conference, Baltimore, Maryland, July 15, 2018), https://www.aallnet.org/recording/aall2018-poweredbyai.
9. Walters, "Powered by AI, Built in the Law Library."
10. Jacques Bughin et al., *Skill Shift Automation and the Future of the Workforce* (2018), McKinsey Global Institute, 2018.
11. Paul Daugherty, Eva Sage-Gavin, Madhu Vazirani, and Miguel Padro, *Advancing Missing Middle Skills for Human-AI Collaboration* (2018), Accenture and Aspen Institute Business & Society Program, 4–11.
12. Daugherty et al., 3.
13. Andy Betts, "Building an AI Mindset: Time to Identify and Develop Skill Sets Now," *MarTech Today*, March 21, 2018, https://martechtoday.com/building-ai-mindset-time-identify-develop-skill-sets-now-212672.
14. Framework for steps based on Singh, Tarry, "Skill Up Your Career for the New AI Economy," *Forbes*, September 19, 2018, https://www.forbes.com/sites/cognitiveworld/2018/09/19/skill-up-your-career-for-the-new-ai-economy.
15. Hichman, *Law Firms*, 16.
16. Ed Walters, "Read/Write: Artificial Intelligence Libraries," *AALL Spectrum*, September/October 2017, 23.
17. LawGeex, *In House Counsel's Legal Tech Buyers Guide* (2018), 9, https://www.lawgeex.com/resources/buyersguide.
18. Crunchbase fundraising tearsheets.
19. Walters, "Read/Write," 22.
20. Margaret Hagan, "Justice Innovation with Law School Design Labs," *Dialogue* (ABA Division of Legal Services), June 15, 2018, https://www.americanbar.org/groups/legal_services/publications/dialogue/volume/21/spring-2018/iolta-design-labs.

21. "Project: Caselaw Access Project," Harvard Law Library Innovation Lab, accessed February 27, 2019, https://lil.law.harvard.edu/projects/caselaw-access-project.
22. Erika Richard and Lester Bird, "How Artificial Intelligence Could Improve Access to Legal Education," *The PEW Charitable Trusts*, January 24, 2019, https://www.pewtrusts.org/en/research-and-analysis/articles/2019/01/24/how-artificial-intelligence-could-improve-access-to-legal-information.
23. Roy Strom, "Wilson Sonsini Launches Software Developer Subsidiary to Automate Legal Services," *The American Lawyer*, February 5, 2019, https://www.law.com/americanlawyer/2019/02/05/wilson-sonsini-launches-software-developer-subsidiary-to-automate-legal-services.
24. Gregg Wirth, "KM, AI & Client Engagement: The Changing Role of Law Firm Librarians, Part 1," *Legal Executive Institute* (blog), http://www.legalexecutiveinstitute.com/changing-role-law-firm-librarians-lowry-bakerhostetler-part-1.
25. "Spotlight on Innovation in Law Firm Knowledge Management," *On Firmer Ground* (blog), April 20, 2018, https://firmerground.wordpress.com/2018/04/10/spotlight-on-innovation-in-knowledge-management.
26. Ava Chisling, "The Many New Faces of Law," *Ross Intelligence* (blog), December 13, 2017, https://blog.rossintelligence.com/post/many-new-faces-law.
27. Karen Anello (Machine Learning Knowledge Analyst, Kira Systems), in discussion with the author, February 2019.
28. Jean O'Grady, "Kira Is Hiring a Librarian – I Mean – A Machine Learning Knowledge Analyst," *Dewey B Strategic* (blog), February 14, 2018, https://www.deweybstrategic.com/2018/02/kira-is-hiring-a-librarian-i-mean-a-machine-learning-knowledge-analyst.html.

JAMIE J. BAKER

7

AI and Legal Research

The use of artificial intelligence (AI) in legal research is increasing as more legal technology companies with products powered by AI enter the market. These companies hope to gain a market share by disrupting the field and revolutionizing the way that law librarians and lawyers conduct legal research.

While these new systems create unprecedented efficiencies in the legal research process, law librarians and lawyers relying on AI must be cognizant of performing ethical legal research in light of the ABA's Duty of Technology Competence. This will be difficult as proprietary algorithms are used to determine relevant results with a lack of transparency that does not allow the end user to understand how the algorithms generated the results.

In addition, as algorithms are used to select relevant case precedent that is used to advance the law, there is a substantial risk of

JAMIE J. BAKER is an associate dean and director of the Texas Tech University School of Law Library, and the author of *The Ginger (Law) Librarian.*

underlying biases becoming embedded in the law. Lawyers must take into account the pitfalls associated with blindly relying on AI to perform legal research and act in their fiduciary capacity to create the best legal arguments for their clients that are the result of their own independent, educated judgment.

Definition of AI Used in Legal Research

AI encompasses a wide subset of technology tools; therefore, it is helpful to start with a basic definition. The *MIT Technology Review* defines AI broadly as "machines that can learn, reason, and act for themselves. They can make their own decisions when faced with new situations, in the same way that humans and animals can."[1]

When it comes to AI used in legal research, the focus is often on the algorithms powering the legal research databases with "the vast majority of the AI advancements and applications . . . refer[ing] to a category of algorithms known as machine learning. These algorithms use statistics to find patterns in massive amounts of data. They then use those patterns to make predictions . . . ."[2]

To better understand how algorithms work, it is helpful to look to a common search engine: Google.

> Google uses a trademarked, [proprietary – mostly secret –] algorithm called "PageRank" that assigns each webpage a relevancy score based on factors, such as:
>
> - The frequency and location of keywords within the webpage. If the keyword only appears once within the body of the page, it will receive a low score for that keyword.
> - How long the webpage has existed: people create new webpages every day. Google places more value on pages with an established history.
> - The number of other webpages that link to the page in question: Google looks at how many webpages link to a particular site to determine its relevance.
>
> Out of these three factors, the third is considered the most important.[3]

While Google is a common search engine that provides a good example of how algorithms work, it is also heavily used for legal research. Time after time, when asking lawyers about the electronic resource that they primarily use for legal research, the overwhelming response is Google.

Much like Google, traditional legal research algorithms use relevancy rankings based on a set of factors. Similar to the factors listed for Google, legal research algorithms utilize keywords as an important factor in their relevancy rankings with statutes and cases containing more keywords given a higher relevancy ranking, for example. The legal research databases also use citation counts to help determine relevancy. Beyond some of these basic patterns that a user can easily discern while using the legal research algorithms, the full set of factors used to determine relevancy are left unknown to the user because of the proprietary nature of the algorithms.

The algorithms are increasing in sophistication beyond mere relevancy ranking, and one of the more well-known software systems employed for legal research is IBM Watson, which is powered by DeepQA technology.[4]

> The key difference between QA technology and document search is that document search takes a keyword query and returns a list of documents, ranked in order of relevance to the query (often based on popularity and page ranking), while QA technology takes a question *expressed in natural language*, seeks to understand it in much greater detail, and returns a precise answer to the question. DeepQA goes well beyond simple question reformulation or keyword analyses. Queries that include disambiguation, unfamiliar syntax, spatially or temporally constrained questions—or simply bad question framing—require a deeper level of content and text analysis.[5]

Taking into account current natural language processing (NLP) capabilities, DeepQA purports to allow "legal search engines to eliminate the guessing game by potentially understanding the legal question being posed."[6] And instead of typing in a search term using Boolean connectors, the lawyer will simply ask a natural language question.[7]

Because of the current limitations of NLP, however, "during the early stages, it is unlikely that a search engine will be able to determine, on its own, the one case that is most on point."[8] Instead, as McGinnis & Wasick state, "the search engine will likely use competing algorithms to 'score' each possible case for how well it lines with the search query and come up with a short list of the top-ranked cases."[9]

While "the algorithm [will] . . . also take into account non-language-related factors, such as whether the opinion was heavily cited to or searched for," it is, at this point, impossible for the legal search engines to choose the best case to make the most creative legal argument.[10]

Current Legal Research Tools Employing AI

Every major legal research vendor is employing some form of AI in their processes, with the most common AI being the algorithms powering the various legal research databases. And there are new vendors popping up all the time. For a thorough listing of legal research companies, see the Codex Techindex, which currently lists upwards of 70 companies specific to legal research.[11]

The rest of this section showcases a few of these companies to provide a sampling of the various ways that AI is being used for legal research. These companies include Westlaw, Lexis, Ravel Law, Lex Machina, Casetext, and ROSS Intelligence.

Westlaw and Lexis

The algorithmic advances, in particular, have been a work in progress as research tools get to practical implementation against good data on a large scale. "The 'Big 2,' Lexis and Westlaw, have applied natural language processing (NLP) techniques to legal research for ten-plus years . . . after [t]he core NLP algorithms were all published in academic journals long ago . . . ."[12] These systems are continuously refining processes as computing power allows for a transition from natural language processing to natural language *understanding*.[13] To that end, Lexis uses IBM Watson technology, and Westlaw's latest iteration is with Westlaw Edge.

Westlaw Edge's promotional materials highlight the refined "WestSearch Plus," stating that it provides "superior predictive research suggestions as [a user] start[s] typing [the] query in the global search bar."[14] Further, it states that "WestSearch Plus applies state-of-the-art AI technologies to help you quickly address legal questions for thousands of legal topics without needing to drill into a results list."[15]

There has also been incremental progress toward practical implementation against good data on a large scale through various vendors such as Lex Machina and Ravel Law, as they have created a legal analytics subfield powered by AI.

Litigation Analytics: Lex Machina and Ravel Law

In Lexis's push to sift through massive amounts of data and provide meaningful results, it has acquired both Lex Machina and Ravel Law (relaunched under the name Context). Lex Machina mines litigation data, revealing insights never before available about judges, lawyers, parties, and the subjects of the cases themselves, culled from millions of pages of litigation information.[16]

As an example of this tool used in practice, after Lex Machina built a large set of intellectual property (IP) case data, it used the corresponding data mining and predictive analytics techniques to forecast outcomes of IP litigation.[17]

Ravel View builds on legal analytics to provide additional metrics of and a visual, data-driven view for legal-research results. Ravel View showcases a truly innovative step in legal-research visualization that meets users where they are likely to look. The beauty of this type of case visualization is the ability to quickly and easily identify key cases that might not have been uncovered in traditional list view, such as spotting key Supreme Court decisions.

It also shows, in context, why the cases are important.[18] For example, after using Ravel View, a user was able to identify an important Supreme Court decision that was buried deep in the traditional list view of results sorted by relevance. Ravel View made it easy to identify the decision visually and showed how often lower courts had cited the case. Ravel View clearly demonstrates that this is a case to review, which the user might have missed otherwise.[19]

Casetext and ROSS Intelligence

Casetext and ROSS Intelligence are both newer legal research vendors that are quickly disrupting the traditional legal research landscape by utilizing AI for legal research.

Casetext is interesting for its drag-and-drop research functionality. From its promotional materials:

> Casetext's AI search, CARA, finds cases on the same facts, legal issues, and jurisdiction as your matter.
>
> Just drag and drop a complaint or brief from your matter, enter a few search terms, and let CARA A.I. find you cases and other authorities that share the context of your matter, including facts, legal issues, and jurisdiction.[20]

Casetext is also utilizing algorithms and Big Data to creatively harvest content. As Pablo Arredondo, Casetext's cofounder and chief product officer, explains in his article "Harvesting and Utilizing Explanatory Parentheticals":

> Explanatory parentheticals—the concise summaries neatly packaged alongside case citations—are ubiquitous, easily harvested, and grossly underutilized. This Paper describes what is believed to be the first instance of harvesting explanatory parentheticals and utilizing them on a mass scale. Specifically,

> this Paper describes how hundreds of thousands of parentheticals were identified, mined from case law, and then integrated into Casetext, a free legal research platform. The value that parentheticals add to research is explored, including enhancing the value of citatory.[21]

Arredondo provides, "[i]n sum, the common law is teeming with concise case law summaries, and leveraging the *Bluebook*-decreed consistency of the explanatory parenthetical format enables an immense set of these summaries to be harvested algorithmically."[22]

ROSS Intelligence, powered by IBM Watson for legal research, is also doing interesting things in the area of AI and legal research. ROSS Intelligence has broken down its AI Search process into three main categories: understanding, retrieval, and ranking.

According to ROSS's website, when it comes to understanding, after "you submit your query, ROSS analyzes the words using our own proprietary natural language processing algorithms. The algorithms understand the time period and jurisdiction of interest and automatically apply filters to focus your query on those places and dates."[23]

As to retrieval:

> Now that ROSS has identified the appropriate date and jurisdiction filters in your query, it will retrieve the passages from our comprehensive corpus of U.S. case law that are most similar to the meaning of your query. We find those passages by using a combination of industry standard search functions and proprietary algorithms. You may have noticed that instead of looking for cases ROSS is looking for passages within cases. We do that because answers to legal research questions are found within passages of text, not the case as a whole. We aim to find precise answers to questions and not just keywords within documents.[24]

And lastly, ranking:

> Once we've retrieved all the cases relevant to your query we use our industry-leading AI algorithms to rank them so that you see the best cases first. ROSS does not limit your search by merely counting the keywords in your query. Emphasizing keyword matches is an outdated and inferior way to rank search results because it often misses the point and intent of your question.[25]

ROSS Intelligence uses these AI tools to "complete [a] holistic set of feature analyses for each case passage [then uses] another machine-learned model to combine each feature into a single score. ROSS uses the score to determine the relevance of a case to [the] query and order [the] search results."[26]

While ROSS is certainly driving innovation in the area of AI and legal research, in January 2017, Blue Hill Research Group released a benchmark report financed by ROSS, Inc., titled *ROSS Intelligence and Artificial Intelligence in Legal Research*, with the main objective to "assess the impact of ROSS-assisted use cases in bankruptcy law research with respect to: information retrieval quality, usability and user confidence, and research efficiency."[27] Ultimately, the benchmark report found that when users conduct searches by entering questions in plain language, "ROSS's cognitive computing and semantic analysis capabilities permit the tool to understand the intent of the question asked and identify answers 'in context' within the searched authorities."[28]

However, based on the results:

> Blue Hill noted that none of these findings indicate that AI-assisted legal research constitutes a dramatic transformation in the use of technology by legal organizations. Rather, the use cases and impact reviewed indicate that tools like ROSS Intelligence more closely represent a significant iteration in the continuing evolution of legal research tools that began with the launch of digital databases of authorities and have continued through developments in search technologies.[29]

As AI continues to be heavily incorporated into the various legal research tools, the ways that users perform legal research must adjust to ensure compliance with the new duty of technology competence that has been adopted in a majority of states.

The Duty of Technology Competence as Applied to AI and Legal Research

As Will Knight noted in the *MIT Technology Review*, "[i]n principle, [AI] is very powerful. But there are many, many technical challenges."[30] At this point in law, lawyers should take care to understand the challenges associated with AI to comply with the ethical duty to understand the risks and benefits associated with the relevant technology.[31]

The Duty of Technology Competence requires lawyers to keep abreast of "changes in the law and its practice, including the benefits and risks associated with relevant technology."[32] While the duty has not, yet, been formally interpreted as applying to the use of AI or algorithms in law, a lawyer should understand the benefits and risks associated with the use of algorithms to ensure competent representation.[33]

The major benefit of using AI for legal research is the efficiency gains. There is recent case law from Canada that focuses on the benefits of using algorithmic results to perform legal research. This case law, in fact, may even be interpreted as *requiring* the use of algorithmic results when ethically performing legal research.[34]

> In both *Cass v. 1410088 Ontario Inc.* ("Cass") and *Drummond v. The Cadillac Fairview Corp. Ltd.* ("Drummond"), justices of the Ontario Superior Court made comments about AI and legal research.
>
> The *Cass* case was a slip and fall in which the defendant prevailed. The plaintiff, who was liable for costs, argued that defendant counsel fees were excessive and unnecessary. One issue raised was a $900 fee for case precedents, which the plaintiff argued are available for free through CanLII or publicly accessible websites. Justice Whitten, perhaps also a lover of legal tech, agreed. He stated in relation to both the excessive amount of time counsel had spent on legal research, as well as the fee that, "[i]f artificial intelligence sources were employed, no doubt counsel's preparation time would have been significantly reduced." The defendant's claims for disbursements were ultimately reduced from $24,300.67 to $11,404.08.
>
> In *Drummond,* the defendant objected to the $1,323 claimed for legal research costs incurred using WestLaw. Justice Perell commented that the law is divided regarding whether a disbursement for legal research is a recoverable cost. One view is that legal-research tools are simply part of a lawyer's overhead and not recoverable, another is that they are a reasonable and recoverable disbursement.
>
> . . . In allowing the $1,323 disbursement for legal research he commented that, "computer-assisted legal research is a necessity for the contemporary practice of law and computer-assisted legal research is here to stay with further advances in artificial intelligence to be anticipated and to be encouraged." He further noted that, "computer-assisted legal research provides a more comprehensive and more accurate answer to a legal question in shorter time than the conventional research methodologies."[35]

This case law provides insights into the foundation of modern legal practice. All lawyers perform some type of legal research when preparing a case. The major benefit of using algorithmic results for legal research is the efficiency and comprehensiveness associated with the results. If done properly, legal research performed on databases powered by algorithms takes much less time and is generally more comprehensive than performing research in print.[36]

In accordance with the Duty of Technology Competence, algorithms should absolutely be used for the utmost benefit, but lawyers must also understand the risks associated with the use of algorithms for legal research and use reasonable care when relying on the results.[37]

While Justice Perrell in the *Drummond* case mentioned that "computer-assisted legal research provides a . . . more accurate answer to a legal question," which might not be true in every instance. Lawyers must not blindly rely on an algorithm to provide an accurate result. Competent lawyers must use their legal training and independent judgment to test and carefully review the results to determine any anomalies.[38]

> As lawyers increasingly rely on algorithms in the everyday practice of law, the legal profession must take active steps to ensure competent use of algorithms to temper the risks associated with their use. "[I]n chasing the amazing possibilities, the profession must not forget the fundamentals. In our race to use technology to be better, faster and cheaper, we must not forget that the law's effect will always be endured by humans. . . . [W]e cannot ignore the danger of a failure of competence."[39]

A major impediment to a lawyer complying with the Duty of Technology Competence when performing legal research using AI is the lack of transparency for users to understand how the algorithm generated its results—results that could be biased.

> Invisible to the user, these products could be subject to intentional or unintentional biases. For example, a product relying on Big Data analysis and statistical correlation might give different advice in response to a criminal charge if race or income were a variable, embedding, unknown to the consumer, historic biases in the information given. With the algorithm hidden, the bias would be, as a practical matter, undetectable. In order for digital legal services to achieve their potential, these issues need careful thought. Given the lack of transparency, it cannot be assumed that the market will provide a sufficient check as consumers may not even realize the issue exists, and most likely will be unable to evaluate the options, even if they recognize the general issue of private algorithms.[40]

Currently, the ML algorithms used for legal research lack the transparency required to fully understand the results. Without an understanding of how the algorithms generate results, it will be difficult, if not impossible, for attorneys to vet the information.

Given the lack of transparency and other issues with blindly relying on algorithms, lawyers might be at a loss as to how to competently use this ubiquitous technology. Without formal guidance on point, lawyers should draw parallels to the current guidance documents pertaining to the Duty of Technology Competence.

For example, the Washington Bar Association states that "[a] lawyer using [a third-party] service must . . . conduct a due diligence investigation of the provider and its services and cannot rely on lack of technological sophistication to excuse the failure to do so."[41] Additionally, we know from the Washington Bar Association opinion that a lawyer's ethical duty regarding technology does not stop after initial due diligence. It is an ongoing duty that requires long-term reasonable care.[42]

> Analogously, competent lawyers must continuously monitor their use of a vendor and the corresponding algorithms to ensure that they use reasonable care when relying on the algorithm's results. We also know that a lawyer's lack of technological sophistication is no excuse, so the lawyer must at least have a basic understanding of the pitfalls associated with using algorithms to be able to vet the content.[43]

When drawing parallels to New York's social media guidance, particularly as it pertains to research, we see that "[i]f an attorney cannot ascertain the functionality of a website, the attorney must proceed with great caution in conducting research on that particular site."[44] Similarly, as noted in *Beyond the Information Age: The Duty of Technology Competence in the Algorithmic Society*, "when a lawyer is using an algorithm but cannot ascertain the functionality, the lawyer must proceed with great caution when relying on the results."[45]

Lastly, from a California Bar opinion, we see "three options from which a lawyer should choose when confronted with unfamiliar technology: (1) become familiar with the technology, (2) consult with or delegate to someone who is familiar with the technology, or (3) decline to represent the client."[46] Although California's hypothetical applies specifically to e-discovery, its conclusions can be read as applying to all of the benefits and risks of technology as defined in comment 8. Likewise, a competent lawyer, when confronted with an unfamiliar algorithm, will become familiar with it by looking for patterns, such as biased results or recognizing foundational cases, for example. If the lawyer cannot confidently ascertain the legitimacy of the results, the lawyer should consult with or delegate to someone who can.[47]

While the parallels to the various guidance documents provide some insight into the competent use of algorithms in law, the underlying principle is that a lawyer, at a minimum, must be aware of the issues surrounding the use of algorithms and use reasonable care. A lawyer might be able to recognize anomalies due to his or her legal training and know enough to test the answer, ask a different question, or adjust the data. If the lawyer is looking for such things, that is.[48]

Research Habits of the Google Generation Creating Electronically Manufactured Law

AI in legal research continues to increase in sophisticated ways, and the Duty of Technology Competence guides lawyers to ethically use the various tools to perform legal research while competently representing clients. However, as the "Google Generation," born in 1993 and later, starts to practice law, they must take great care not to fall back on the research habits that they have likely developed through years of keyword searching and allowing the algorithms to do the heavy lifting for them with little attention paid to the quality of results.

> [T]here have been some interesting findings about [the Google Generation's] information behavior. As early as 2008, studies show that "the speed of young people's web searching means that little time is spent in evaluating information, either for relevance, accuracy, or authority." Additionally, "[f]aced with a long list of search hits, young people find it difficult to assess the relevance of the materials presented and often print off pages with no more than a perfunctory glance at them." Also, "[y]oung scholars are using tools that require little skill: they appear satisfied with a very simple or basic form of searching."[49]

While there has been little discussion of the research habits of law students' use of algorithms to conduct research, it is likely that law students will fall back on research techniques that they know and feel comfortable with. As part of the Google Generation and beyond, it means that these students, unless taught otherwise, will rely heavily on the algorithms to select relevant material after performing basic searches, and they will also spend little time evaluating the results.[50]

Accordingly, as we know, Westlaw and Lexis are using search algorithms to provide a better user experience. From a recent empirical study, it has been shown that the legal database algorithms have a surprising amount of variation in case law results that each algorithm deems relevant for a particular search query.[51] Therefore, a user relying on the first page of results in the legal databases could get significant variation in the relevant cases on a particular topic. The user, through hasty searching and vetting of results, has just allowed the algorithm to have a significant role in selecting the cases that the algorithm deems should advance the law.[52]

It is inevitable that algorithms will increasingly be used to govern populations.[53] The underlying data and algorithms will be used to understand, analyze, control, direct, order, and shape society. "Because the relationship is one of governance, the obligations are fiduciary."[54] Without algorithmic accountability and transparency, the very people who create laws to govern will not be able to act in their fiduciary capacity.

Because an algorithm's results are only as good as the underlying data, as we move toward an algorithmic society that relies heavily on algorithmic decision-making, any errors could have consequences on the development of the law. To that end, law librarian Mary Matuszak collects the errors that she finds during the legal research process in the various databases and distributes them via the Law-Lib listserv as "Error of the Day." While these errors are seemingly minute individually, the consequences are greater in the aggregate.

"The legal . . . industry [is], by nature, [an industry] of precision. A small typographical error in a legal document could result in a malpractice lawsuit."[55] Most tasks in this industry require meticulous attention to detail. Delegating the tasks to a computerized program involves a significant amount of trust. Given the various ethical duties and the precision necessary to practice law, if the algorithms do not provide the requisite transparency, these duties, when violated, may go undetected or open lawyers up to malpractice claims.

Law librarians are in the best position to teach on the various issues surrounding the use of algorithms in law because we are often on the frontlines of teaching future lawyers how to use the very technologies that employ the use of algorithms in legal research. With so much at stake, law librarians must take their role of assessing and curating quality information seriously and teach prospective lawyers to do the same.[56]

Conclusion

While law librarians and lawyers are using many various forms of AI to conduct legal research, it will be quite some time before high-level legal research is susceptible to automation. This is because it requires the type of creative analysis that is better suited to the human brain.

The type of high-level legal research that will be difficult for a computer to replicate goes beyond logical or scientific reasoning, which AI is currently better suited, to more pragmatic level thinking, where "[t]he goal is not to reach the right decision but to make the best argument for one side."[57] Creating the best argument for a client requires a level of analytical, pragmatic thinking that is inextricably linked to legal research process.[58]

Legal research when performed properly is highly sophisticated and "[r]equires an ability to sort through and correctly spot the issues provoked by a given set of facts; the ability to formulate a research plan; knowledge of how to find, read, and update primary authority; knowledge of the available secondary sources and when and how to use them to educate oneself on the issue; an understanding of jurisdiction and the nature of precedent so as to recognize the applicable primary authority; an ability to understand citation; the capacity to synthesize and apply the information found to the original issue; and an ability to recognize when the research process is complete."[59]

This sophisticated legal research process requires the highest level of NLP because as Professor Sarah Valentine states, it "cannot be mechanically divorced from legal analysis and reasoning."[60] In fact, Professor Kris Franklin emphasizes that "[u]nderstanding how legal authorities are most effectively deployed to build legal arguments requires mastery of all of the most fundamental components of legal reasoning: reading sources of law meticulously, interpreting them critically, and applying them strategically."[61] Ultimately, Valentine concludes that it is "impossible to do legal research without analyzing, synthesizing, and applying the information found, both to the original issue and to the research plan developed to address the issue."[62]

Now this is not to say that all legal research is high level. Some types of legal research could and should be automated for efficiency. When competently performing legal research under the guidelines of the Duty of Technology Competence, the efficiency gains are a major benefit of using the associated technology. Although only some jurisdictions adhere to the formal duty, all lawyers should now use reasonable care and remain cognizant of the ethical implications of the technology that they use in the practice of law. Not only are there very real issues regarding the lack of transparency and potential bias that could be perpetuated through blindly relying on algorithms, there are also theoretical issues in giving independent judgment over to machines.[63]

As we move to a time in law when algorithms will increasingly be used to create greater efficiencies and govern populations, lawyers must act as information fiduciaries for their clients and protect them from the potential risks. This will be an uphill battle as the Google Generation enters the legal field, as they have generally become comfortable with incompetent research skills that have them relying on the top few results generated by algorithms with little thought given to evaluating the content. Legal educators, including librarians, must capitalize on moments to discuss the issues surrounding the use of algorithms with their students to ensure that the students have an understanding of the benefits and risks associated with the relevant technology.

NOTES

1. Karen Hao, "What is AI? We drew you a flowchart to work it out," *MIT Technology Review.* "The Algorithm." (2018) https://www.technologyreview.com/s/612404/is-this-ai-we-drew-you-a-flowchart -to-work-it-out/.
2. Hao, "What is AI?"
3. Jonathan Strickland, "How Google Works," How Stuff Works, accessed April 18, 2019, https://computer.howstuffworks.com/internet/basics/google1.htm.
4. Sherry Xin Chen and Mary Ann Neary, "Artificial Intelligence: Legal Research & Law Librarians," *AALL Spectrum,* May 2017, https://lawdigitalcommons.bc.edu/cgi/viewcontent.cgi?article=2077&context =lsfp.
5. Craig Rhinehart, "10 Things You Need to Know About the Technology Behind Watson," Craig Rhinehart (blog), January 17, 2011, https://craigrhinehart.com/2011/01/17/10-things-you-need-to-know-about-the-technology-behind-watson/.
6. Jamie J. Baker, "2018: A Legal Research Odyssey: Artificial Intelligence as Disruptor," *Law Library Journal* (2018).
7. Baker, "2018: A Legal Research Odyssey."
8. Baker, "2018: A Legal Research Odyssey."
9. John O. McGinnis and Steven Wasick, "Law's Algorithm," *Florida Law Review* (2014).
10. McGinnis and Wasick, "Law's Algorithm."
11. Codex, "TechIndex," https://techindex.law.stanford.edu/categories/4.
12. Michael Mills, "Artificial Intelligence in Law: The State of Play 2016," Thomson Reuters Legal, March 24, 2016, https://www.neotalogic.com/wp-content/uploads/2016/04/Artificial-Intelligence-in-Law-The-State-of-Play-2016.pdf.
13. Mills, "Artificial Intelligence in Law."
14. Jamie J. Baker, "Error of the Day & Maintaining Integrity of Algorithmic Results," Ginger (Law) Librarian (blog), November 9, 2018, http://www.gingerlawlibrarian.com/2018/11/error-of-day-maintaining-integrity-of.html.
15. Baker, "Error of the Day."
16. Lex Machina, "What We Do," https://lexmachina.com/what-we-do/whats-unique/.
17. Mills, "Artificial Intelligence in Law."

18. Jamie J. Baker, "Ravel View for Lexis Advance Visually Showcases Case Data for Faster Searching," Ginger (Law) Librarian (blog), June 28, 2018, http://www.gingerlawlibrarian.com/search?q=ravel+view.
19. Baker, "Ravel View for Lexis Advance."
20. Casetext, "Product," https://casetext.com/product.
21. Pablo Arredondo, "Harvesting and Utilizing Explanatory Parentheticals," *South Carolina Law Review* (2018), https://heinonline.org/HOL/LandingPage?handle=hein.journals/leinforv1&div=6&id=&page=.
22. Arredondo, "Explanatory Parentheticals."
23. ROSS Intelligence, "Why ROSS," https://rossintelligence.com/why-ross.html.
24. ROSS Intelligence, "Why ROSS."
25. ROSS Intelligence, "Why ROSS."
26. ROSS Intelligence, "Why ROSS."
27. David Houlihan, "ROSS Intelligence and Artificial Intelligence in Legal Research," *Blue Hill Research,* January 17, 2017, http://bluehillresearch.com/ross-intelligence-and-artificial -intelligence-in-legal-research/.
28. Houlihan, "ROSS Intelligence and Artificial Intelligence in Legal Research."
29. Baker, "2018: A Legal Research Odyssey."
30. Will Knight, "Google and Others Are Building AI Systems That Doubt Themselves, *MIT Technology Review,* January 9, 2018, https://www.technologyreview.com/s/609762/google-and-others-are-building-ai-systems-that-doubt-themselves/?utm_source=newsletters&utm_medium=email&utm_content=2018_01_09&utm_campaign=the_algorithm.
31. Jamie J. Baker, "Disruption in Law: Algorithms that Doubt Themselves," Ginger (Law) Librarian (blog), January 16, 2019, http://www.gingerlawlibrarian.com/2018/01/disruption-in-law-algorithms-that-doubt.html.
32. Jamie J. Baker, "Beyond the Information Age: The Duty of Technology Competence in the Algorithmic Society," *South Carolina Law Review* (2018).
33. Baker, "Beyond the Information Age."
34. Jamie J. Baker, "Are Algorithms Required for Ethical Legal Research?,"Ginger (Law) Librarian (blog), February 1, 2019, http://www.gingerlawlibrarian.com/2019/02/are-algorithms-required-for-ethical.html.
35. Lisa Stam & Hilary Page, "Costs and Legal Tech," Lexology (blog), January 10, 2019, https://www.lexology.com/library/detail.aspx?g=bca77e2e-ddf7-42cc-b3f8-a0ef82725afc.
36. Baker, "Are Algorithms Required for Ethical Legal Research?"
37. Baker, "Are Algorithms Required for Ethical Legal Research?"
38. Baker, "Are Algorithms Required for Ethical Legal Research?"
39. Baker, "Beyond the Information Age"; Wendy Wen Yu Chang, "Time to Regulate AI in the Legal Profession? (Perspective)," Big Law Business, July 12, 2016, https://biglawbusiness.com/time-to-regulate-ai-in-the

-legal-profession-perspective/, quoted in Baker, "Beyond the Information Age."

40. Ray Worthy Campbell, "The Digital Future of the Oldest Information Profession," SSRN, January 17, 2016, https://papers.ssrn.com/sol3/papers.cfm?abstract_id=2716972.
41. Washington Bar Association Opinion 2215 (2012).
42. Washington Bar Association Opinion 2215 (2012).
43. Baker, "Beyond the Information Age."
44. New York Bar Social Media Ethics Guidelines, June 9, 2015.
45. Baker, "Beyond the Information Age."
46. California Bar Opinion: Cal. State Bar, Formal Op. 2015-193 (2015) quoted in Baker, "Beyond the Information Age."
47. Baker, "Beyond the Information Age."
48. Baker, "Beyond the Information Age."
49. Baker, "Beyond the Information Age," 16; Ian Rowlands, et.al., "The Google Generation: The Information Behaviour of the Researcher of the Future," *Aslib Proceedings* 60, no. 4 (2008): 290, quoted in Baker, "Beyond the Information Age."
50. Baker, "Beyond the Information Age."
51. Susan Nevelow-Mart, "The Algorithm as Human Artifact: Implications for Legal (Re)search," 109 *Law Library Journal* 387 (2017), available at http://scholar.law.colorado.edu/articles/755.
52. Baker, "Beyond the Information Age."
53. Jack Balkin, "The Three Laws of Robotics in the Age of Big Data," *Ohio State Law Journal* (2017).
54. Balkin, "The Three Laws of Robotics."
55. Baker, "2018: A Legal Research Odyssey."
56. Baker, "2018: A Legal Research Odyssey."
57. Phoebe C. Ellsworth, *Legal Reasoning: Cambridge Handbook of Thinking and Reasoning,* (New York: Cambridge University Press, 2005).
58. Sarah Valentine, "Legal Research as a Fundamental Skill: A Lifeboat for Students and Law Schools," *University of Baltimore Law Review* 39 no. 2 (Winter 2010): 175-227.
59. Valentine, "Legal Research as a Fundamental Skill."
60. Valentine, "Legal Research as a Fundamental Skill."
61. Valentine, "Legal Research as a Fundamental Skill."
62. Valentine, "Legal Research as a Fundamental Skill."
63. Baker, "Beyond the Information Age."

THERESA TARVES

8

AI in Legal Education

Law students are often overwhelmed with the legal research resources available to them and the volume of legal information that they must sift through in order to conduct legal research. Those who teach legal research at law schools—often academic law librarians—are also faced with limited time available to introduce students to the legal research databases and the skills they will need when they begin their careers as lawyers. However, artificial intelligence (AI) tools are becoming widespread in legal research databases and providing instruction related to AI tools can help support and enhance a law student's legal research. Further, students often do not recognize the difference between research results that have been cultivated and edited by skilled attorney editors and those that were generated by an AI tool. And while each of these—attorney editors and AI tools—have their positives and negatives, it is imperative to teach students to think

THERESA TARVES is the associate director of the law library, director of the Legal-Tech Virtual Lab, and professor of legal research at Penn State Law Montague Law Library.

critically about their legal research, their research results, and how these results are generated by the research databases.

There are two parts of teaching AI to law students. The first part involves the AI tools that are being used for legal research and in the practice of law. The second part involves the legal issues surrounding AI. This includes, among other things, the liability when a tool that uses AI is wrong or makes a mistake, such as when an autonomous vehicle gets in a car accident or when a robotic AI machine used in surgery makes a medical mistake. While the legal issues surrounding AI are interesting and worthy of including in the law school curriculum where they fit based on their relevant practice area, this chapter will focus on the AI tools being used primarily for legal research and in the practice of law.

Today's Students: Learning Styles, Technology, and Legal Research

It is often assumed that, because today's students are considered "digital natives," they either do not need instruction on how to use technology or they will pick it up so quickly that instruction is unnecessary. However, among educators, it quickly becomes clear that while students are adept at using their smartphones and social media, they struggle with more "traditional" technologies like email and lack information literacy because they consume it so quickly that they often do not consider the source or know how to determine if a source is legitimate.[1] Most law students entering law school in 2019 are from Generation Z[2], although there are still a fair amount of Millennials[3], and they are defined by a set of characteristics that are different from many of us who are teaching law students today, but are representative of most digital natives.

First, digital natives tend to have short attention spans and lack an ability to focus on tasks.[4] Instead, they are prone to skimming or "power-browsing" through information and will read a complex document in the same way that they might scroll through a social media site.[5] Second, digital natives learn best when they are presented with both traditional classroom teaching techniques combined with new technologies to support their learning of a subject.[6] It can be difficult for educators to introduce technologies that complement their traditional classroom practices especially when it can be hard to see how these new technologies will actually benefit our students.[7] Further, there is a danger in introducing too many technologies so that the new tools actually detract from student learning rather than enhancing it. Third, while digital natives do not typically have trouble locating relevant information, they tend to struggle with evaluating the quality of information.[8] Because of this, they often cannot readily "distinguish legitimate sources (primary authority, or law review articles from prominent legal scholars, for example) from non-legitimate sources (blog posts written by law students, or articles in Wikipedia, for example)."[9]

These last two characteristics are critical characteristics that all legal researchers need. Anyone familiar with legal documents knows how difficult they can be to read, especially for law students who are still learning how to understand legal language and the ways that cases, statutes, and regulations are written. Further, even those who are not law librarians or experts in legal research know the skill that it takes to locate the most relevant sources, be able to analyze all of your research results, narrow them down to those most relevant sources, and formulate a legal argument to best advocate for your client. In addition, with the sheer volume of legal information being produced today and the ease of accessing this information online through free and paid resources with differing degrees of credibility, it becomes even more critical for law students today to understand how to differentiate between credible and non-credible sources.

Educators who are teaching legal research therefore must not only teach law students how to use legal research databases and analyze research results, but also how to evaluate the quality of information and distinguish between legitimate and non-legitimate sources.

AI and Legal Research Tools

A common complaint among those who teach legal research is that students often think that legal-research databases like Lexis Advance, Westlaw Edge, and Bloomberg Law operate exactly the same way as Google. While the databases do try to mimic the feel of Google by allowing for natural language searches in the main search box, some of their features that look Google-like do not operate in the same way that Google does. For example, when starting to type a search in the main search box of either Lexis Advance, Westlaw Edge, or Bloomberg Law, all three databases begin to show suggestions, as does Google. Google's drop down shows suggested searches, so when a user clicks on one of the drop-down suggestions, Google runs this as a search and brings up a result page. However, in Lexis Advance, Westlaw Edge, and Bloomberg Law, the suggestions are often suggested documents, not just suggested searches, as the students typically believe. This can cause the students to click on these suggestions and then either experience confusion because the resulting document is not what they were looking for or assume that the research result is actually the correct "answer" for their research. This can then cause students to provide a result from outside of their jurisdiction or to give a secondary source when they were looking for primary authority. This occurs not only because they are still learning about types of sources, but also because they have trouble distinguishing suggested searches from the suggested documents, which might not be related or relevant to their research issue.

Legal research educators who are very familiar with these databases can often feel frustrated at the students' lack of attention to detail, as well as students' assumptions about the databases—with students failing to turn a critical eye to the research results in front of them. But it is precisely for these reasons that it is critical to teach law students about AI and legal research tools. AI is becoming particularly prevalent in the context of legal research. There are "new players" on the market solely touting their AI-led legal research tools, as old players are adding new AI tools and resources to their databases to compete with these new players and with each other. If legal-research instruction does not begin to address the way that AI is affecting legal research, then our students, who are already struggling with evaluating information and determining what information is credible, will be unprepared to practice when they enter the job market. Further, these tools can be used to enhance a student's understanding and learning of legal-research techniques, as long as we teach the students to understand what tools are available, how they work, and how the students can think critically to use AI-driven tools to support and enhance their legal research, rather than control it.

Overview of AI Legal Research Tools

There are three main categories of AI legal-research tools that students should be exposed to in law school: (1) AI tools in traditional legal research databases; (2) "brief-analyzing" tools; and (3) legal-analytics tools. Each of these uses AI in a different way, and each has varying degrees of transparency for law school users.

AI Tools in Traditional Legal Research Databases

Lexis Advance, Westlaw Edge, and Bloomberg Law each have developed their own AI-driven tools as part of their research databases. See table 8.1 for a list of these tools.

The most prevalent AI tools in the legal-research databases are Lexis Advance's Lexis Answers and Westlaw Edge's WestSearch Plus.

TABLE 8.1
AI tools integrated in legal research databases

Lexis Advance	*WestlawEdge*	*Bloomberg Law*
▪ Lexis Answers ▪ Legal Research Assistant Chatbot (forthcoming) ▪ Context Analytics	▪ WestSearch Plus ▪ Folder Analysis ▪ KeyCite Overruling Risk ▪ Statutes and Regulations Compare ▪ Litigation Analytics	▪ Points of Law

Both tools provide AI-generated suggested questions while a user is typing search queries, and both display an AI-generated answer on the results page before the actual results of the search are displayed. In both databases, the AI-generated answer appears on the result page if the user either clicks on a suggested question or runs a natural language search. If the user runs a terms and connectors or Boolean search, the AI-generated answer does not immediately appear on the result page. But in Lexis Advance, there is also text at the top of the result page that says, "View an answer to the question: What are the elements of defamation?" with a link to the Lexis Answers.

Lexis Answers provides users with AI-generated answers to common legal questions, such as legal definitions, standards of review, elements of a claim or defense, burden of proof, and legal doctrine with more question types coming. Users can also scroll through additional sources showing an answer by clicking on the "Next" link at the top right of the answer box.

WestSearch Plus, which incorporates the tool previously known as "Westlaw Answers" and together are referred to as "Law Summaries," also provides answers to common legal questions and suggests searches based on West Key Numbers. A list of questions or types of questions that WestSearch Plus will answer is not available because the tool can now answer thousands of questions. However, it seems from sample searches that it goes beyond standard legal questions about elements of a claim or standards of review. (See table 8.2 for sample searches and corresponding suggested questions.) One or two AI answers generated by WestSearch Plus are displayed above the research results, and users can click a "Show More" button at the bottom of the box to see additional results. For both Lexis Answers and WestSearch Plus, it is best to choose a jurisdiction so that users can get answers from within it. If a jurisdiction is not chosen, then the AI-generated answers could come from any jurisdiction.

Both Lexis Answers and WestSearch Plus suggest questions that the AI-tool thinks a researcher might be asking while the user is typing in

TABLE 8.2
Westsearch Plus—Sample searches and suggested questions

Sample Search	*WestSearch Plus Suggested Questions*
Employment discrimination	▪ What is pretext in employment discrimination? ▪ Is summary judgment appropriate in employment discrimination cases? ▪ How does an employee show pretext in a discrimination claim?
Defamation	▪ When does a cause of action for defamation accrue? ▪ Can a statement of opinion be defamatory? ▪ Is truth an affirmative defense to defamation?
Eminent domain	▪ When can the government take private property for public use by eminent domain? ▪ Must the government compensate a property owner for a taking by eminent domain? ▪ What is eminent domain?
NOTE: The jurisdiction for all sample searches was set to All Federal	

his or her search. This can be very helpful for law students who are not yet very familiar with legal terminology, but it can also create confusion. As previously mentioned, law students often believe that suggested questions or sources that drop down from the Lexis Advance and WestlawEdge search bars are suggested *searches* since this is what drops down while a user is searching Google. They don't always realize that the suggestions are not necessarily searches; furthermore, they might not realize that the suggested questions are from Lexis Answers and WestSearch Plus AI tools. A law student who is not yet savvy in using legal research databases might click on the question and see one or two answers from these tools based on one or two primary sources, and they might conclude that these are the final "answers" to their legal issue. They might lead them to think that their research is complete, without exploring the results further.

Lexis Advance's other prevalent AI tool that will be released soon is the Lexis Research Assistant, a chatbot that will bring a conversational approach to legal research. It is not yet available in Lexis Advance, but once it is, users will be able to click an icon to access it. It will keep track of recent searches and remind users that they have already researched a topic. It will also suggest filters based on recent searches and activity, as well as Lexis Answers based on what the user is searching. The goal of the Lexis Research Assistant is to make legal research more conversational for users.

Westlaw Edge also has a few other notable AI tools. One of these tools is Folder Analysis, which reviews what a user has saved to a folder and suggests potential legal issues and additional search results based on what is saved in the folder. Westlaw Edge also added the KeyCite Overruling Risk citator to identify a case that might not have been directly overruled, but has been undermined because it relies on another case that has been overruled or otherwise invalidated. Finally, Westlaw Edge also has a "compare statutes and regulations" AI tool that allows users to compare current and historical versions of statutes and regulations to see specifically what language has changed version to version.

Bloomberg Law's main AI tool is "Points of Law." This tool identifies key legal language in a case and makes a generalized statement of law. It then allows users to see the top three cases cited for a particular point of law at issue and see related points of law that are frequently cited by courts that have referenced the original point that the user is viewing. Users can also run a Points of Law search to find all points of law based on the user's search.

AI Tools for Brief Analyzing

Another category of AI legal research tools are those that analyze briefs to recommend research results based on an entire legal document. While there are several of these on the market, two are the most well known and are available for free to law students: Casetext's CARA A.I. and ROSS's EVA. CARA A.I. allows a user to upload any document with factual or legal issues, such as a brief or a complaint, and enter in additional search terms related to the user's legal research issue. It then produces ranked results based on the specific legal issues it identifies from the user's uploaded document. Users can also upload a brief or other legal document into EVA, and it will identify negatively cited cases, as well as suggest additional cases that might be on point for the user's legal issues. Users can also run natural language searches to locate additional cases.

These tools can be enormously helpful to a law student, especially to help quell fears that their research is complete. However, as with all research tools, the results tend to be only as good as the document uploaded or the search entered. With traditional legal-research tools, if a user enters a bad search, they are likely to get bad results. If a law student, who is still learning how to form legal arguments and develop legal-writing techniques, uploads a document that is not yet well developed and is missing key legal issues, then these tools are not likely to suggest the most relevant cases to better support the legal issues. This is not because the tools themselves are not good at what they do, but rather because the user of the tool is still learning how to do effective legal writing. Therefore, it is important to teach students the benefits and potential drawbacks of using these tools, so that students understand that the tools themselves are only as good as the information that the students have inputted into the tool.

AI and Legal Analytics

While legal analytics is not brand new, there are many new products and features coming from existing products that leverage AI and the sheer amount of legal data available to assist with legal research. Lexis recently released Context, which analyzes language that judges find most compelling and persuasive, as well as a judge's propensity to grant or deny motions by type. It also analyzes expert witness-related documents to determine how frequently an expert is challenged and whether or not their testimony has been excluded or admitted. Westlaw Edge also recently made litigation analytics available through its main platform. Its product analyzes likely case outcomes, timelines, and costs, as well as patterns in judicial rulings, expert witness challenges, and potential information about opposing counsel. Bloomberg Law has long included litigation analytics within its platform, which allows users to evaluate litigation patterns for companies, law firms, judges, and attorneys. There are also several standalone legal analytics tools (like Lexis-owned Lex Machina and Intelligize), but law students tend to be most familiar with the resources available to them via Lexis Advance, Westlaw Edge, and Bloomberg Law.

For law students, these tools are best used for interview prep, as students can look up firms and attorneys for whom they are interviewing to be a summer associate, as well as for judges that they are interviewing with to be a clerk.

Benefits of Teaching AI Tools to Law Students

Those of us who teach legal research want our law students to be well prepared to practice law when they enter the job market. We also want our law students to be critical thinkers who can understand the source of their research results, judge the credibility of that source, and analyze their results to formulate them in a way that adequately supports their view of their client's legal issues. We certainly want all law students to know how to begin a search and also to become comfortable enough with legal research to know when they have exhausted their resources and their research is complete.

The latter is usually the biggest challenge for law students, because most of the things that they are researching have no right answer. Since this is different than many other kinds of research that they have previously done before entering law school, students often struggle with it greatly. Even when their research is complete, students still feel like it's not. Students often feel that they must find the "right" answer or a "final" answer, and when they are unable to find this, they think that they must have missed something. Tools like CARA A.I. and EVA can help students confirm that they have, in actuality, not missed anything with their research. Likewise, these tools can also identify areas where the student might need to do further research. Having access to AI tools that support legal research can go a long way in helping students feel more comfortable that their research is truly complete—that they have exhausted all resources and that they have double-checked their research to ensure that they are not missing any key primary sources.

The good news is that AI tools that are either part of Lexis Advance or Westlaw Edge, as well as those that are standalone tools (like CARA A.I. and ROSS's EVA), are easy to use. The more complex features that traditional legal research databases use have been stripped away to make them more streamlined and more like the familiar Google interface. These tools can allow for efficiency in legal research by providing an extra assist at the front end (like Lexis Answers and WestSearch Plus), to help a user find an answer to a legal question more quickly, or to help on the back end (like CARA A.I. and EVA), by doing a final check of a written document to ensure that all relevant results have been found.

Further, when law students begin their summer jobs or graduate and begin their careers, many of them will have access to AI tools to assist with their legal research. In order to ensure that our law students are prepared for practice, it is to their benefit to teach them how to use these tools adequately, so that they feel comfortable using them before they get into practice. In addition, the more comfortable that law students are with using AI tools as part of their legal research, the better they will be able to quickly adapt to using and recognize the legitimacy of the standalone AI tools that they do not have access to in law school or new tools that are brought to the market after they graduate from law school. Those of us who teach legal research can then feel comfortable knowing that we are arming our students with the best set of legal research strategies and tools possible.

The Potential Drawbacks of Teaching AI Tools to Law Students

While there are many benefits to teaching law students how to use AI tools for legal research, there are some drawbacks as well that should be highlighted, so that those choosing to add it to their curriculum can tailor their efforts accordingly.

First, if students rely too heavily on AI tools to supplement their own legal research, it can prevent them from learning how to do complex legal research on their own. While we want to give students as many tools as possible to help them be better legal researchers, we do not want them to become dependent on those tools at the expense of learning how to research without them. While the AI tools in Lexis Advance, Westlaw Edge, and Bloomberg Law are built into the platform, students might find themselves working for an employer that only has access to one of these platforms.

Furthermore, many of the standalone AI legal research tools are free for law students, but not free to practicing attorneys. If a student begins to rely heavily on CARA A.I. while in law school but his or her future employer does not subscribe to this tool, the student might struggle when approached with complex legal research.

Also, students who understand the foundational aspects of legal research and develop strong research competencies while in law school will better understand the types of sources they find in the future and the way those sources intersect to create a legal argument. These students will be better legal researchers overall and be better able to use AI tools to enhance their research, rather than direct it.

Along the same lines, if a student relies on an AI tool too early in his or her research, there is a danger that he or she will have the false sense that his or her research is complete, when in reality, it is not. If the user submits something that is not well developed and is missing legal issues or key legal arguments, the tool might not pick up on the additional legal issues to complete the legal argument, and therefore, the tool will not suggest additional relevant case law. These tools work best when there is a clear picture of the legal issues in question, because they will suggest research results to supplement the user's research based on what the user submits or enters as a search into the tool or database.

Finally, just like humans, these AI tools are not perfect. There is the very real possibility that additional suggested research results will not enhance the student's analysis of the legal issues. An experienced attorney is likely to recognize when results are incorrect or irrelevant for the legal issue at hand. A law student, on the other hand, might assume that anything the database tells them must be correct—and then erroneously use incorrect results to formulate a legal analysis.

To prevent this, students must be taught to critically evaluate the results from AI tools, just as they should be taught to critically evaluate *all* research results. However, there is a bigger teachable moment here: the opportunity to make sure students realize that they are responsible for the results of AI tools and to discuss the legal ethics (and potential malpractice) of errors. As an instructor, this is your chance to help students better understand why it is important to critically evaluate both the information they have located as well as the AI tools they use. (For more information on this subject, see "Teaching Students to Critically Evaluate AI Legal Research Tools" later in this chapter.)

AI Tools in the Curriculum

Because AI tools for legal research are increasingly becoming available to law students, it is important to expose students to these tools on some level. Ideally, students should receive instruction on how to recognize when these tools are most useful and how to critically review the results from these tools, so that they are not blindly relying on them without understanding their potential drawbacks. AI tools are likely best introduced in an advanced legal research course to upper-level students, who have learned some legal research basics and hopefully have had at least one summer of on-the-job legal research experience. Upper-level law students will benefit from adding these resources to the legal research skills that they have already learned and will have the foundational legal research knowledge to use AI tools to enhance their research rather than control it.

However, the reality in legal education is that many law schools do not include much time in the curriculum for legal research instruction. Even schools that do offer research courses (whether required or elective) have limited time for teaching tools and resources outside of the foundational legal research basics.

So what if a law school does not present the opportunity for all law students to be exposed to AI tools at an upper level? In this case, it is best to introduce students in whatever format makes most sense for an academic law library. Those of us who teach required first year legal research courses should include teaching these tools in the first-year curriculum to help expose students to the tools and hopefully teach the students to use them with a critical eye. While not the ideal time to introduce them, since first year law students are still learning the basics, it is still better to expose students to these tools than to leave them out of the course entirely. Teaching the AI tools toward the end of a course will help ensure that the students have spent most of the course learning the basics of legal research before being exposed to AI tools so that they use them to enhance their research. Finally, many law librarians run library-led workshops. While drumming up people to attend can be a challenge, holding workshops specifically on AI tools for legal research can draw in students who are interested in new legal technologies and, at the very least, expose students to these tools.

Teaching Students to Critically Evaluate AI Legal Research Tools

There are several AI tools for legal research, and as such, wading through the different tools to determine how to best teach them and their applications to students can be hard to do. Given the time (or lack thereof) devoted to legal research instruction in law schools, it might be too difficult to teach students about *all* the tools available. Instead, try focusing on a few key tools, such as those available in Lexis Advance, Westlaw Edge, and Bloomberg Law. Brief analyzers that are available for free to law schools (such as Casetext's CARA A.I.) and legal-analytics resources can help students understand that these tools exist and how to navigate new tools that they might later encounter in practice. Luckily, many of these tools operate similarly to others already available, so students—especially those who are digital natives—rarely have trouble translating their existing skills to the AI research tools.

The most important thing to teach students about AI tools is how to use them effectively. Many legal-research instructors are already teaching students the differences between natural language searches and terms and connectors searches, particularly as it relates to the relevancy rankings of the algorithms' search results for natural language searching.[10] Students should also be taught the difference between AI-led searches and search results. It's important to stress to students that AI-led searches and results must be evaluated critically. Students need to understand which results were provided using an AI tool so that they can better discern how the database delivered that result. These results might differ from those in the search results using natural language or terms and connectors searching.

Students should also be taught that any results—whether from natural language, a terms and connectors search, or an AI tool—can contain mistakes. Over numerous years of using legal-research databases, many law librarians have found inaccuracies in search results, as well as the documents themselves. This has been no different when using AI tools. Within several minutes of trying AI tools in Lexis Advance and Westlaw Edge, users might notice that some of the answers or results vary across the databases. If law students are not wary of these potential discrepancies and possible mistakes, they might assume that the database has correctly provided the answer and move on with their research. While in many cases the answer is likely correct, in the cases where it is not, real issues can arise for a presumptuous researcher.

As such, students in law school should be strongly encouraged to check results across databases with AI tools—and have access to these resources without the burden of costs. If students are taught to double-check their research across platforms (no matter how they arrived at the results) and get comfortable with all available research databases, they will likely begin to understand which AI tools are the most reliable, and when and how to best use them to enhance their research. Students should be taught never to rely solely on the AI tool alone or, for that matter, one type of search.

A common question that law students have is how they can know that they have completed their research. Double-checking using different search strings, different types of searches, and different databases to see if the results of a search are consistent is a great way to confirm this. AI tools can help students understand their research and get to an answer sooner but should always be double-checked against other types of searches.

Conclusion

AI tools for legal research are a great way for users to enhance their research when used effectively. They can help lead law students to the relevant primary authority and provide clearer information sooner than traditional legal research. They can assure a law student that his or her research is complete by providing a way to double-check and confirm research results. However, these tools work best when used with critical thinking skills to evaluate the information provided by the AI tool to ensure relevance and correctness. The tools should enhance research rather than control it. Because these tools are becoming so prevalent in legal-research databases that are accessible to and even free for use by law students, it is important to introduce these tools to them and teach them how to use them effectively. That way, students will be better prepared to use them properly once they get into practice.

RECOMMENDED READING

Davies, Alex, ed. *AI in Application: An In-Depth Examination from the Legal Profession*. London: ARK Group, 2018.

Diamond, Randy J., Darin Fox, Kenneth J. Hirsh, Heidi Frostestad Kuehl, Michael Robak. "Let's Teach Our Students Legal Technology: But What Should We Include." *AALL Spectrum* 23, no. 1 (September/October 2018): 23–28.

Goodman, Joanna. *Robots in Law: How Artificial Intelligence Is Transforming Legal Services*. London: ARK Group, 2016.

Mart, Susan Nevelow. "The Algorithm as a Human Artifact: Implications for Legal [Re]Search." *Law Library Journal* 109, no. 3 (Summer 2017): 387–422.

Talley, Nancy B. "Imagining the Use of Intelligent Agents and Artificial Intelligence in Academic Law Libraries." *Law Library Journal* 108, no. 3. (Summer 2016): 383–402.

NOTES

1. Corey Seemiller and Meghan Grace, *Generation Z Goes to College* (California: John Wiley & Sons, Inc., 2016), 60, 66, 203–4.
2. "Generation Z refers to those born from 1995 through 2010. Having their world completely shaped by the Internet, they are often also aptly referred to as digital natives. . . ." Seemiller and Grace, 6.
3. "Generation Y, more commonly known as Millennials, falls between Generation X and Generation Z. Although the dates of their birth years range depending on what source is used, one could put it as encompassing the 1980s and early 1990s." Seemiller and Grace, 4.
4. Laura P. Graham, "Generation Z Goes to Law School: Teaching and Reaching Law Students in the Post-Millennial Generation," *University of Arkansas at Little Rock Law Review*, 2019, Forthcoming, draft September 2018, https://ssrn.com/abstract=3271137, 25–26.
5. Graham, 26.
6. James B. Levy, "Teaching the Digital Caveman: Rethinking the Use of Classroom Technology in Law School," *Chapman Law Review* 19, no. 1 (Winter 2016): 246, 277–79.
7. Levy, 253.
8. Kurt Meyer, "Teaching Legal Research to Today's Digital Natives," *AALL Spectrum* 21, no. 4 (March/April 2017): 14.
9. Laura P. Graham, "Generation Z Goes to Law School," 39.
10. For more information, see Susan Nevelow Mart, "The Algorithm as a Human Artifact: Implications for Legal [Re]Search," *Law Library Journal* 109, no. 3 (Summer 2017): 387–422.

TAWNYA K. PLUMB

9
Access to Justice in the Age of AI

Technology as an Access to Justice Solution

For those unfamiliar with the concept of "Access to Justice" (A2J), it can be defined in notions of legal rights, availability of legal resources, assistance to unrepresented litigants, and the physical ability to access the courthouse.[1] Technology has historically intersected these notions by providing services to those in need. Basic phone service enabled legal-aid hotline services to serve the poor. More recently, phone systems have delivered text messages to defendants, reminding them of their court dates. This is significant, because the delivery of text reminders is reducing the number of bench warrants issued and curtailing costly jail time.[2] The personal computer empowered with the internet shared a plethora of free legal information, including details on how to find a lawyer, how to learn more about a legal issue, and where and when to connect with a volunteer reference attorney. Further technological

TAWNYA K. PLUMB is an associate law librarian and the head of electronic and digital services at George W. Hopper Law Library, University of Wyoming College of Law.

advances led to online, fillable, free legal forms, live chat legal help, and legal-document services, including LegalZoom and Rocket Lawyer.

RECAP is another example of technology developed under A2J notions. Federal court documents are customarily available on PACER (Public Access to Court Electronic Records) for a fee, but advocates argue that the federal courts are in violation of the E-Government Act by unfairly charging more for documents than is required to cover operating costs.[3] Current litigation or proposed legislative changes could resolve this dispute, but in the meantime, RECAP, a freely available web extension for Chrome and Firefox browsers, provides complimentary access to selected PACER court documents.[4] While paying a few dollars for a court filing might not seem a great burden to some, the required registration and payment could prevent access to others and contributes to the digital divide.

The digital divide—a gap distinguishing those who have access to technology from those who do not—became a topic of conversation in the mid-1990s. The National Telecommunications and Information Administration's report, *Falling Through the Net: A Survey of the "Have Nots" in Rural and Urban America,* prompted many discussions on computer access and ownership.[5] Libraries and librarians have assisted in reducing the digital divide by applying for and receiving grant funding and then providing free access to computers and training on usage. Tablets and smart phones grew in popularity, and again, libraries and librarians offered access and training. The latest opportunity for librarians to lessen the digital divide is to advocate for A2J solutions using artificial intelligence (AI).

AI and Its A2J Implications

Defining AI is complex, as Chapter 1 of this text explores. This chapter compartmentalizes AI into categories of machine learning (ML), natural language processing (NLP), cognitive systems, and robotics and smart machines. Definitions for each concept will be followed by examples of AI-inspired technology and their implications in meeting A2J goals.

Machine Learning (ML)

Machine learning—the ability of a machine to learn (often referred to by its initials, ML)—forms the basis of AI but in some definitions might not technically be considered intelligent.[6] ML is characterized by the study of algorithms and the refined ability to predict outcomes; those in the legal field covet this predictive nature. Legal database vendors have gathered data and are providing products that predict judicial analytics, recidivism, and neighborhood crime. There are both opportunities and detriments to these technologies when viewed through the A2J lens.

Opportunities are found in many legal research platforms, including Fastcase's Docket Alarm, Lexis Advance's incorporation of Lex Machina and Ravel Law, Westlaw Edge's Litigation Analytics, and Gavelytics, a newcomer to the field. These products predict the success of a motion in front of a particular judge, the laws a judge will likely cite, the length of time a case will take, and the anticipated outcome. In order to meet client demand for "better results for lower, more predictable fees," law firms are starting to rely on data-driven products to ensure higher quality assistance.[7] If anyone is in need of better results at a lower cost, it is the pro se litigant tackling a legal issue without an attorney. In an A2J win, law librarians in a position to deliver public access to these data-driven applications would arm unrepresented library users with the same predictive technology available to lawyers in top firms. If products are not readily licensed for public access, law librarians should negotiate with vendors to find access solutions.

Predicting judicial analytics is uncontentious, as its data usage does not raise ethical issues. Companies, however, have created ML, data-driven products that are raising ethical flags. One such product is COMPAS (Correctional Offender Management Profiling for Alternative Sanctions). Developed by Northpointe (now named "equivant"), COMPAS offers risk-assessment software to courts to predict an individual's risk of recidivism when making determinations about bond settings, sentencing, and release options. Public interest nonprofit organization ProPublica investigated COMPAS and discovered racial disparities likely to falsely flag black defendants almost twice as often as white defendants and to label white defendants as low risk more often than black defendants.[8] This is a concern for law librarians who serve diverse populations.

PredPol, which has trademarked itself as "The Predictive Policing Company," was designed by the Los Angeles Police Department in collaboration with mathematicians and behavioral scientists from UCLA and Santa Clara University, and is another product built on a biased ML algorithm .[9] The creators pulled available data on crime type, location, and day and time to create and sell a product to police departments that publishes frequent updates anticipating where crime will happen. Police departments then use this information to make decisions on where to dispatch police officers. Although PredPol has been named to the GovTech 100 List for the fourth straight year and has been adopted by a number of police departments nationwide, there is a steady stream of protests blasting the program for inherent bias. After investigating

Oakland Police Department's use of PredPol, statisticians affiliated with the Human Rights Data Analysis Group concluded, "If biased data is used to train these predictive models, the models will reproduce and in some cases amplify those same biases. At best, this renders the predictive models ineffective. At worst, it results in discriminatory policing."[10] The nonprofit group determined that the complex interaction between criminality, policing strategy, and community-police relations (which includes judgments on race and ethnicity) is what actually measures crime, rather than police records.[11] Another critic refers to PredPol as a "WMD" (a "weapon of *math* destruction") and concludes, "The result is that we criminalize poverty, believing all the while that our tools are not only scientific but fair."[12] There are similar predictive products used by other police departments. New York City uses CompStat, and Philadelphia uses HunchLab, a locally developed service.[13] These products enable AI to work against A2J missions.

Predictive products that include biased algorithms pose a challenge to the A2J notion of legal rights. What can law librarians do to help? Inspired advocates could support nonprofits, such as ProPublica and Human Right Data Analysis Group in identifying and combating bias. Community activists can implement and educate on AI Now's Algorithmic Impact Assessment with four goals of 1) publicly listing and describing algorithms used by a community's agencies, 2) providing an opportunity for algorithm audit, 3) increasing public agency expertise to evaluate their systems, and 4) offering opportunities for the public to respond and dispute an agency's approach to accountability.[14] Law librarians savvy with data collection and statistics can do their own investigations on ML algorithms to spot and call out bias. Public law librarians working in software-targeted neighborhoods could encounter increased visits and requests for help that result in extra pressure placed on A2J services and resources. Law librarians can actively promote A2J resources in their libraries, perhaps seeking grant funding, to ensure that all patrons have their legal-research needs met.

Natural Language Processing (NLP)

Natural language processing (NLP) is "the ability of a computer program to understand human communication in written and oral forms."[15] The innovative legal-research engine, ROSS Intelligence, runs on NLP and attempts to answer legal research questions directly. NLP "gives AI-powered applications immediacy and intimacy... You can just talk to it—you don't need to search what you need in a particular way."[16] While law librarians are experts in complex Boolean searching, many attorneys are not, which could result in more billed time to clients for complicated legal research tasks. If ROSS Intelligence can intuitively guide lawyers to precise answers efficiently, and if lawyers can pass the savings on to their clients, perhaps more pro se litigants could afford attorneys. Ideally, ROSS Intelligence will become accessible to public law library users, and not just attorneys and law firm librarians. Providing public access to this advanced searching platform would be an A2J success.

Voicea's EVA (Enterprise Voice Assistant) is an NLP product that could improve law office efficiency. EVA accepts voice commands to create action items, set calendar reminders, email meeting attendees, transcribe, and even tell jokes.[17] EVA is one of several digital assistants touting AI capabilities. Attorneys and law firm librarians, however, must recognize confidentiality issues when using EVA or similar products. From an A2J perspective, these assistants can save time and money, while creating more cost-effective workflows that could result in lower billable rates for those in need.

Legal academic institutions are developing NLP products as well, with A2J missions in mind. Stanford's Legal Design Lab and Suffolk's Legal Innovation and Technology Lab (with funding from The Pew Charitable Trusts) have built "Learned Hands," a game and a research project inspiring to be a Rosetta stone for legal help.[18] Learned Hands is an issue-spotting game for attorneys, law students, and others with some law background. Players are given stories and are asked to identify legal issues. Behind the scenes, responses are being used to train natural language ML models on how to identify legal issues.[19] Once a sufficient taxonomy is created, the data can then be turned over to legal-aid organizations to improve the quality of their legal help portals.

Cognitive Systems

A cognitive system enables users to interact with machines and has the ability to learn, model, and generate a hypothesis.[20] Alarmists have raised concerns that this type of AI technology could be disruptive to the lawyer and law librarian professions, since learning and decision-making are high-level intellectual skills. While still in development, the technology has not yet reached a level of interaction to compete with the quality of personal, human service. Yet, some in legal need might find it intimidating to speak directly with an attorney or a law librarian. Some might also not feel comfortable visiting a law library. These individuals could benefit from a neutral tech intermediary, such as a chatbot. Legal chatbots built using cognitive analysis are beneficial to the A2J cause, because they remove the intimidation factor in asking questions.

TABLE 9.1
2019 Legal chatbot snapshot

Chatbot	*Legal Expertise*	*Creator*	*Availability*
coParenter	custody mediator	family law experts	downloadable app $12.99 per month $119.99 per year
DoNotPay	parking tickets divorce, data breaches, small claims	British-American entrepreneur	free app for iOS devices
Driver Bot	traffic accidents	British law firm	website serving the UK
PatBot	workers compensation	private law firm	website serving Washington State
Procezeus	landlord-tenant	Concordia University & Université de Montréal	still in development
SoloSuit	debt	LawX (BYU Law School)	website serving Utah
Visabot	US residence permits	entrepreneurs	now part of the DoNotPay platform

Many law librarians are familiar with chatbots, also known as chatterboxes or conversation agents, and might already be using them in their libraries to respond to general questions about library hours, directions, and book renewals. Those unfamiliar with chatbot technology might appreciate the following perspective: "Bots flatten a website; when someone chats with a bot, they do not need to know the layout of the website, or the resources available to them. The chatbot is programmed with that information and pulls together the necessary sources."[21] Now imagine a legal chatbot that could converse with an information seeker, sort through dense content hidden behind links and layers of legal information, and provide streamlined answers. This is where legal cognitive computing technology is today. Table 9.1 lists popular chatbots that are helping the public solve their basic legal issues.

The table is labeled a "snapshot," as the chatbot development scene is volatile. Former legal chatbots AasthaBot (wills and trusts), DivorceBot, Larissa (divorce), LawBot (criminal law), and Lexi (privacy policies) pushed the legal chatbot dialog forward, but no longer exist. One might ponder the fate of the 2019 chatbots listed. If the volatility of chatbots continues, this could be a detriment to A2J progress.

The snapshot also illustrates a diversity of chatbot developers. Internationally, entrepreneurs, lawyers, and students are developing chatbots to streamline legal access. A current Stanford student and nonlawyer founded DoNotPay, perhaps the most known legal chatbot. Driver Bot's creator, a lawyer, "wants to stop nonlawyers from deciding the direction of legal technology."[22] This sentiment could elicit more chatbot development from attorneys. Students working in law school innovation labs are contributing to legal chatbot development as well.

Law librarians might already be taking part in legal chatbot development in their law schools, law firms, courts, or bar associations. For those new to chatbots, there are opportunities for law librarians to participate. Presenters are instructing on how to build chatbots at national law library conferences, and chatbot building software (such as Chatfuel) is readily available to use in conjunction with Facebook. Those with a bit of funding might opt to employ Law Droid or Josef as their legal chatbot development company. Academic law librarians are in a position to collaborate with law school clinics to build bots to serve the public. Law firm librarians are well placed to evaluate attorney and industry needs and innovate. Public law librarians could develop chatbots to expand legal research service to those unable to visit a law library. Tech-savvy law librarians could also serve as a resource to anyone interested in developing a chatbot, by providing how-to library guides and resource leads.

Robotics and Smart Machines

Literature, movies, cartoons, and other media have presented images over the years of robots functioning within society. Some of these robots have been helpful around the house, some fall in love, others become self-aware, questioning their humanity and purpose, and at least one becomes defiant and murderous. Within the context of AI, robotics "combines hardware (mechanical parts, sensors, screens, etc.) with intelligent software and data, to perform a task for which a certain level of intelligence is required (e.g., orientation, motion, interaction, etc.)."[23] Smart machines, which include robots, have the ability to make decisions without human input.[24] While legal products use creative marketing to claim to be "robot lawyers," these tend to be document-generating applications that do not take a physical form and are not autonomous. There are a few physical robots entering library spaces, however, and these come with A2J opportunities.

Libraries are primarily testing physical robots to assist with collection maintenance. The Max Planck Institute for Procedural Law in Luxembourg invited Tory, an autonomous robot developed by MetraLabs, for a library visit. Tory successfully completed a full collection inventory in one hour (an exercise that could take a staff person 400-1,000 hours) and identified eight missing books (often an impossible task).[25]

AuRoSS (an Autonomous Robotic Shelf Scanning system) is capable of similar library tasks and is supported by Singapore's Agency for Science, Technology and Research. These robots rely on RFID (radio-frequency identification) technology.

Max Planck Institute librarian Juja Chakarova further theorizes on how robots could be used to offer library maps in real time, share building temperature control data, and even interact with library users. She cites "Pepper," a robot manufactured by SoftBank Robotics, formerly Aldebaran Robotics. Pepper is showing promise as a "night-shift librarian" and will be deployed in 500 Japanese libraries.[26]

As law libraries struggle with budget cuts and staff reductions, a robot law librarian could streamline tasks and improve services to the public, especially the poor and middle class. Using robots to complete collection maintenance tasks can shift professional focus from time-consuming administrative tasks to service-oriented projects. Improved maps could better direct all library users to the resources they need and eliminate needless frustration. Employing a night-shift law librarian capable of human interaction could greatly extend library hours, offering flexibility to library visitors in need of self-help legal resources. Should technology advance into the realm of autonomous legal smart machines, one could hope that any efficiencies found could result in a less expensive legal world.

Opportunities for Law Librarians to Advance A2J Initiatives Using AI

Law Librarians as A2J Guardians

Presidential candidate Donald Trump used the phrase "extreme vetting" when describing his proposed immigration policies. In this spirit of his campaign rhetoric, President Trump's Immigration and Customs Enforcement agency held an "industry day," attended by legal research pioneer LexisNexis, to ask big data vendors to build a new tool for Homeland Security to use as its extreme vetting software.[27] CUNY School of Law librarians Sarah Lamdan and Yasmin Sokkar Harker called out LexisNexis for their support of an extreme vetting initiative and reminded law librarians of their responsibilities to protect personally identifiable information and honor the Association of College and Research Libraries (ACRL) and American Association of Law Libraries (AALL) standards regarding the ethical use of information.[28] Sarah and Yasmin serve as excellent examples of law librarians challenging a vendor and serving as A2J guardians of the legal right to privacy.

Protecting privacy is not the only ethical obligation of law librarians. A recently shared AALL committee email proposes new ethical principles, which now include a statement opposing discrimination based on immutable and personal characteristics, including but not limited to age, citizenship, gender, gender transition status, marital status, military status, origin, physical or mental ability, political beliefs, race, religion, sexual orientation, or socio-economic status.[29] This proposed principle places a responsibility on law librarians to guard patrons from discrimination within libraries; this includes making sure that AI technologies implemented in libraries are free from AI bias. One way to keep track of offending vendors is to follow ProPublica's *Machine Bias: Investigated Algorithmic Injustice* newsletter and then publically condemn legal vendors using discriminatory AI systems.[30]

Another approach to combat discrimination would be to propose and advocate for laws that regulate AI bias and offer algorithmic transparency. President Obama's administration started down this path with an AI report considering big-data challenges and opportunities within the credit industry, employment, higher education, and criminal justice.[31] More recently, bipartisan members of the house introduced a resolution to establish a Federal Advisory Committee on the Development and Implementation of Artificial Intelligence, citing the "Fundamentally Understanding The Usability and Realistic Evolution of Artificial Intelligence Act of 2017," or for short, the "FUTURE of Artificial Intelligence Act of 2017."[32] Introduced in both the House and Senate, the act has not been engrossed. Several state legislatures have been successful in passing limited AI legislation to date, but there are plenty of proposed bills for state legislatures to consider. Law librarians in positions to monitor and progress legislation could help the A2J cause by advocating for non-discriminatory data in AI algorithms and demanding transparency. A Brookings Institute author notes that "incorrect social inferences can be mitigated by giving consumers control over their digital footprint."[33] If transparency can be built into legislation, the public would be empowered to view their digital footprint, see how their data is used, and identify if discrimination is in play.

Law Librarians as AI Creators and Promoters

At last count, 26 law schools had already developed innovation centers within their buildings to explore AI and other emerging technologies.[34] Academic law librarians are supporting and, in some cases, running these innovation centers. Brigham Young University's LawX lab designed the SoloSuit chatbot to help pro se Utahns navigate the debt collection process. Michigan State University College of Law's curriculum includes a course called Artificial Intelligence and Law to support their LegalRnD Center for Legal Services Innovation. Many of these law school labs are already developing technology with A2J missions in mind, but academic law librarians have an opportunity to propose new A2J ideas and follow up on their implementation.

Law librarians are in a great position to advertise A2J trainings. The ATJ Tech Fellows program trains law students on how to develop their technological skills and then use their skills to improve access to legal services. In 2018, 23 law students earned an ATJ Tech Fellowship and were placed with a partnering legal services organization.[35] A 2017 student fellow, Chad Au from the William S. Richardson School of Law at the University of Hawai'i at Mānoa, used his fellowship to develop a chatbot to answer legal questions posed by visitors to the Legal Aid Society of Hawai'i's website.[36] Neota Logic, an AI drag-and-drop platform, offers a program to train law students and nonprofit organization staff on their Neota Logic System to develop A2J applications for their clients.[37] Law librarians have great marketing avenues to promote these opportunities.

Conclusion

This chapter began with an abbreviated history of law librarian involvement in technologies that progressed A2J causes. As technologies have evolved from corded phones and personal computers to smart phones and interactive devices, law librarian commitment to employing emerging technologies and supporting A2J initiatives remains a constant. Law librarians will master and instruct on the use of AI-inspired research tools, help develop and promote chatbots, and work robots into library workflows. Law librarians will be on the lookout for AI algorithms built with discriminatory bias that impacts communities. Law librarians will continue to safeguard patron privacy and promote access to legal services. Librarian R. David Lankes once said, "To be a librarian is not to be neutral, or passive, or waiting for a question. It is to be a radical positive change agent within your community."[38] Law librarians have opportunities to be radical positive change agents in providing access to justice in the age of AI.

RECOMMENDED READING LIST

Chakarova, Juja. "I, Robot, Can Help You, Librarian: MPI Luxembourg Library is paving the way." *MPI Luxembourg Library*. January 2, 2018, https://

www.mpi.lu/fileadmin/mpi/medien/library/News_and_Events/2018/BuB_Robots_in_Libraries.pdf.

Goodman, Joanna. *Robots in Law: How Artificial Intelligence Is Transforming Legal Services*. Peoria, IL: ARK Group, 2016.

O'Neil, Cathy. "Civilian Casualties: Justice in the Age of Big Data," in *Weapons of Math Destruction*, 84-104. New York: Crown, 2016.

Turner Lee, Nicol. "Detecting Racial Bias in Algorithms and Machine Learning." *Journal of Information, Communication, and Ethics in Society* 16, no. 3 (June 2018): 252–60.

Walters, Ed. *Data-Driven Law: Data Analytics and the New Legal Services.* Boca Raton, FL: CRC Press, 2019.

NOTES

1. J.J. Prescott, "Improving Access to Justice in State Courts with Platform Technology," *Vanderbilt Law Review* 70 (November 2017): 1994–1995.
2. Jason Tashea, "Text-message Reminders are a Cheap and Effective Way to Reduce Pretrial Detention," *ABA Journal*, July 17, 2018, http://www.abajournal.com/lawscribbler/article/text_messages_can_keep_people_out_of_jail.
3. *National Veterans Legal Services Program v. United States*, 291 F.Supp.3d 123 (D.C. Cir. 2018).
4. "RECAP Project - Turning PACER around since 2009," Free Law Project, accessed February 27, 2019, https://free.law/recap.
5. U.S. Department of Commerce, *Falling Through the Net: A Survey of the 'Have Nots' in Rural and Urban America,* (National Telecommunications and Information Administration, July 1995), https://www.ntia.doc.gov/ntiahome/fallingthru.html.
6. Stefan van Duin and Naser Bakhshi, "Artificial Intelligence Defined," Deloitte, March 2017, https://www2.deloitte.com/se/sv/pages/technology/articles/part1-artificial-intelligence-defined.html.
7. Ed Walters, *Data-Driven Law: Data Analytics and the New Legal Services* (Boca Raton, FL: CRC Press, 2019), 4.
8. Julia Angwin et al., "Machine Bias," ProPublica, May 23, 2016, https://www.propublica.org/article/machine-bias-risk-assessments-in-criminal-sentencing.
9. "Overview," PredPol, https://www.predpol.com/about.
10. K. Lum and W. Isaac, "To Predict and Serve?," *Significance* 13 (October 2016): 15.
11. Lum and Isaac, 16.

12. Cathy O'Neil, "Civilian Casualties: Justice in the Age of Big Data," in *Weapons of Math Destruction* (New York: Crown, 2016), 91.
13. O'Neil, 85.
14. AI Now Institute, "Algorithmic Impact Assessments: Toward Accountable Automation in Public Agencies," Medium, April 9, 2018, https://medium.com/@AINowInstitute/algorithmic-impact-assessments-toward-accountable-automation-in-public-agencies-bd9856e6fdde.
15. Walters, *Data-Driven Law*, 46.
16. Joanna Goodman, *Robots in Law: How Artificial Intelligence Is Transforming Legal Services* (Peoria, IL: ARK Group, 2016), 7.
17. "Welcome to the 'Voice Command Center,'" Voicea, accessed February 27, 2019, https://help.voicea.com/features/welcome-to-the-voice-command-center.
18. "Learned Hands," Learned Hands, https://learnedhands.law.stanford.edu.
19. "Learned Hands," https://learnedhands.law.stanford.edu.
20. Marcia Kaufman Hurwitz, Adrian Bowles, and Judith Hurwitz, "The Foundation of Cognitive Computing," in *Cognitive Computing and Big Data Analytics* (Indianapolis, IN: John Wiley & Sons, Incorporated, 2015), 1, http://ebookcentral.proquest.com/lib/uwy/detail.action?docID=1895129.
21. DeeAnn Allison, "Chatbots in the Library: Is It Time?," *Library Hi Tech*, 30, no. 1 (2011): 96.
22. Dan Bindman, "Regional Firm's Motoring Law Chatbot 'First of Many,'" legalfutures, August 17, 2018, https://www.legalfutures.co.uk/latest-news/regional-firms-motoring-law-chatbot-first-of-many.
23. Duin and Bakhshi, "Artificial Intelligence Defined."
24. Duin and Bakhshi, "Artificial Intelligence Defined."
25. Juja Chakarova, "I, Robot, Can Help You, Librarian: MPI Luxembourg Library is paving the way," *MPI Luxembourg Library*, January 2, 2018, https://www.mpi.lu/fileadmin/mpi/medien/library/News_and_Events/2018/BuB_Robots_in_Libraries.pdf.
26. Chakarova, "I, Robot, Can Help You, Librarian."
27. Sam Biddle and Spencer Woodman, "These are the Technology Firms Lining Up to Build Trump's 'Extreme Vetting' Program," *The Intercept*, August 7, 2017, https://theintercept.com/2017/08/07/these-are-the-technology-firms-lining-up-to-build-trumps-extreme-vetting-program.
28. Sarah Lamdan and Yasmin Sokkar Harker, "LexisNexis's Role in ICE Surveillance and Librarian Ethics," *Law Librarian Blog*, December 11, 2017, https://llb2.com/2017/12/11/ice.
29. Amy Wharton, "Comments Sought —Revised Ethical Principles Committee Draft," AALL Members Open Forum list archives, February 22, 2019, https://community.aallnet.org/communities.

30. *Machine Bias: Investigating Algorithmic Injustice,* ProPublica, https://www.propublica.org/series/machine-bias.
31. Executive Office of the President, "Big Data: A Report on Algorithmic Systems, Opportunity, and Civil Rights," The White House: President Barack Obama, Archives, May 2016, https://obamawhitehouse.archives.gov/sites/default/files/microsites/ostp/2016_0504_data_discrimination.pdf.
32. Fundamentally Understanding The Usability and Realistic Evolution of Artificial Intelligence Act of 2017, H.R. 4625, 115th Cong. (2017).
33. Nicol Turner Lee, "Detecting Racial Bias in Algorithms and Machine Learning," *Journal of Information, Communication, and Ethics in Society* 16, no. 3 (2018): 257.
34. "Directory of Law School Innovation Centers," Above the Law 2020, accessed February 27, 2019, https://abovethelaw.com/law2020/directory-of-law-school-innovation-centers.
35. "Fellowship Overview," ATJ Tech Fellows Program, https://www.atjtechfellows.org/overview.
36. Patrick Palace, "Chatbots for Justice! Is That a Thing?," American Bar Association Solo, Small Firm and General Practice Division, December 18, 2018, https://www.americanbar.org/groups/gpsolo/publications/gpsolo_ereport/2018/december-2018/chatbots-justice-is-that-thing.
37. "Law School & Pro Bono Programs," Neota Logic, https://www.neotalogic.com/pro-bono.
38. R. David Lankes, "Success through Collaboration," January 16, 2013, https://davidlankes.org/success-through-collaboration.

JAMES M. DONOVAN

10
Benefits, Drawbacks, and Risks of AI

The specter of the impact of artificial intelligence (AI) on law and legal education casts a long and uncertain shadow. Its mix of enthusiasm and trepidation can arise from a thin idea of what the label means. Four components differentiate AI from even high-end automation: big-data and predictive analytics, deep-learning software, cloud computing, and natural language processing (NLP).[1] The perspective of the person on the street, though, is captured as "the art of creating machines that perform functions that require intelligence when performed by people," centering on the ability to make independent choices.[2] While that gloss might fail as a technical specification, it appears to capture the ordinary meaning and will suffice for the purposes of this chapter, with only one additional clarification.

In the following discussion, we focus on what exists today: narrow (or weak) AI. Narrow AI refers to algorithms that are application-specific, as compared to the generalized AI that mimics the human

JAMES M. DONOVAN is the director of the law library and James and Mary Lassiter associate professor of law at the University of Kentucky College of Law Library.

ability to learn and perform on any topic. Generalized (or strong) AI does not currently exist, and some experts are skeptical that it ever will.[3] If society decides that even this limited version of AI is undesirable, all things considered, then that determination should preclude any need to separately evaluate the general variety. For the time being, therefore, we are justified in considering only the narrow version.

By that definition, we are already immersed in an AI-rich environment. The appeal is obvious: A dispassionate computer algorithm returns lower error rates when compared to humans, in part because it reasons from data without being swayed by emotions or preferred outcomes. A common example of everyday AI application occurs whenever Amazon shoppers find book recommendations based on their past views and purchases. AI's ability to find hidden patterns received a powerful demonstration when Target identified a young customer whose shopping habits signaled a pregnancy that was unknown to her parents, who had complained when the store started sending baby-related coupons.[4] AI helps spam filters learn to exclude emails of a certain kind and not just those that contain certain words. Our phones work to understand our individual dialects. With the development of self-driving cars, intelligent refrigerators, and medical diagnostics, it will be a rare individual who can claim that they have insulated themselves from this new world of nonhuman thinking and learning. Such a ubiquitous impact cannot help but reach into the practice of law.

Benefits of AI

Always seeking to gain a competitive advantage, law firms have a tradition of being early adopters of new technology (perhaps second only to health care). Legal professionals had earlier demonstrated their openness to cutting-edge methods with their quick acceptance in the seventies of one of the first full-text data services developed by LEXIS. In keeping with that pragmatism, the field has implemented a range of useful AI applications to assist in the efficient performance of routine tasks. The following are representative examples of these valuable benefits.

Legal Research

The major commercial platforms have incrementally incorporated AI into their existing tools. Most apparent to users will be the improved ability for the system to comprehend natural language, both in the queries and in the documents. This achievement expands legal research results by the identification of patterns of conceptual use and other variables beyond the strict keyword or headnote analysis that was the standard only a short time ago. Further functionality analyzes past searches and retrievals to identify the kinds of materials of interest to the patron, and then suggests additional items the algorithm concludes as being helpful. These improvements have resulted in more efficient searching, capable of identifying relevant authorities in a fraction of the time when applying traditional Boolean techniques.

Jury Selection

The hallmark of AI is the use of "Big Data"—the manipulation of large, complex datasets, too unwieldy for even simple processing by ordinary applications—to identify hidden patterns as described in the Target anecdote. This represents a qualitative change: We don't just know the usual things better and faster, but we have access to new and different kinds of relationships than were discernible just a few years ago.

Voltaire (https://voltaireapp.com/) is a legal AI company that leverages this potential to give litigators deep insights in real time into the psyches of potential jurors. As described by the company, the service "explores all public data related to the potential juror, correlates the data against known patterns in human behavior, and then produces a detailed profile, with indications of the type of person they are and how their views and biases may be a positive or negative factor as part of a jury."[5]

Outcome Prediction

For several years, attorneys have had the ability to examine how certain kinds of cases typically fare in specific jurisdictions or before certain judges, although without offering a determination on how one's current case might fit into this pattern. Because it can access more data and identify hidden patterns not readily discernible to the human expert, AI makes possible that critical last step. For example, the London firm of Hodge Jones & Allen invested in a tool to predict likely outcomes of personal injury cases in order to help decide whether to settle.[6] Additional work is begin pursued that will allow similar determinations, but at the level of the deciding judge.[7]

E-Discovery

Empirical research has demonstrated that technology-assisted review of large document sets to find relevant documents is both more effective at finding desirable items and accomplishes this superior result more efficiently—and more cheaply—than traditional manual review.[8] Beyond the search for mere keywords, AI identifies context, concepts, and tone through the application of predictive coding. Predictive coding—the marking by experts of sample documents that the program employs to identify similar items—enjoys official judicial approval after it was declared that "computer-assisted review is an available tool and should be seriously considered for use in large-data-volume cases where it may save the producing party (or both parties) significant amounts of legal fees in document review."[9]

Contracts

The first successful use of AI in the law firm was LONald in 2015 by the firm of Berwin Leighton Paisner for the purpose of contract due diligence.[10] Because AI is able to manipulate concepts as well as words, it has proven to be a valuable tool to generate consistent agreements. Although the greater speed and accuracy of AI systems as compared to human performance is often taken as given, contract analysis is one of the few areas in which the two sides have directly competed. When evaluating five Non-Disclosure Agreements for problematic issues, the AI "achieved an average 94 percent accuracy rate, ahead of the lawyers who achieved an average rate of 85 percent."[11] The time required to reach these results was even more dramatically different: "On average, it took 92 minutes for the lawyer participants to complete all five NDAs. . . . In contrast, the AI engine completed the task of issue-spotting in 26 seconds."

Personnel

As the results of the head-to-head comparison suggest, a key benefit of the new technology is that the proven superiority in performing the routine tasks of legal practice can help firms to control personnel costs. Although several authors have been predicting that AI will result in major disruptions in the legal market—and despite clients pushing firms to adopt these tools to realize lower charges on their service bills—thus far, the rise in AI applications has not directly impacted the numbers finding legal employment.[12]

Still, fear of displacement could lead practitioners to dismiss the benefits of AI. One of the authors of the e-discovery effectiveness study, Maura Grossman, has acknowledged that some attorneys harbor a resistance to admitting that a machine can do a task better than humans. She described an experiment showing that, even after a demonstration that the algorithm can better predict outcomes, subjects bet against it in favor of their own judgments. Grossman interprets this pattern as illustrating a tendency of some lawyers to be more critical of machine failures but highly tolerant of human error, perhaps feeling that "there but for the grace of God. . . ."[13]

Instead of real numbers declining, what we have seen are changes in the kinds of work that attorneys now are able to do. Freed from rote tasks, attorneys will have more opportunity to undertake creative tasks that provide an intellectual and professionally stimulating challenge. The avoidance of unnecessary stress and frustration can lead to fewer attorneys experiencing burnout.[14]

Drawbacks of AI

Benefits of the thoughtful development and deployment of AI applications accrue to almost every fact of legal practice. However, we must also recognize that even when AI performs as intended, it can generate negative repercussions. These drawbacks require that AI not merely be adopted solely for the upside; a cost-benefit analysis should be performed in each case to determine if benefits outweigh the possible costs.

Potential problems associated with the introduction of AI into daily legal practice arise at two discrete levels of concern. The first considers how AI can create challenges within law, while the second acknowledges that society at large has its own interests in such developments. Whether new applications that offer clear benefits to the profession should be shelved because of the broader ramifications remains a legitimate question. The following are examples of the potential drawbacks.

Costs

Most products must be developed inside each firm to take advantage of its specific expertise. Creation of AI utilities can be expensive in terms of both time and money. One vendor estimates that a typical AI application can cost up to $300K to create and train.[15] The firm's expectation is that in the long run, it will be able to recoup this expenditure: Businesses making this investment are estimated to realize a 38 percent revenue boost.[16] This view, however, ignores the opportunity costs that can be required. The machine learning (ML) that is at the core of successful AI development requires that experts who would otherwise spend their time billing for services to clients must instead spend their time training the system by coding documents and evaluating results. Some practices might not be in a financial position to make this investment, putting them at further disadvantage relative to those that are.

Unintended Consequences

A product intended to offer strategic advantage can lead to unexpected outcomes, some of them undesirable. As previously mentioned, many attorneys worry that if research results can now be obtained in minutes rather than hours, this could result in fewer personnel who would otherwise be hired to perform such tasks. Although firm staffing has not significantly seen reductions for this reason, that could change down the road.

The more immediate issue concerns not staffing, but billing. *Cass*, a Canadian case (discussed in chapter 7), denied a research bill as excessive, in light of the fact that "If artificial intelligence sources were employed, no doubt counsel's preparation time would have been significantly reduced."[17] The more efficiently work is performed, the less likely clients are to pay the costs traditionally charged for that work product. Such a change would force a move away from the billable hour and the adoption of alternative arrangements—as yet unspecified—regarding how firms bill for services and, indirectly, how they pay their attorneys.[18]

Compulsory AI

Although few attorneys would mourn the loss of the billable hour, the movement toward the ordinary employment of AI tools points in another direction that they might find less attractive. At last count, 35 states have adopted the ABA Model Rule 1.1 (Duty of Competence) revised Comment 8, which requires technological knowledge for ethical legal practice.[19] The rule encourages attorneys to have comparable relevant expertise as those with whom they frequently interact (e.g., C-level executives) and to ensure that client services are streamlined to maximize efficiency, privacy, and cost effectiveness.

When first proposed in 2012, the understanding of the standard focused on the lawyer's understanding of matters such as how cloud computing can be ethically utilized to store client documents, proper management of social media, or how to strip inappropriate metadata from electronic documents before sharing.[20] Today, though, reasoning in cases like *Cass*, which underscores the efficiency of AI-powered researching, can, when paired with the duty of technological competence, lead to the further conclusion that the use of AI is not merely desirable and beneficial, but actually necessary to the competent practice of law.[21] There have been hints that a similar progression is already gaining ground in the practice of medicine.[22] Should the adoption of AI tools become not a strategic option but either formally or de facto compulsory for the ethical and competent practice of law, the impact would fall heaviest on smaller practices that lack the resources to create their own tools or find the subscriptions to proprietary applications prohibitively expensive.

Lack of Creativity

Earlier it was mentioned that today's AI is of a narrow or weak variety. In other words, it is able to handle only a well-defined set of tasks. An AI trained in contract evaluations, for example, is unable to function on predicting litigation outcomes. Importantly, this is not simply due to a lack of training; the tool lacks the infrastructure to recognize and process the relevant data, even if exposed. Strong or general AI, on the other hand, would be able to process whatever the request, in much the same manner as a human can perform nearly any task required.

Although narrow AI is sufficient for many purposes, we should be aware of what its functional limitations include. AI (at least thus far) can only tell us, given past examples of applying current rules, what will be the likely legal solution to a query.[23] What it cannot tell us, though, is the *right* thing to do. For example, given the parameters under which the platform operates, almost by definition it can never counsel that the situation requires altering the system itself, perhaps by jury nullification or by arguing to reject the doctrine of stare decisis. Consequently, an AI-driven legal system will, on the whole, tend to further entrench the status quo.

One might respond to this observation by noting that AI only offers recommendations and that it is always up to the practitioner's professional judgment as to what should actually be done. In practical terms, as already suggested, professionals are often ill-advised to not contradict the AI system because it normally performs better than people. However, problem solving by humans frequently requires more than the mere application of rules, often needing creative connections and insights built upon cross-disciplinary knowledge that is inaccessible to the narrow AI. Although most legal tasks do not require such expansive resources, we might not be well served by growing too dependent on a system that excludes them.

Not all of the potential drawbacks of an AI-dominated legal industry will fall on the profession itself. Society at large risks exposure to more generalized ramifications.

Overdependence on Automation

A repeated complaint among law librarians is that the "Googlization" of Westlaw and Lexis has resulted in law students increasingly relying on the machine to do work that lawyers should perform. Perhaps much as the use of calculators in math class allowed students to externalize their understanding of the underlying principles, law students, because the discovery of results no longer depends on knowing beforehand exactly where the information sought is likely to reside, tend to come comparatively later to disciplinary defaults (such as that public laws will be found in the *Statutes at Large*). AI functionality promises to exacerbate this reliance. Instead of using the tool as an assist, it threatens to become a substitute for the professional expertise of the attorney.

Recall that algorithms cannot make strategic decisions for the case, but only assign a statistical likelihood to the differing options that satisfy the search criteria. Final decision falls to human consumers, who, if they are to remain sufficiently skilled to make that call, must retain the same level of material and methodological expertise as existed in the pre-AI environment. Yet the effort to learn something that a machine will normally do better will prove a poor enticement, with perhaps little reward, not only in law, but in all manners of professional and technical expertise. Society must be aware of the altering incentives for training and education, and shape its curricula and incentives accordingly.

Professional Status

While the unsettling impact of AI on the legal profession is frequently discussed, the effects of this disruption are not a purely internal concern. Law must maintain not only an actual level of efficiency and expertise, but be perceived as doing so. Otherwise the social contract that underlies its distinctive status as a profession might be deemed void. As already mentioned, overreliance on automated legal expertise could advance far enough that it impacts what attorneys are expected to know for themselves. The resulting changes in perceptions as to what it means to be a "lawyer" could lead to a decreased respect and a grant of self-regulation, should practitioners come to be viewed as mere technicians, while the machines do most of the serious work. Without prudent integration of these powerful knowledge tools into the practice of law, the field could risk losing recognition as one of the archetypical professions, with all that flows from that status.

Legal Diversity

One of the lessons from legal anthropology concerns the unintended consequences of a well-intentioned change in the accessibility of legal information. For example, when Botswana was a part of the British Empire, the administrators asked Isaac Schapera to collect the oral legal traditions of the local peoples. To his disappointment, the resulting descriptive ethnography came to be applied as a prescriptive code of what the law should be, thereby freezing in place what to that point had been a fluid and flexible system of law.[24]

Because law is fundamentally a set of rules and procedures, in theory the entire judicial process should be ideal for intelligent automation. In practice, however, laws exist to govern human behavior and form a framework for society. While consumers can hope that AI would be capable of recognizing and reflecting local variation on legal norms, the more likely outcome is that the algorithms will be trained on data from a specific jurisdiction. Exposing them to all regional variations, with a corresponding ability to limit analysis to a subset thereof, might not always be practical. Increased legal automation could therefore result in an unplanned legal homogenization. To the extent that we judge as desirable variations around what society considers acceptable or unacceptable, we can debate whether automating justice should be allowed to outpace our ability to program that diversity into the algorithm.

Even functioning as designed, AI can create problems while solving others. Now that a sizeable record of AI performance is available, the discussion has occasionally turned to risks arising when AI operations deviate from their designed parameters. They will still be following their programming, but not always performing in the manner the creators intended.

Bias

The marquee benefit of AI algorithms—the ability to predict future outcomes based on past events—has a dark side. Given the way in which AI self-programs, the means by which it arrives at its decisions cannot be fully known. In the literature, this is known as "the black box" problem, which became an issue in *State v. Loomis.*[25] In that case, a defendant who was sentenced based on a recidivism assessment derived from a commercial algorithm called "COMPAS" (an acronym for Correctional Offender Management Profiling for Alternative Sanctions). The court held that the use of an automated assessment was not a violation of his due-process rights, even though neither the court nor the defendant had access to the algorithm to better understand how it had arrived at its determination that the defendant was at risk to recommit.

It is worth noting that the EU has chosen a different route than the USA. Its newly effective General Data Protection Regulation explicitly limits the extent to which a person can be subject to automated judgments, going further to incorporate a right to explanation concerning any such automated decision when it occurs.[26] How this second rule will be applied is yet unknown given that, due to the black box problem, it might not be physically possible to offer the explanation that the law requires and which the subject needs to mount a meaningful rebuttal.

In any event, the *Loomis* court's certainty that no rights were violated by the procedural reliance upon automated risk assessments should be questioned in light of ProPublica's finding that COMPAS reported that "black defendants were far more likely than white defendants to be incorrectly judged to be at a higher risk of recidivism, while white defendants were more likely than black defendants to be incorrectly flagged as low risk."[27] In other words, AI algorithms have proven capable of being as biased as the societies that created them, contrary to the expectations of their programmers.

Bias of one kind or another is a common result, certainly not limited to this one product. The factors that skewed the COMPAS predictions have impacted other systems as well, such as one used to predict child abuse.[28] Hewlett Packard computers equipped with facial-tracking software that functioned with white faces proved unable to recognize African Americans; similarly, an AI-judged beauty pageant appeared unfavorable to nonwhite contestants.[29] Google was shown to display fewer employment ads for higher paying jobs when the user was marked as female than as male.[30] The list of similarly disturbing AI examples of the irrelevant biases of humans could be greatly expanded.

These are all examples of inaccurate biases due to training on historical data that incorporates those biases. Those assumptions then become part of the pattern learned by the system to interpret future cases. Even when overt markers of race, sex, etc., are removed in an attempt to guide the algorithm away from considering those variables, the system can discover proxy indicators (e.g., ZIP codes for race) that yield the same outcomes.

The risk for the profession, as well as for society in general, is that these biases might not be recognized. If, as considered earlier, attorneys tend to defer to the system's suggestions, we could find these biases not only propagated but also routinized for the future.

To avoid such cases, it has been suggested that we should create an "FDA"-type watchdog for algorithms.[31] In line with that idea, the previous Congress saw the introduction of the "FUTURE of Artificial Intelligence Act of 2017," which had as one purpose to study "how bias can be identified and eliminated in the development of artificial intelligence."[32] Although national legislation on this problem remains a distant prospect, New York City has become the first jurisdiction to require that all automated decision systems be reviewed for "equity, fairness, and accountability."[33]

Legal Responsibility

In 2015, a factory robot grabbed and killed a man.[34] A self-driving car killed a pedestrian in 2018.[35] Who bears legal responsibility for these acts? The machine? The programmer? The owner or user?

Jacob Turner's recent book, *Robot Rules*, considers these alternatives in some detail. The issues are complex and will require attorneys and policy makers to think more deliberately about assumptions they had previously taken as self-evident. Unlike other machines, AI is exceptional because it makes moral choices and can develop independently.[36] The second feature especially suggests that the existing product liability regimes cannot be extended to encompass the bad actions of AI.[37]

Alternatively, we must consider whether the AI itself should be held responsible. Nonhuman entities can already have legal standing and responsibility. Corporations are perhaps the most obvious example, and some advocate for the legal personality of animals. Where will AI fall in this continuum, especially given developments such as Saudi Arabia's grant of "citizenship" to a humanoid robot?[38] To the extent that legal responsibility follows choice and understanding of consequences, AI seems quite close to what we require of humans when holding them liable for actions.

If those questions seem a ways off for legal practices, we can begin with a relatively simple problem closer to home, such as who is responsible for a false positive or negative produced by the AI engine upon which the attorney subsequently relies? If it veers toward malpractice to fail to use AI, as the direction we are headed in suggests, who is ultimately responsible for the bad decision?

Even in his text, Turner is unable to definitively answer such questions, but he reminds us that as we work to create tools whose primary quality is their approximation of human intelligence, they might also come to shoulder some of the burdens of that accomplishment. It will fall to lawyers using good reasons to draw the necessary distinctions and stake out the defensible boundaries.

NOTES

1. Joanna Goodman, *Robots in Law: How Artificial Intelligence Is Transforming Legal Services* (London: Ark, 2016), 7.
2. Ray Kurzweil, *The Age of Intelligent Machines* (Cambridge, MA: MIT Press, 1992), 14; Jacob Turner, *Robot Rules: Regulating Artificial Intelligence* (London: Palgrave Macmillan, 2019), 15.
3. Turner, *Robot Rules,* 6.

4. Charles Duhigg, "How Companies Learn Your Secrets," *New York Times,* February 16, 2012, https://www.nytimes.com/2012/02/19/magazine/shopping-habits.html?pagewanted=1&_r=1&hp.
5. "Voltaire Uses AI and Big Data to Help Pick Your Jury," *Artificial Lawyer,* April 26, 2017, https://www.artificiallawyer.com/2017/04/26/voltaire-uses-ai-and-big-data-to-help-pick-your-jury/.
6. Michael Cross, "Role of Artificial Intelligence in Law," *Raconteur,* February 19, 2015, https://www.raconteur.net/risk-management/time-for-technology-to-take-over.
7. Daniel L. Chen, "Machine Learning and the Rule of Law," in *Computational Analysis of Law,* eds. M. Livermore and D. Rockmore (Santa Fe, NM: Santa Fe Institute Press, 2019).
8. Maura R. Grossman and Gordon V. Cormack, "Technology-Assisted Review in E-Discovery Can Be More Effective and More Efficient Than Exhaustive Manual Review," *Richmond Journal of Law & Technology* 17, no. 3 (2011), 11.
9. *Da Silva Moore v. Publicis Groupe & MSL Grp.,* 287 F.R.D. 182 (2012).
10. Goodman, *Robots in Law,* 30.
11. Lawgeex, *Comparing the Performance of Artificial Intelligence to Human Lawyers in the Review of Standard Business Contracts* (New York: Lawgeex, 2018), https://images.law.com/contrib/content/uploads/documents/397/5408/lawgeex.pdf.
12. John O. McGinnis and Russell G. Pearce, "The Great Disruption: How Machine Intelligence Will Transform the Role of Lawyers into the Delivery of Legal Services," *Fordham Law Review* 82, no. 6 (2014), 3041. See also Richard Suskind, *Tomorrow's Lawyers: An Introduction to Your Future* (2d ed., Oxford: Oxford University Press, 2017); Richard Suskind and Daniel Suskind, *The Future of the Professions: How Technology Will Transform the Work of Human Experts* (Oxford: Oxford University Press, 2016); Sam Skolnik, "Artificial Intelligence Creeps into Big Law, Endangers Some Jobs," *Bloomberg Law Big Law Business,* January 22, 2019), https://biglawbusiness.com/artificial-intelligence-creeps-into-big-law-endangers-some-jobs.
13. Maura Grossman, Ralph Losey, and Geoffrey Kingsporn, "E-Discovery," *Exterro EdTalks,* May 18, 2018, https://www.exterro.com/resources/edtalks-presentations-5/.
14. Leslie Gordon, "How Attorneys Can Avoid Burnout and Debilitating Anxiety," *ABA Journal* 101, no. 7 (July 2015): 59.
15. "How Much Does Artificial Intelligence (AI) Cost in 2019?," *Azati Software Blog,* January 23, 2019, https://azati.com/how-much-does-it-cost-to-utilize-machine-learning-artificial-intelligence/.
16. Ellyn Shook and Mark Knickrehm, *Reworking the Revolution* (New York: Accenture, 2018), 3, https://www.accenture.com/t20180613T062119Z_w_/nl-en/_acnmedia/PDF-69/Accenture-Reworking -the-Revolution-Jan-2018-POV.pdf#zoom=50.

17. *Cass v. 1410088 Ontario Inc.,* 2018 ONSC 6959 (2018) (CanLII), 34 http://canlii.ca/t/hw728.
18. Geordie Clark, "Billable Hour 'Makes No Sense' in an AI World," *Raconteur,* November 27, 2018, https://www.raconteur.net/risk-management/ai-analytics-billable-hour.
19. Robert Ambrogi, "Tech Competence," *LawSites* (blog), https://www.lawsitesblog.com/tech-competence.
20. Jamie J. Baker, "Beyond the Information Age: The Duty of Technology Competence in the Algorithmic Age," *South Carolina Law Review* 69, no. 3 (2018): 557.
21. Jamie J. Baker, "Are Algorithms Required for Ethical Legal Research?," *The Ginger (Law) Librarian,* February 1, 2019, http://www.gingerlawlibrarian.com/2019/02/are-algorithms-required-for-ethical.html.
22. Matthew Turner, "Does a Doctor's Failure to Use AI to Diagnose a Patient Constitute Medical Malpractice?," *Sommers Schwartz Blog,* April 20, 2018, https://www.sommerspc.com/blog/2018/04/does-a-doctors-failure-to-use-ai-to-diagnose-a-patient-constitute-medical-malpractice/.
23. Legal philosophers may note that this observation suggests that law will increasingly resemble Justice Holmes's observation that law is whatever the courts are willing to enforce. Oliver Wendall Holmes, Jr., "The Path of Law," *Harvard Law Review* 10, no. 8 (1897): 457, 461.
24. Suzette Heald, "The Legacy of Isaac Schapera," *Anthropology Today* 19, no. 6 (Dec. 2003): 18.
25. Nizan Geslevich Packin and Yafit Lev Aretz, "Learning Algorithms and Discrimination," in *Research Handbook of Artificial Intelligence and Law,* eds. Woodrow Barfield and Ugo Pagallo (Northampton, MA: Edward Elgar, 2018), 88, 92. *State v. Loomis,* 881 N.W.2d 749 (Wis. 2016).
26. Art. 22: "The data subject shall have the right not to be subject to a decision based solely on automated processing, including profiling, which produces legal effects concerning him or her or similarly significantly affects him or her," https://gdpr-info.eu/art-22-gdpr/; Art 13(2)(f): "The controller shall, at the time when personal data are obtained, provide the data subject with the following further information necessary to ensure fair and transparent processing . . . the existence of automated decision-making, including profiling, referred to in Article 22(1) and (4) and, at least in those cases, meaningful information about the logic involved, as well as the significance and the envisaged consequences of such processing for the data subject," https://gdpr-info.eu/art-13-gdpr/.
27. Jeff Larson, Surya Mattu, Lauren Kirchner, and Julia Angwin, "How We Analyzed the COMPAS Recidivism Algorithm," ProPublica, May 23, 2016, https://www.propublica.org/article/how-we-analyzed-the-compas-recidivism-algorithm.
28. Virginia Eubanks, "A Child Abuse Prediction Model Fails Poor Families," *Wired,* January 15, 2018, https://www.wired.com/story/excerpt-from-automating-inequality/.

29. Brian X. Chen, "HP Investigates Claims of 'Racist' Computers," *Wired,* December 22, 2009, https://www.wired.com/2009/12/hp-notebooks-racist/; Sam Levin, "A Beauty Contest Was Judged by AI and the Robots Didn't Like Dark Skin," The Guardian, September 8, 2016, https://www.theguardian.com/technology/2016/sep/08/artificial-intelligence-beauty-contest-doesnt-like-black-people.
30. Amit Datta, Michael Carl Tschantz, and Anupam Datta, "Automated Experiments on Ad Privacy Settings," *Proceedings on Privacy Enhancing Technologies* 1 (2015), 92, https://content.sciendo.com/view/journals/popets/2015/1/article-p92.xml.
31. "New York Bulletin – AI Workshop + Do We Need an FDA for Algorithms," *Artificial Lawyer,* January 29, 2019, https://www.artificiallawyer.com/2019/01/29/new-york-bulletin-ai-workshop-do-we-need-an-fda-for-algorithms/.
32. H.R. 4625, 115th Cong. (2017).
33. New York City, Office of the Mayor, "Mayor de Blasio Announces First-In-Nation Task Force To Examine Automated Decision Systems Used by the City," News, May 16, 2018, https://www1.nyc.gov/office-of-the-mayor/news/251-18/mayor-de-blasio-first-in-nation-task-force-examine-automated-decision-systems-used-by.
34. Associated Press, "Robot Kills Worker at Volkswagen Plant in Germany," *The Guardian,* July 1, 2015, https://www.theguardian.com/world/2015/jul/02/robot-kills-worker-at-volkswagen-plant-in-germany; see also James Temperton, "When Robots Kill: Deaths by Machines Are Nothing New But AI Is About to Change Everything," *Wired,* March 17, 2017, https://www.wired.co.uk/article/robot-death-wanda-holbrook-lawsuit.
35. Troy Griggs and Daisuke Wakabayashi, "How a Self-Driving Uber Killed a Pedestrian in Arizona," *New York Times,* March 21, 2018, https://www.nytimes.com/interactive/2018/03/20/us/self-driving-uber-pedestrian-killed.html?mtrref=www.google.com.
36. Turner, *Robot Rules,* 64.
37. Turner, *Robot Rules,* 91.
38. Zara Stone, "Everything You Need to Know about Sophia, the World's First Robot Citizen," *Forbes,* November 7, 2017, https://www.forbes.com/sites/zarastone/2017/11/07/everything-you-need-to-know-about-sophia-the-worlds-first-robot-citizen/#5da9179a46fa.

SCOTT BAILEY, HUU NGUYEN, SASKIA MEHLHORN,
STEVE LASTRES, STEVE DELCHIN, and JANINE CERNY

11

Ethics in the Use of AI

A Lawyer's Perspective

At a time when legal applications of artificial intelligence (AI) were no more than a distant thought, other industries were already in the midst of the adoption of AI-driven technologies. Financial institutions, health-care providers, and the automotive industry were among the first to dive into the world of AI and show other industries the possibilities and restrictions of adopting new technologies.

Skip a few years forward, and today the legal industry is increasingly using artificial intelligence in its practices to improve the efficiency and accuracy of legal services offered to clients. But while AI offers cutting-edge advantages and benefits, it also raises complicated questions implicating professional ethics. Law librarians must be aware

SCOTT BAILEY is the director of research services at Eversheds Sutherland (U.S.) LLP. **HUU NGUYEN** is a partner at Squire Patton Boggs (U.S.) LLP and a member of ABA Board for Robotics and AI. **SASKIA MEHLHORN** is the U.S. director of knowledge services at Norton Rose Fulbright U.S. LLP. **STEVE LASTRES** is the director of knowledge management services at Debevoise & Plimpton LLP. **STEVE DELCHIN** is a senior attorney at Squire Patton Boggs (U.S.) LLP. **JANINE CERNY** is an associate at Squire Patton Boggs (U.S.) LLP.

of the ethical issues involved in using (and not using) AI, and they must have an awareness of how AI might be flawed or biased.

How AI Is Being Used in the Practice of Law

AI is not the "robot lawyer" of popular imagination. It is, however, a powerful tool for finding patterns and perceiving connections within those collections that might be overlooked by humans. As Bryan Cave litigation partner and Chief Information Officer Kathryn DeBord says,

> At root, AI processes a lot of information and identifies patterns within that information. And the more humans interact with it, the more it can learn, suggest, and identify new patterns. Right now, AI is used in the legal field primarily to facilitate document review and to conduct due diligence as well as legal research.[1]

Unlike traditional legal search tools such as Westlaw or Lexis, which rely on keyword searching to extract information, AI searches conceptually. Using sophisticated algorithms that combine linguistic analysis, statistical probability and prediction, and initial guidance from human experts, AI seemingly "understands" documents by evaluating the relationships among words and the documents that contain them. No longer constrained by literal-minded keyword searching, AI software can make effective and reliable inferences into which documents are likely responsive to a specific question, with a remarkable degree of accuracy. As AI becomes even more advanced in the coming years, it fundamentally will transform the practice of law. Lawyers who do not adopt AI-driven tools will be left behind.

There are many different ways that lawyers are using AI to improve productivity and provide better legal services to their clients. The following are several of the main examples.

Electronic Discovery/Predictive Coding

Law firms, predictably, use AI for electronic discovery. In the past, the primary use case was the technology-assisted review (TAR), in which a lawyer trained the computer how to categorize documents in a case. Through a method of predictive coding, the AI technology is able to classify documents as relevant or irrelevant, among other classifications, after extrapolating data gathered from a sample of documents classified by the lawyer.[2] TAR itself has undergone an evolution and now incorporates an approach that is called "continuous active learning."[3]

Document review lawyers start to code documents with the computer sitting in the background, analyzing their entries and providing the reviewers documents deemed important. With this approach, no initial seed set of documents has to be determined, leading to a considerable increase in accuracy and speed.

Another AI-driven development in e-discovery is the use of technology in the extraction and presentation of text messages. Statista statistics predicts that, by 2020, approximately 2.34 billion consumers will be using mobile messaging apps,[4] which will lead to an increased need to extract this information and make it available in court proceedings. Traditionally, extraction was a complex, time-consuming process mainly dependent on prior knowledge and extensive domain proficiency. With the consistent development of deep learning and representation learning, this has been replaced by an automated method that relies on the identification and extraction of unstructured data sets and further classifying those sets.[5]

Litigation Analysis/Predictive Analysis

AI is changing the way lawyers think, the way they do business, and the way they interact with clients. AI is more than legal technology. It can now be used to predict the outcome of litigation through the method of predictive analytics. AI tools utilize case law, public records, dockets, and jury verdicts to identify patterns in past and current data.[6] The AI then analyzes the facts of a lawyer's case to provide an intelligent prediction of the outcome.[7]

Virtually all of the major legal-research vendors now provide litigation analytics tools. LexisNexis acquired RavelLaw and LexMachina and recently integrated both platforms into the Lexis Advance platform, which now provides data analytics on case law, expert witnesses, judges, motions, and law firms, as well as by practice area. Similarly, Thomson rolled out Westlaw Edge, which has competing litigation analytics. Not to be left behind, Bloomberg Law deployed its own litigation analytics module.

We are now seeing the rise of niche startups in the litigation analytics space. For example, Casetext can ingest a legal brief, and then identify and suggest relevant cases that could strengthen the brief. Similarly, a lawyer can have Casetext ingest an opposing counsel's brief, to help discover what cases were omitted from it.

As adoption rates for legal analytics tools rise, there will certainly be pressure for all lawyers to adopt litigation analytics tools. The data-driven lawyer of tomorrow will be able to be more persuasive in court, do a better job identifying a reliable expert witness, and know more about their own firm and attorneys. As technology continues to improve, the ability to extract and classify legal language will improve, and the types of questions legal analytics can answer will continue to multiply. Questions that once seemed impossible to answer are now answered with a quick dashboard lookup. With strong adoption at the largest law firms already, the legal market is poised to continue to incorporate more quantitative tools into both the business and practice of law.

Contract Management

Law librarians use AI tools to assist with contract management. This fact is particularly valuable to anyone who quickly needs to identify important information in contracts. For example, AI tools can flag termination dates and alert the information professional about deadlines for sending a notice of renewal. The AI tools also can identify important provisions in contracts, such as most-favored-nation clauses, indemnification obligations, and choice of law provisions.[8] In general, this area can be divided into two larger use cases: on the one side, the administration of contract creation through collaboration platforms, and, on the other, the management of the contract through the incorporation of proofreading tools and clause library integration.

Collaboration platforms at their core are not AI tools but instead, a way to manage cases through one platform that allows communication among clients and lawyers, document editing, calendaring, etc. The incorporation of AI applications does, however, allow a deeper integration between the client and the law firm. One of the scenarios is the integration of predictive analytics, where the connection between client data and outside intelligence allows the firm to foresee potential threats in the future. [9]

The other side of contract management is the incorporation of AI-driven algorithms into document proofreading and clause library capabilities, which is of special interest for law firms. One of the vendors in this sphere has delivered different contract tools that are of interest across practice areas, with one reducing the time spent on proofreading by reportedly up to 90 percent, and the other by providing automated development and access to the firm's clause library. Both tools are part of an integrated matter management process that is possible through ML and content analytics.

Due Diligence Reviews

AI is being used to assist in automated due diligence review for corporate transactions to reduce the burden of reviewing large numbers of documents.[10] Similar to contract management, a due diligence review involves the computer identifying and summarizing key clauses from contracts.[11]

Easing the time-consuming and costly burden of due diligence and enhancing the accuracy of the process have long been management goals in law firms—and the ability to do both is considered to be one of the primary efficiencies illustrating the potential of AI. Companies including Kira Systems, LawGeex, Luminance, eBrevia, ThoughtRiver, iManage RAVN, and Leverton aim to analyze transactional documents and instantly identify clauses of concern. Highlighting these clauses in contracts and transactional documents allows the attorney to immediately begin substantive work, rather than spend hours reading, analyzing, and searching. The extent of this benefit to law firms is hard to estimate, but saving time and money is typically expressed in hundreds of hours and millions of dollars for major firms and transactions. These software companies tout intelligent "extraction" of the exact clauses and concepts needed within very large document sets, saving hours of document review for the attorneys at rates of $350 per hour and above. This translates to significant savings for the client and allows law firms to elevate their level of work toward a more-customized model. Driving the value of work from the more-commodified document review and due diligence processes toward a "bespoke" high-value level of service delivery is a key differentiator for the world's top firms. In many cases, tools such as these due diligence AI software platforms allow firms to forgo contracting with lower-cost contract attorneys or alternative-service providers for their "lower value" document review work. This is also a major savings for the firm and their clients.

The primary differentiator between an AI due diligence review and an automated textual search is that this technology uses machine learning (ML) to identify clauses of concern rather than just strictly looking for matching text. These systems learn from human requirements to turn unstructured data in a mass of corporate documents into structured data for rapid analysis.

As a result of this technological leap for document review and due diligence, firms are aiming to be more global and service oriented, increasing their volume and breadth of selling services to clients across the world. With added efficiency built into their due diligence processes due to the strength of these AI platforms, firms can service a client more deeply with more attention to the higher-value, sophisticated work, while offering the ability to do more-commodified work at a substantial volume discount. The competitive advantage for those implementing this technology effectively is clear, and the market for these services will only strengthen as their widespread use and quality improve.

"Wrongdoing" Detection

For a number of years, corporations have used the concept of predictive coding to search their internal records in order to detect bad behavior preemptively and avoid public scrutiny. AI-driven technology is able to see beyond attempts to disguise wrongdoing and identify code words[12] and can further review employee emails to determine morale, which could lead to identification of wrongdoing.[13] For example, in one test using emails of Enron executives, AI was able to detect tension amongst employees that was correlated with a questionable business deal.[14]

For law firms, this is not only of interest as they are scrutinizing their own employees' behavior, but furthermore as they work with clients on domestic and international deals that require extensive investigation of all parties involved. AI can be used to detect bribery, fraud, compliance issues, and potential litigation—and furthermore, to extract the essence of conversations.

Legal Research

Legal research has always been core to the practice of law. AI technology was infused a decade ago into research tools to provide natural language searching, but it is becoming increasingly sophisticated. With AI, lawyers can rely on natural language queries—rather than simple Boolean queries—to return more meaningful and more insightful results.[15] AI also can be used to produce basic legal memos. One AI program, ROSS Intelligence, which uses IBM's Watson AI technology, can produce a brief legal memo in response to a lawyer's legal question.[16] Over time, such AI technology will become more and more powerful.

Unlike traditional legal-search tools such as Westlaw or Lexis, which rely on keyword searching to extract information, AI searches conceptually. Using sophisticated algorithms that combine linguistic analysis, statistical probability and prediction, and initial guidance from human experts, AI seemingly understands documents by evaluating the relationships among words and the documents that contain them. No longer constrained by literal-minded keyword searching, AI software can make effective and reliable inferences as to which documents are likely responsive to a specific question with a remarkable degree of accuracy.

Today's AI-infused legal-research tools not only return relevant cases and secondary sources, but also provide highly responsive suggestions that answer thousands of types of black-letter-law questions. In fact, both Lexis and Westlaw are working on the ability for researchers to ask digital assistants such as Alexa and Siri their legal-research questions and obtain answers immediately on a smart phone, iPad, or other smart device. Further, as AI gets better at linguistically analyzing searches, it can determine user intent to serve up exactly what a researcher might be looking for. It doesn't take a lot of imagination to see that AI-infused legal research tools can be far more efficient at answering legal questions and also at providing insight and context.

However, using these AI tools does not come without risk. There are some AI methods that are much more of a black box (such as deep learning), while other methods are much more explainable. A lawyer must be an educated consumer and be aware of the important differences in AI technologies that could lead to different results depending on the tool that is relied upon.

Law librarians, who have managed print collections and provided legal research instruction to lawyers for over a century (first in books and then using computer-assisted legal research platforms), are best qualified to now extend instruction to AI legal-research platforms. The construction of virtual collections that include an AI corpus can be strengthened with law librarian expertise. Further, law librarians can play a critical role in helping lawyers to both reduce AI-related risks and become more information and technology literate, in order to fulfill their ethical duties.

AI to Detect Deception[17]

Finally, as AI becomes more advanced, lawyers can use it to detect deception. Researchers, for example, are working on developing AI that can detect deception in the courtroom. In one test run, an AI-system performed with 92 percent accuracy, which researchers described as "significantly better" than humans.[18] While AI is still being developed for use in courtrooms, it already is being deployed outside the practice of law. For example, the United States, Canada, and European Union have run pilot programs using deception-detecting kiosks for border security.[19]

Being Aware of AI

The bottom line is that it is essential for any information professional to be aware of how AI can be used in their day-to-day work. AI translates into better, faster, and more-efficient legal services to companies and organizations. The end result is that lawyers using AI are better counselors for their clients. In the next few years, the use of AI by law firms will be no different than the use of email—an indispensable part of the practice of law.[20]

Not surprisingly, given its benefits, more and more business leaders are embracing AI, and they naturally will expect both their in-house team and outside service providers to embrace it as well. Those who already are experienced users of AI technology will have an advantage and will be viewed as more valuable to their organizations and clients. From a professional development standpoint, legal professionals need to stay ahead of the curve when it comes to AI. But even apart from the business dynamics, professional ethics requires them to be aware of AI and how it can be used to deliver client services. As explored next, a number of ethical rules apply to lawyers' use and non-use of AI.

The Legal Ethics of AI

To date, neither the American Bar Association (ABA) nor any of the state bars have published formal opinions addressing the ethical use of AI by lawyers. Given the transformative nature of AI, it is perhaps not surprising that there are no opinions on ethics. But even so, there are several rules of ethics that apply to the use of AI.

Several Ethics Rules Apply to Lawyer's Use (And Non-Use) of AI

There are a number of ethical duties that apply to the use of (and non-use of) AI by lawyers, including the duties of: (1) competence (and diligence), (2) communication, (3) confidentiality, and (4) supervision.

Duty of competence

Under Rule 1.1 of the ABA Model Rules, a lawyer must provide competent representation to his or her client. The rule states that "[c]ompetent representation requires the legal knowledge, skill, thoroughness, and preparation reasonably necessary for the representation."[21] The duty of competence requires lawyers to be informed and up to date on current technology. In 2012, this was made clear when the ABA adopted Comment 8 to Rule 1.1, which states that "[t]o maintain the requisite knowledge and skill, lawyers should keep abreast of changes in the law and its practice, including the benefits and risks associated with relevant technology. . . ."[22]

As one author points out, there does not appear to be any instance "in which AI represents the standard of care in an area of legal practice, such that its use is necessary."[23] Nonetheless, lawyers generally must understand the technology available to improve the legal services they provide to clients. Lawyers have a duty to identify the technology that is needed to effectively represent the client, as well as determine if the use of such technology will improve service to the client.[24]

Under Rule 1.1, lawyers also must have a basic understanding of how AI tools operate. While lawyers cannot be expected to know all the technical intricacies of AI systems, they are required to understand how AI technology produces results. As one legal commentator notes, "[i]f a lawyer uses a tool that suggests answers to legal questions, he must understand the capabilities and limitations of the tool, and the risks and benefits of those answers."[25]

Duty to communicate

ABA Model Rule 1.4 governs a lawyer's duty to communicate with clients and requires a lawyer to "reasonably consult with the client about the means by which the client's objectives are to be accomplished."[26] A lawyer's duty of communication under Rule 1.4 includes discussing with his or her client the decision to use AI in providing legal services. A lawyer should obtain approval from the client before using AI, and this consent must be informed. The discussion should include the risks and limitations of the AI tool.[27] In certain circumstances, a lawyer's decision *not* to use AI also might need to be communicated to the client if using AI would benefit the client.[28] Indeed, the lawyer's failure to use AI could implicate ABA Model Rule 1.5, which requires lawyer's fees to be reasonable. Failing to use AI technology that materially reduces the costs of providing legal services arguably could result in a lawyer charging an unreasonable fee to a client.[29]

Duty of confidentiality

Under ABA Model Rule 1.6, lawyers owe their clients a general duty of confidentiality. This duty specifically requires a lawyer to "make reasonable efforts to prevent the inadvertent or unauthorized disclosure of, or unauthorized access to, information relating to the representation of a client."[30] The use of some AI tools requires client confidences to be "shared" with third-party vendors. As a result, lawyers must take appropriate steps to ensure that their clients' information is appropriately safeguarded.[31] Appropriate communication with the client also is necessary.

To minimize the risks of using AI, a lawyer should discuss with third-party AI providers the confidentiality safeguards in place. A lawyer should inquire about "what type of information is going to be provided, how the information will be stored, what security measures are in place with respect to the storage of the information, and who is going to have access to the information."[32] AI should not be used in the representation unless the lawyer is confident that the client's confidential information will be secure.

Duty to supervise

Under ABA Model Rules 5.1 and 5.3, lawyers have an ethical obligation to supervise lawyers and nonlawyers who are assisting lawyers in the provision of legal services, to ensure that their conduct complies with the Rules of Professional Conduct.[33] In 2012, the title of Model Rule 5.3 was changed from "Responsibilities Regarding Nonlawyer Assistants" to "Responsibilities Regarding Nonlawyer Assistance."[34] The change clarified that the scope of Rule 5.3 encompasses nonlawyers, whether human or not. Under Rules 5.1 and 5.3, lawyers are obligated to supervise the work of the AI utilized in the provision of legal services, and understand the technology well enough to ensure compliance with the lawyer's ethical duties. This includes making sure that the work product produced by AI is accurate and complete, and does not create a risk of disclosing client confidential information.[35]

There are some tasks that should not be handled by today's AI technology, and a lawyer must know where to draw the line. At the same time, lawyers should avoid underutilizing AI, which could cause them to serve their clients less efficiently.[36] Ultimately, it's a balancing act. Given that many lawyers are focused on detail and control over their matter, it is easy to see why "the greater danger might very well be underutilization of, rather than overreliance upon, artificial intelligence."[37]

Key Practical Takeaways Relating to the Ethics of AI

There clearly are a number of ethical rules that apply to lawyers' use and non-use of AI technology, and they have real-world applications. Lawyers must be informed about AI's ability to deliver efficient and accurate legal services to clients, while keeping in mind the ethical requirements and limitations. Ultimately, lawyers must exercise independent judgment, communicate with clients, and supervise the work performed by AI. In many ways, the ethical issues raised by AI are simply a permutation of ethical issues that lawyers have faced before with regard to other technology. It shows that the legal ethics rules are adaptable to new technologies, and AI is no exception.

Bias in the AI Context

There is a final, often overlooked consideration in a lawyer's use of AI technology, and that is the problem of bias. For all the advantages that AI offers lawyers, there also is a genuine concern that AI technology could reflect the biases and prejudices of its developers and trainers, which in turn could lead to skewed results. It is critical for lawyers using AI to understand how bias can impact AI results.

The problem of bias in the development and use of AI potentially implicates professional ethics. In August 2016, the ABA adopted Model Rule 8.4(g), which prohibits harassment and discrimination by lawyers against 11 protected classes.[38] Rule 8.4(g) states that it is professional misconduct for a lawyer to "engage in conduct that the lawyer knows or reasonably should know is harassment or discrimination on the basis of race, sex, religion, national origin, ethnicity, disability, age, sexual orientation, gender identity, marital status, or socioeconomic status in conduct related to the practice of law."[39] About 20 states already have some variation of ABA Model Rule 8.4 on the books, and several other states are considering whether to adopt ABA's new expansive rule. Lawyers in jurisdictions that have adopted some form of Rule 8.4 must consider whether their use of AI is consistent with the rule. Moreover, even in jurisdictions that have not adopted some form of Rule 8.4, lawyers must consider how bias in the use of AI could create risks for clients.

Bias in AI technology stems from the nature of AI tools, which involve machine training rather than programming. If the data used for training is biased, the AI tool will produce a biased result. Microsoft, for example, recently launched an AI tool that could have text-based conversations with individuals.[40] The tool continuously learned how to respond in conversations based on previous conversations. Unfortunately, the tool began to mimic the discriminatory viewpoints of the people it previously engaged in conversation.[41]

As yet another example, the Correctional Offender Management Profiling for Alternative Sanctions (COMPAS) software used by some courts to predict the likelihood of recidivism in criminal defendants has been shown by studies to be biased against African-Americans.[42] For these reasons, it is important to have diverse teams developing AI to ensure that biases are minimized. The data used for training AI should also be carefully reviewed in order to prevent bias.

In the AI world, there has been a movement away from "black-box" AI, in which an AI model is not able to explain how it generated its output based on the input.[43] The preferred model is now "explainable AI,"[44] which is able to provide the reasoning for how decisions are reached. Governments are beginning to recognize the importance of transparency in the use of AI. New York City, for example, recently passed a law that requires creation of a task force that monitors algorithms used by its government, such as those used to assign children to public schools.[45] One of the task force's responsibilities is to determine how to share with the public the factors that go into the algorithms.[46]

Ultimately, the need for lawyers to understand how AI generates results is important for combatting bias and providing good counsel to clients. And it could be required by legal ethics. As detailed above, lawyers have a duty to communicate with clients, and explaining why AI generates a particular outcome could be included as part of that duty. The good news is that while AI has the potential to be biased, AI is much more predictable than humans. It is easier to remedy bias in machines than it is in humans. Given their role as officers of the court, it is critical for lawyers to be on the forefront of understanding how bias in the use of AI can impact outcomes achieved by the legal profession and society as a whole.

Conclusion

Without a doubt, AI promises to fundamentally transform the practice of law. AI holds out the promise of freeing lawyers from mundane tasks and allowing them to devote more of their time to counseling clients, which after all is the core of what lawyers do. Lawyers should not fear AI, but rather should embrace it. Professional ethics requires them to do so.

NOTES

1. "Artificial Intelligence: Imagining the Possibilities in Litigation," Bloomberg Big Law Business, October 26, 2016, https://bol.bna.com/artificial-intelligence-imagining-the-possibilities-in-litigation-perspective/.
2. David L. Gordon and Rebecca L. Ambrose, *The Ethics of Artificial Intelligence*, The Jackson Lewis Corporate Counsel Conference (2017), https://www.jacksonlewis.com/sites/default/files/docs/Final_The%20Ethics%20of%20Artificial%20Intelligence_Gordon%20and%20Ambrose.pdf.
3. "What is technology-assisted review or Tar?," Aug. 15, 2018, https://www.zapproved.com/blog/what-is-technology-assisted-review-tar/.
4. "Number of mobile phone messaging app users worldwide from 2016 to 2021," https://www.statista.com/statistics/483255/number-of-mobile-messaging-users-worldwide/.
5. Liang, Hong et al., "Text feature extraction based on deep learning: a review," *EURASIP Journal on Wireless Communications and Networking* 2017, no. 1 (2017), https://www.ncbi.nlm.nih.gov/pmc/articles/PMC5732309/.

6. Max Tegmark. *Life 3.0: Being Human in the Age of Artificial Intelligence* (New York, NY: Random House, 2017).
7. Tegmark, *Life 3.0.*
8. Tegmark, *Life 3.0.*
9. Ericka Chickowski, "Success of AI and enterprise collaboration tools depends on the ecosystem," TechTarget (Spring 2019), https://searchcontentmanagement.techtarget.com/feature/Success-of-AI-and-enterprise-collaboration-tools-depends-on-ecosystem.
10. Chickowski, "Success of AI and enterprise collaboration tools."
11. Lauri Donahue, "A Primer on Using Artificial Intelligence in the Legal Profession," *Harvard Journal of Law and Technology* (Jan. 3, 2018), https://jolt.law.harvard.edu/digest/a-primer-on-using-artificial-intelligence-in-the-legal-profession.
12. Sterling Miller, *Artificial Intelligence and its Impact on Legal Technology: To Boldly Go Where No Legal Department Has Gone Before*, Thomson Reuters, https://legal.thomsonreuters.com/en/insights/articles/AI-and-its-impact-on-legal-technology.
13. Frank Partnoy, "What Your Boss Could Learn by Reading the Whole Company's Emails," *The Atlantic,* Sep. 2018, https://www.theatlantic.com/magazine/archive/2018/09/the-secrets-in-your-inbox/565745/.
14. Partnoy, "What Your Boss Could Learn."
15. Tegmark, *Life 3.0.*
16. Steve Lohr, "A.I. Is Doing Legal Work. But It Won't Replace Lawyers, Yet," *New York Times*, Mar. 9, 2017, https://www.nytimes.com/2017/03/19/technology/lawyers-artificial-intelligence.html.
17. Shivali Best, "The Robot That Knows When You're Lying," *Daily Mail,* Dec. 20, 2017, http://www.dailymail.co.uk/sciencetech/article-5197747/AI-detects-expressions-tell-people-lie-court.html.
18. Best, "The Robot That Knows When You're Lying."
19. Jeff Daniels, "Lie-detecting Computer Kiosks Equipped with Artificial Intelligence Look Like the Future of Border Security," CNBC, May 15, 2018, https://www.cnbc.com/2018/05/15/lie-detectors-with-artificial-intelligence-are-future-of-border-security.html.
20. Tegmark, *Life 3.0.*
21. ABA Model Rule 1.1.
22. Hedda Litwin, "The Ethical Duty of Technology Competence: What Does It Mean for You?," National Association of Attorneys General, https://www.naag.org/publications/nagtri-journal/volume-2-issue-4/the-ethical-duty-of-technology-competence-what-does-it-mean-for-you.php.
23. James Q. Walker, "What's Artificial About Intelligence? The Ethical and Practical Considerations When Lawyers Use AI Technology," Bloomberg Law (2018), https://www.rkollp.com/newsroom-publications-443.html.
24. Stone et al., "Artificial Intelligence and Life in 2030."

25. David Lat, "The Ethical Implications of Artificial Intelligence," Above the Law: Law2020, https://abovethelaw.com/law2020/the-ethical -implications-of-artificial -intelligence/.
26. ABA Model Rule 1.4.
27. Stone et al., "Artificial Intelligence and Life in 2030."
28. Stone et al., "Artificial Intelligence and Life in 2030."
29. "Ethical Use of Artificial Intelligence in the Legal Industry: The Rules of Professional Conduct," *Emerging Industries and Technology Committee Newsletter*, (March 2018), https://insolvencyintel.abi.org/bankruptcy articles/ethical-use-of-artificial-intelligence-in-the-legal-industry-the-rules -of-professional-conduct.
30. ABA Model Rule 1.6.
31. Stone et al., "Artificial Intelligence and Life in 2030."
32. Stone et al., "Artificial Intelligence and Life in 2030."
33. Stone et al., "Artificial Intelligence and Life in 2030."
34. *Variations of the ABA Model Rules of Professional Conduct*, ABA CPR Policy Implementation Committee, Sep. 29, 2017, https://www.americanbar .org/content/dam/aba/administrative/professional_responsibility/mrpc _5_3.pdf.
35. Stone et al., "Artificial Intelligence and Life in 2030."
36. Kaplan, *Artificial Intelligence*, 28.
37. Kaplan, *Artificial Intelligence*, 28.
38. "ABA Rule 8.4 Finding Few Followers, but Sparking Lots of Encouraging Discussion," ABA, Aug. 3, 2018, https://www.americanbar.org/news/ abanews/aba-news-archives/2018/08/aba_rule_8_4_finding/.
39. ABA Model Rule 8.4(g).
40. Jonathon Vanian, "Unmasking A.I.'s Bias Problem," *Fortune*, June 25, 2018, https://www.fortune.com/longform/ai-bias-problem/.
41. Vanian, "Unmasking A.I.'s Bias Problem."
42. Julia Angwin, et. al., "Machine Bias," ProPublica, May 23, 2016, https:// www.propublica.org/article/machine-bias-risk-assessments-in-criminal -sentencing.
43. Jason Bloomberg, "Don't Trust Artificial Intelligence? Time to Open the AI 'Black Box,'" *Forbes*, Sep. 16, 2018, https://www.forbes.com/sites/ jasonbloomberg/2018/09/16/dont-trust-artificial-intelligence-time-to -open-the-ai-black-box/#56c1d9a3b4a7.
44. "Opening AI's Black Box Will Become a Priority," PwC, https://www.pwc .com/us/en/services/consulting/library/artificial-intelligence-predictions/ explainable-ai.html.
45. Elizabeth Zima, "Could New York City's AI Transparency Bill Be a Model for the Country?," *Government Technology*, Jan. 4, 2018, https://www .govtech.com/policy/Could-New-York-Citys-AI-Transparency-Bill-Be-A -Model-for-the-Country.html.
46. Zima, "Could New York City's AI Transparency Bill Be a Model for the Country?"

12 The Future of AI in Law Libraries

The future is already here —it's just not very evenly distributed.
—William Gibson, author and futurist

Having been tasked with writing here about the future of artificial intelligence (AI) in law libraries, let me say at the outset that I am neither a futurist nor a law librarian. Further, I subscribe to the popular saying—often credited to Yogi Berra but apparently more accurately attributed to Danish politician Karl Kristian Steincke[1] —that it is difficult to make predictions, especially about the future. But when it comes to the future of AI in libraries, I echo the quote at the start of this chapter from William Gibson in believing that the future can be found today, if one only looks around a bit. In the issues libraries face today, I believe glimpses of the futures they face tomorrow and beyond can be found.

Today, the legal profession is witnessing a time of unprecedented innovation, in which AI is a significant factor. With that come both opportunities and challenges for law libraries. Once upon a time not so long ago, it was largely just a handful of well-established companies that drove the development of new products in legal. Now, the internet

ROBERT J. AMBROGI is a lawyer and journalist who tracks legal technology and innovation through his blog *LawSites* and his podcast *LawNext*.

and advances in technology have changed the formula. We have transformed from a time when legal technology and legal information were products driven almost exclusively by large companies to a time when anyone with a good idea to make things simpler and smarter can—at least potentially—succeed.

Consider Daniel Lewis. He was midway through his second year at Stanford Law School when he decided there was a better way to do legal research. He began discussing his idea with various people at Stanford, including Jeffrey Heer, a computer science professor and expert who introduced Lewis to concepts of data visualization, which helped give shape to his idea. By the time he graduated from law school in 2012, Lewis and classmate Nicholas Reed, with whom he had partnered, were receiving offers from investors. Barely a month later, just a few days before they were to take the bar exam, they closed an initial round of $1.1 million in financing, and thus was born their legal-research company, Ravel Law. Five years later, Ravel was acquired by LexisNexis.[2]

Once, it would have seemed audacious beyond belief for a second-year law student to think he could take on the legal-research establishment—yet this kind of innovation is now becoming common in law. In 2009, the website "Angel List," which tracks startups in various industries, listed 15 for legal technology. Today, it lists more than 2,000. My review of Angel List indicates that it's overinclusive. My own list of legal-technology startups numbers just over 700—although I know for a fact that is underinclusive. A fair estimate, I would suggest, is that the number of legal-technology startups worldwide is easily 1,000, perhaps closer to 1,200.

Another barometer of the state of legal technology is investment. There was a time when a legal-technology company, especially a startup, couldn't even hope to schedule a meeting with an investment firm. Suddenly, that's changed. Whereas total investment in legal technology in 2017 was $233 million, a year later, in 2018, it rose to more than $1 billion. Among the investors who have "discovered" legal technology are several of the biggest venture capital firms in Silicon Valley—including Andreessen Horowitz, a combination law firm and legal-technology company, founded by Silicon Valley serial entrepreneur Justin Kan, that invested $65 million in Atrium.

Not surprisingly, much of that investment money is landing in the laps of companies developing AI applications for law. Among the major investments in 2018 were $50 million to Kira Systems, a Toronto-based developer of machine learning (ML) software for contract review and analysis; $30 million to Seal Software, a developer of AI-powered content discovery and analytics products; $25 million each to two e-discovery companies, Everlaw and Logikcull, both of which use AI in their document-review technologies; and $12 million to LawGeex, a company whose AI product automates the review and approval of contracts.[3]

Against this backdrop of accelerated growth, legal-technology companies—both established and startups —are increasingly using AI to bolster legal research. Both Thomson Reuters and LexisNexis have long used natural language processing (NLP)—a form of AI—in their research platforms. But in recent years, both have advanced their use of AI—Thomson Reuters with its release of Westlaw Edge and LexisNexis with its suite of Lexis Analytics. Meanwhile, startups in this space are doing much more than tilting at windmills, with Casetext's CARA winning the American Association of Law Libraries' product of the year in 2017[4] and Judicata developing an application, called Clerk, that predicts a brief's likelihood of success.[5]

Concerns Over AI's Impact

Amidst this surge in the numbers and variety of legal-technology products—and especially in the emerging varieties of AI products—those who work in law libraries might wonder what the future bodes for them. In the popular and public consciousness, librarians were long defined by and associated with the physical place in which they worked—the library. But as technology rendered the physical space of the library less relevant (or too expensive), some wondered what it meant for those who worked in law libraries. As a 2014 *New York Times* article described, "Shelves full of uniformly bound legal volumes—beloved of any photographer, videographer or cinematographer who needs a background that instantly proclaims 'law office'—are headed to oblivion in the digital era."[6]

AI raises that concern to another level. Not only are the physical libraries shrinking or disappearing, but now many fear AI will eventually take over the jobs of those currently working in libraries.

Already, we know of at least one chatbot that is doing some of the work of a law librarian. During an innovation tournament at the 2017 AALL annual meeting, Katherine Lowry, Director of Practice Services at Baker Hostetler, won the $2,500 top prize for her "Attorney Facing Chatbot." The chatbot was able to field questions from attorneys at her firm that they previously would have directed to the knowledge desk. The service proved particularly useful in off hours, when the desk was unstaffed. Of course, clever as it was, the bot would never replace an actual librarian or knowledge professional; to the contrary, it required a professional to program and train it.

What else might be the future roles of chatbots in legal research? Another glimpse came at a program in January 2019, when LexisNexis revealed that it was developing chatbots to be included in the Lexis Advance legal research platform as a way of helping guide users in their research. "What if legal research was more human, more like a conversation, the kinds we have among ourselves?" teased Serena Wellen, Senior Director of Research Information at LexisNexis. "Our goal is to make legal research more guided in a more conversational experience," Wellen said.[7]

LexisNexis said the bot, called Lexis Research Assistant, would be released within the Lexis Advance platform sometime in 2019. Eventually, the company said, users would be able to interact with multiple sub-bots for various tasks related to their research workflow. The bot would retain an activity stream of all a user's research, and at any time, the user would be able to click a thread within this stream to engage conversationally with the bot. The bot would help users remember prior relevant research, suggest applicable filters to refine research, help users pick up lost trains of thought, and offer suggestions of shortcuts to possible answers and overviews.

This bot suggests a broader theme for the future of legal research. "We see in the future an interaction with Lexis Advance that is highly conversational," said Jeffrey S. Pfeifer, Vice President and Chief Product Officer, North America, at LexisNexis. "You ask a question, we present results. The interaction becomes more humanlike."[8]

The Evolving Role of Librarians

Meanwhile, even as chatbots begin to take on roles in legal research, legal-research companies have taken to giving their products anthropomorphic names such as CARA (from Casetext), EVA (from ROSS Intelligence) and Vincent (from vLex). Is it any wonder that some information professionals might feel threatened by a robot revolution?

Yet the reality might be precisely the opposite of what people fear. In the future, technology will not diminish the role of the information professional. Rather, it will make it more important than ever before. If the present is any indicator of the future, then—as Mark Twain might have said—any suggestions of the death of the information professional have been greatly exaggerated. To the contrary, there has never been a more exciting time to be a legal-information professional—and never has the role of the legal-information professional been more important or essential.

Sure, the internet and online research have made it enormously easier to find information and evolving AI tools are further easing the path to finding the answers we need. But even as technology has eased research in some respects, it has raised new obstacles to finding information:

1. There is such a glut of information available to researchers that it can be difficult for them to sort the wheat from the chaff.
2. In an era of rampant "fake news" and digitally altered media, it is increasingly more difficult to assess the quality and reliability of information.
3. It remains difficult to find many forms of very specific information—the very kinds of information lawyers often need.
4. The nature of information is changing. In particular, data is now information, and in this era of Big Data, many are struggling with how to manage and make sense of it.

Added to that, AI presents unique problems of its own. Most significant of these, perhaps, is the dicey matter of the algorithms that power AI technologies and the biases inherent in them. These can include "social-neutral" biases that skew a particular research platform's results in a particular direction or socially harmful biases that skew certain technologies to deliver biased results.

Thus, in this rapidly evolving and frequently challenging environment of AI and new technologies, the role of the law library and of the law librarian has never been more important or more diverse. As Steve Lastres, director of knowledge management services at Debevoise & Plimpton, put it: "Our work has gone beyond research and into AI, data analytical tools, and business development. We are providing a level of service and customization that we have never offered before."[9]

Here is where the future of law libraries becomes crystal clear, because as lawyers continue to grapple with the challenges of technology, and particularly of information technology, no one is better situated to guide them than law librarians.

> Libraries have a unique institutional advantage. Who will take the time to learn and use AI tools in the firm? Will it be senior partners? Junior associates trying to make their hours? Law professors trying to teach, publish, and grade? Information professionals in the library have the unique background and skills to master these tools.[10]

What does AI mean to the future of law libraries? It means new roles and responsibilities for law librarians. Those roles, as I will discuss further, include:

- Gatekeeper
- Guide
- Ethicist
- Interpreter

Librarian as Gatekeeper

Now and into the future, law librarians must wear a variety of hats. Increasingly, one of those is legal technologist. These days, one can hardly be an information professional without also becoming a technology professional, because the two disciplines overlap in almost every way. For that reason, law librarians increasingly serve the role of technology "gatekeeper" within their firms and organizations. I hear this repeatedly, directly from vendors themselves. Law librarians get it. They understand the importance of technology in advancing the legal profession, and they are more likely than other legal professionals to understand the mechanics of technology, to be able to get under the hood and size up whether a product is what it claims to be.

We see this at law firms as well, where law librarians are often the gatekeepers for new technology, helping to vet and evaluate products before their firms plunk down precious dollars. We see this at law schools, where law librarians are often at the forefront of pushing for teaching and program initiatives in technology innovation and competence. We see this in court systems and government agencies, where law librarians are often helping to lead the charge for expanding access to justice.

Increasingly, librarians play a critical role in the legal profession. They are the gatekeepers. They are, if you will, the technology police. They have the skill and the savvy to scrutinize vendors' claims and make sure the reality comports with the marketing. In this way, librarians—maybe more so than any other role in the legal profession—are critical to keeping the industry honest.

These days, it seems that every new product is baiting its hook with claims of being innovative and practice-changing. More to the point, it sometimes seems that virtually every new product claims to use AI or have an AI component. (A 2019 survey found that 40 percent of AI startups in Europe did not, in fact, use AI.[11]) Law firms, pressured to adopt new technologies, are quick to bite. Someone needs to serve as the gatekeeper. Someone needs to keep companies honest. Increasingly, that someone is a law librarian.

While that is happening already, the future role of the librarian as gatekeeper will become only more important. Because of their distinctive knowledge of legal research and information systems, librarians will be the point persons within their organizations for evaluating and selecting AI-driven research and analytics tools. Their knowledge of AI will carry over to give them a central role in also evaluating and selecting AI systems for other purposes within their organizations, such as contract review.

Librarian as Guide

As discussed earlier, law librarians of the future will come to play a critical role in evaluating and selecting AI technologies, particularly those related to legal research. But that role will extend well beyond selecting AI systems. Law librarians will be called to facilitate the use of AI within their organizations through the training of lawyers and law students, and by continuing the evaluation of AI systems and their use.

In their paper, "Artificial Intelligence: Legal Research and Law Librarians," Mary Ann Neary and Sherry Xin Chen of Boston College Law School describe why law librarians are well suited to this role:

> Librarians, aware of what results can optimally be retrieved by a particular search, can gauge the gaps or weaknesses in an AI system by evaluating search results. Law librarians who train/instruct law students/new practitioners can be an integral part of the AI system construction, implementation, and evaluation team. Librarians' familiarity with law students'/associates' search practices and patterns can be harnessed in teaching AI systems as well.[12]

Beyond training others in the use of AI systems, law librarians could also have an additional training role—that of training and refining the machine learning (ML) systems in use at an organization.

> Librarians know their constituencies' information needs. Librarians in law firms and in corporate special libraries have in-depth knowledge of the sources required for successful practice in those settings. . . . [T]he legal applications of AI systems require constant feeding of current and relevant information. Law librarians, as information professionals with a unique understanding of users' search habits, goals, and available data, can help the institution tailor the application and maximize the benefits of the AI system.[13]

In addition to training third-party AI systems, law librarians will also have a role—perhaps the lead role—in building systems internally. Ed Walters and Morgan Wright make this point in their article, "Putting Artificial Intelligence to Work in Law Firms":

> When law firms harness the vast expertise in their document repositories, billing systems, and human experts, they can create data training sets that are unique. Using AI tools, they can build the next generation of legal services, truly differentiated from the offerings of other firms, and of accounting firms that wish to break into the legal services market but who don't have the historical legal data on which to build.
>
> Who will be the makers in this new era of read/write artificial intelligence? It would be natural for the law firms' experts in legal information, law librarians, to have the central role. Law librarians have expertise with enterprise legal data, great access to KM systems and document management systems, and the training in ontologies and legal information.[14]

Already, we have reached a time when technology is enabling lawyers to work more independently, to work remotely, and to operate in a way that puts a premium on mobility. In the future, AI-driven research tools and technologies will further free lawyers from the traditional constraints of law practice. But if lawyers do not have the skills or understanding they need to use these AI-driven services and tools, they cannot practice effectively, now or a decade from now. In the future, the role of law librarian in training lawyers, associates, and law students will be as important as it ever was—maybe more so.

Librarian as Ethicist

Evolving ethical expectations with regard to lawyers' understanding and use of technology, including AI, pose potential pitfalls for legal professionals. Librarians in the future will serve a valuable role as members of legal teams in helping lawyers navigate new technologies and the ethical requirements surrounding those technologies.

In 2012, something happened that I've called a sea change in the legal profession: The American Bar Association (ABA) formally approved an amendment to the Model Rules of Professional Conduct to make clear that lawyers have a duty to be competent, not only in the law and its practice, but also in technology.

Specifically, the ABA's House of Delegates voted to amend Comment 8 to Model Rule 1.1, which pertains to competence, to read as follows:

Maintaining Competence

> To maintain the requisite knowledge and skill, a lawyer should keep abreast of changes in the law and its practice, *including the benefits and risks associated with relevant technology*, engage in continuing study and education and comply with all continuing legal education requirements to which the lawyer is subject. (Emphasis added.)[15]

As the name indicates, the Model Rules are just a model. They provide guidance to the states in formulating their own rules of professional conduct. Each state is free to adopt, reject, ignore, or modify the Model Rules. For the duty of technology competence to apply to the lawyers in any given state, that state's high court (or rule-setting body) would first have to adopt it. As of this writing, 36 states have done so.[16]

As significant as is Comment 8, it is also somewhat vague. What exactly does it mean for a lawyer to keep abreast of the benefits and risks associated with relevant technology? So far, the best answers we have to that question are found in two major ethics opinions that provide guidance on the meaning of Comment 8. One, from California, considers the duty of technology competence in the context of electronic discovery.[17] The other, from the ABA's Standing Committee on Ethics and Professional Responsibility, discusses technology competence with regard to protecting client confidences when using email and other forms of data transmission.[18]

Although these two opinions concern different contexts for the application of the duty of technology competence, they closely parallel each other in the overarching guidance they provide as to the meaning and application of the duty. Significantly, both opinions make virtually identical points about a lawyer's ethical obligations under Model Rule 1.1, Comment 8. The two opinions agree:

A lawyer has an obligation in every matter, on a case-by-case basis, to make a preliminary assessment of the technology issues that might arise and of the lawyer's competence to handle those issues.

If the lawyer lacks the requisite competence, the lawyer may bring on a third party, such as a consultant or another lawyer, to assist with the technology issues. Alternatively, the lawyer can refer the matter to someone who does have the requisite competence.

Even if the lawyer brings on a third party, the lawyer retains the overall responsibility to ensure that the attorney-client privilege is maintained and that no confidential client information is disclosed to outside parties.

Even if the lawyer brings on a third party, the lawyer retains the overall requirement to supervise the matter and to ensure that all staff working on the matter are properly trained and supervised.

On this latter point, the California ethics opinion said this:

> [The rule] permits an attorney to meet the duty of competence through association with another lawyer or consultation with an expert. . . . Such expert may be an outside vendor, a subordinate attorney, or even the client, if they possess the necessary expertise. This consultation or association, however, does not absolve an attorney's obligation to supervise the work of the expert under [the] rule . . ., which is a non-delegable duty belonging to the attorney who is counsel in the litigation, and who remains the one primarily answerable to the court. An attorney must maintain overall responsibility for the work of the expert he or she chooses, even if that expert is the client or someone employed by the client. The attorney must do so by remaining regularly engaged in the expert's work, by educating everyone involved in the e-discovery workup about the legal issues in the case, the factual matters impacting discovery, including witnesses and key evidentiary issues, the obligations around discovery imposed by the law or by the court, and of any relevant risks associated with the e-discovery tasks at hand. The attorney should issue appropriate instructions and guidance and, ultimately, conduct appropriate tests until satisfied that the attorney is meeting his ethical obligations prior to releasing ESI.[19]

Thus, for the lawyer who lacks technology competence, these requirements create a Catch 22. One cannot manage what one does not understand. Although the opinions allow a lawyer who lacks technological competence to bring on a third-party consultant, they do not relieve the lawyer of the ultimate duty to oversee the case and protect the client.[20]

Needless to say, AI technology is particularly difficult to understand, even for the more tech-savvy among us. Vendors' secrecy around their AI products' algorithms and inner workings render these products a black box, at least in the eyes of many lawyers. Selection, use, and oversight of AI systems are tasks many lawyers see as daunting—and they are tasks that will challenge lawyers' ethical obligations.

Here is where the law librarian of the future will be particularly valuable. As professionals trained in both law and systems, librarians of the future will be essential members of technology-driven legal teams. They will help lawyers understand the ethical obligations implicated in the use of AI systems, and then help lawyers understand best practices in selecting and deploying AI systems.

As Neary and Chen put it:

> In light of the exponential amount of data and the complexity of technology involved in an AI system, both the benefits that can be reaped from an optimal AI application and the dangers that may come from a "false sense of accuracy" are amplified. Law librarians' keen awareness of the pitfalls in similar technology and advocacy in teaching creative and efficient searching strategies are valuable assets in this time of rapid change.[21]

This is not to say that librarians must become ethicists, strictly speaking. But librarians, uniquely among legal professionals, have knowledge and skills that span law, practice, and technology. Likewise, the issues raised by the duty of technology competence span law, practice, and technology. In helping lawyers understand their duties and obligations with regard to technology, while also helping them understand the capabilities and limits of the technology itself, librarians in the future will be essential members of legal teams.

Librarian as Interpreter

The dirty little secret of AI is that it is not actually intelligent. It is the application of mathematical algorithms to data. Those algorithms do not appear out of thin air. They are written by humans. That means that, just as humans have flaws and biases, so do algorithms. But because those algorithms are usually proprietary to the companies that create them, consumers are not privy to the biases within them or even aware of the ways in which those biases might skew results. This is one of the great dangers of AI. AI needs an interpreter, and no one in the legal profession is better situated to serve that role than the law librarian.

Algorithmic biases can manifest themselves in various ways. In his article, "The Digital Future of the Oldest Information Profession," Ray Worthy Campbell, Professor of Law at Peking University School of Transnational Law, describes the potential dangers of hidden biases in products used by corporations offering legal services.

> As routine matter of business, the corporations offering legal services do not share the algorithms which they use to

> provide products or solutions. However, and invisible to the user, these products could be subject to intentional or unintentional biases. For example, a product relying on Big Data analysis and statistical correlation might give different advice in response to a criminal charge if race or income were a variable, embedding, unknown to the consumer, historic biases in the information given. With the algorithm hidden, the bias would be, as a practical matter, undetectable.
>
> In order for digital legal services to achieve their potential, these issues need careful thought. Given the lack of transparency, it cannot be assumed that the market will provide a sufficient check as consumers may not even realize the issue exists, and most likely will be unable to evaluate the options, even if they recognize the general issue of private algorithms. While tight government regulation of the giant Internet companies summons up its own parade of horribles, the issue is too important to ignore.[22]

The biases Campbell describes are unacceptable in a system that purports to mete out equal justice for all. If the system relies on technology that is inherently biased against certain individuals because of their race or income, then it cannot be fair. As Campbell suggests, it is imperative that checks be developed to guard against such outcomes.

More subtle but also significant are the algorithmic biases attached to different legal research platforms. This first struck Susan Nevelow Mart, Director of the Law Library and Associate Professor at the University of Colorado Law School, after receiving an email from Mike Dahn, Senior Vice President for Westlaw product management at Thomson Reuters. In it, Dahn said, "All of our algorithms are created by humans."[23] In that seemingly innocuous statement, Mart saw significance. If search algorithms are built by humans, then those humans made choices about how the algorithms work. Unavoidably, those human choices become the biases and assumptions that get coded into each system and that have implications for the results they deliver.

So Mart set out to study how hidden biases and assumptions affect the results provided by some of the major legal research providers. She chose six to study: Casetext, Fastcase, Google Scholar, Lexis Advance, Ravel, and Westlaw. The results of her study, which she published in the paper, "The Algorithm as a Human Artifact: Implications for Legal {Re} Search," were, in her own words, "a remarkable testament to the variability of human problem solving."[24]

Remarkable indeed. Mart found that there is hardly any overlap in the cases that appear in the top ten results returned by each database. An average of 40 percent of the cases were unique to one database, and only about 7 percent of the cases were returned in search results in all six databases.

One hypothesis Mart wanted to test was whether each algorithm would find the same cases. After all, the search algorithm for each database was trying to achieve the same result in the same pool of information by finding relevant cases. As it turned out, however, the different algorithms found very different cases. In fact, each research platform returned an average of 40 percent unique cases. On average, 25 percent of the cases were in only two databases, 15 percent appeared in three databases, 9.5 percent appeared in four databases, just under 7 percent appeared in five databases, and just under 7 percent appeared in all six databases.

Because the algorithms all rank relevance and the goal is to return relevant cases, another hypothesis was whether the top ten cases would all be relevant. Here again, Mart's study found otherwise. The more-established research providers, Westlaw and Lexis Advance, did better at delivering relevant cases, but no service was perfect. The degree of relevance ranged from 67 percent for Westlaw to 39.7 percent for Casetext.

One further factor Mart examined was the number of unique cases each platform delivered that were also relevant. In other words, given that each platform returned an average of 40 percent unique cases, how many of those unique cases were relevant? Westlaw did the best, she found, with 33.1 percent of its cases both unique and relevant. Casetext fared the worst, with just 8.2 percent of its unique cases found to be relevant.

Mart's research demonstrates why it is important for legal researchers to have at least some understanding of the biases inherent in different systems and not to limit their research to any single system. "Legal research has always required redundancy in searching; one resource does not usually provide a full answer, just as one search does not provide every necessary result," Mart writes. "This study clearly demonstrates that this need for redundancy has not faded with the rise of the algorithm."

Beyond that, Mart believes we should all challenge legal research companies to be much more transparent about the biases in their algorithms.

Algorithmic accountability in legal databases will help assure researchers of the reliability of their search results and will allow researchers greater flexibility in mining the rich information in legal databases. If researchers know generally what a search algorithm is privileging in its results, they will be better researchers.

Whether considering AI in legal research or in legal products more generally, wider adoption of AI in the legal profession will require diligence, scrutiny, and oversight by someone who has the capability to understand the underlying technology and know the questions that need to be asked – an interpreter, if you will, of the language of AI.

In this, who will guide the legal profession if not law librarians? Who will help legal professionals make sense of the potential biases in AI research and practice tools if not law librarians? Who will push vendors for transparency and accountability if not law librarians? When considering AI and the future of law libraries, this could be among law librarians' most important roles—helping to protect legal professionals from the tools they will rely on in the practice of law.

Librarian as Linchpin

The future of AI in law libraries is not to be found in a particular type of AI technology. Neither is it to be found in the particular kind of law library space—or even, necessarily, in a law library at all. The technology will evolve. Libraries will evolve. Rather, the future of AI in law libraries is to be found in the professionals we call by various titles, most commonly law librarian.

"The future is already here," Gibson said. We need only look around at what already is happening within the legal profession to see what lies ahead. Already, law librarians are gatekeepers, helping ensure their firms and organizations make the right decisions about technology. Already, law librarians are guides, training lawyers and others about the use of technology. Already, law librarians are ethicists, helping lawyers understand their professional responsibilities. Already, law librarians are interpreters, using their skills as knowledge professionals to be a bridge between those who develop products and those who use them.

As the pace of technology development and adoption accelerates in the legal profession, the multifaceted role of the law librarian will only accelerate along with it. With greater use of AI and other technologies by legal professionals, the work that law librarians do and the value they provide will become even more important. Already, it is an exciting and challenging time to be a law librarian. In the future, it will be even more so.

NOTES

1. Niel Bohr section, in *The Yale Book of Quotations,* ed. Fred R. Shapiro, (New Haven, CT: Yale University Press, 2006), 92.
2. Robert Ambrogi, "Breaking: LexisNexis Acquires Ravel Law." *LawSites* (blog), June 8, 2017, www.lawsitesblog.com/2017/06/breaking-lexisnexis-acquires-ravel-law.html.

3. Robert Ambrogi, "The 20 Most Important Legal Technology Developments of 2018," *LawSites* (blog), Dec. 26, 2018, www.lawsitesblog.com/2018/12/20-important-legal-technology-developments-2018.html.
4. Robert Ambrogi, "Law Librarians Name Casetext's CARA as New Product of the Year," *LawSites* (blog), May 3, 2017, www.lawsitesblog.com/2017/05/law-librarians-name-casetexts-cara-new-product-year.html.
5. Robert Ambrogi, "Judicata Readies Release of Powerful Tool to Analyze Briefs, Like Moneyball for Motions," Oct. 2, 2017, www.lawsitesblog.com/2017/10/judicata-readies-release-powerful-tool-analyze-briefs-like-moneyball-motions.html.
6. David W. Dunlap, "So Little Paper to Chase in a Law Firm's New Library," *The New York Times*, Oct. 22, 2014, www.nytimes.com/2014/10/23/nyregion/so-little-paper-to-chase-in-a-law-firms-new-library.html.
7. Robert Ambrogi, "Chatbots Are Coming to Lexis Advance, to Help Guide Your Legal Research," *LawSites* (blog), Feb. 6, 2019, www.lawsitesblog.com/2019/02/chatbots-coming-lexis-advance-help-guide-legal-research.html.
8. Ambrogi, "Chatbots."
9. Mary Ellen Egan, "Law Librarian? Try Chief Knowledge Officer," *The American Lawyer*, June 30, 2017, www.law.com/americanlawyer/almID/1202791116149/.
10. Ed Walters, "Read/Write: Artificial Intelligence Libraries." *AAAL Spectrum* 22, no. 1 (2017).
11. Aliya Ram, "Europe's AI Start-ups Often Do Not Use AI, Study Finds," *Financial Times*, March 4, 2019, www.ft.com/content/21b19010-3e9f-11e9-b896-fe36ec32aece.
12. Mary Ann Neary and Sherry Xin Chen, "Artificial Intelligence: Legal Research and Law Librarians." *AALL Spectrum* 21, no. 5 (2017): 16–20.
13. Neary and Chen, "Artificial Intelligence," 16–20.
14. Ed Walters and Morgan Write, "Putting Artificial Intelligence to Work in Law Firms." *AALL Spectrum* 23, no. 1 (2018).
15. Robert Ambrogi, "36 States Have Adopted the Duty of Technology Competence," LawSites (blog), www.lawsitesblog.com/tech-competence.
16. Ambrogi, "The Duty of Technology Competence."
17. State Bar of California, Formal Opinion No. 2015-193 (2015).
18. American Bar Association Formal Opinion 477 (2017).
19. State Bar of California, Formal Opinion No. 2015-193 (2015), supra at 5.
20. Although these opinions explicitly cite, discuss, and interpret Model Rule 1.1, Comment 8, it should be noted that both also cite Model Rule 1.6, pertaining to a lawyer's duty to protect client confidences.
21. Neary and Chen, "Artificial Intelligence."

22. Ray Worthy Campbell, "The Digital Future of the Oldest Information Profession," in *Research Handbook on Digital Transformations*, eds. F. Xavier Olleros and Majlinda Zhegu (Edward Elgar, 2016), available at https://papers.ssrn.com/sol3/papers.cfm?abstract_id =2716972.
23. Susan Nevelow Mart, "The Algorithm as a Human Artifact: Implications for Legal {Re}Search," *Law Library Journal* 109, no. 3 (2017-20):388, http://scholar.law.colorado.edu/articles/755.
24. Mart, "The Algorithm as a Human Artifact," 390.

VIRGINIA A. NEISLER

13

AI Resources

This book was written by law librarians, for law librarians, to help illustrate how we in the profession are leveraging artificial intelligence (AI) tools and cutting-edge technology. But AI is an immense, ever-evolving topic. No single resource can cover *everything* that one might want to know about the topic. If reading this book has piqued your interest in the topic of artificial intelligence, there is a lot more to learn!

In order to accommodate readers with varying backgrounds and differing levels of technical expertise in coding, computing, scripting, and data science, this chapter includes a wide array of materials. While the majority of items highlighted in this chapter are appropriate for all readers, descriptions will indicate whether items are particularly good for true beginners or if an item is really only appropriate for those with advanced technical skills.

This chapter is laid out in three parts. Part I provides some broad educational resources for readers looking for an overview or survey

VIRGINIA A. NEISLER, JD, MLS, is a faculty services and reference librarian at the University of Michigan Law School Library.

treatment of AI. Part II contains a selected list of some of the best current awareness tools along with tips for utilizing those tools to their best advantage. Finally, Part III consists of in-depth resources that delve deeply into various topics associated with artificial intelligence.

Check out the following list of resources to continue your AI education.

Part I: Basic Education

Items highlighted in this section all look at the big picture of AI. Each is designed to help readers learn more about the basics of AI, including machine learning (ML), algorithms, neural networks, and other computing processes that form the mechanics by which AI is created.

Quick Reads

DeBrule, Sam. "What is Artificial Intelligence?" *Machine Learnings (blog)*, April 5, 2017, https://machinelearnings.co/how-to-prepare-your-career-for-artificial-intelligence-driven-automation-1bb153759b3b.

This quick article is written in a casual, conversational tone and deals with the basics of AI from a very high-level beginner perspective.

Sheffer, Ryan. "How to Train Your Robot: A Beginner's Guide to Machine Learning." *Chatbot News Daily,* July 6, 2016, https://chatbotnewsdaily.com/how-to-train-your-robot-21361b297ba0.

This very brief, illustrated article lays out the basics of ML in less than five minutes.

Longer Resources

Frankish, Keith, and William M. Ramsey. *The Cambridge Handbook of Artificial Intelligence*. Cambridge: Cambridge University Press, 2014.

This handbook is distinctly academic in nature, with a focus on the theoretical and philosophical applications of cutting-edge AI research, rather than on technical or applied issues. Each chapter, authored by leaders in AI research, delivers a survey-level overview of a different thematic point relating to state-of-the-art research in their field. Although not suitable for a true beginner, it is an excellent resource for those with a basic understanding of AI and a taste for academic exploration.

Gerrish, Sean. *How Smart Machines Think*. Cambridge, MA: The MIT Press, 2018.

Have you ever wondered how your Netflix recommendation, new self-driving cars, neural networks, and chess-playing programs work? In this work, Sean Gerrish explores each of those systems and more. Although an expert in the field, Gerrish keeps the math to a minimum to appeal to a broad audience. He reviews ground-breaking research in successive chapters, collecting new and expanding knowledge about AI, all in one source.

Mueller, John Paul, and Luca Massaron. *Artificial Intelligence for Dummies*. Hoboken, NJ: Wiley, 2018.

Though readers might hesitate to pick up any book aimed at "dummies," this work is quite valuable for true beginners to the field. It transitions smoothly from understanding AI and how it is used today, to looking at future uses, before taking a deeper dive into how AI will impact us in the future. The book includes real-world examples to bring abstract AI applications to life and is an excellent starting place for beginners.

Russell, Stuart J. and Peter Norvig. *Artificial Intelligence: A Modern Approach*, 3rd edition. Boston: Pearson, 2016.

This leading AI textbook provides two introductory chapters—written largely in plain language—which give an overview of the AI with some figures and general principles. There are learning cues as well, such as vocabulary in the margins. Later chapters and the companion website—http://aima.cs.berkeley.edu/—are significantly more advanced, and those with coding skills or slightly more advanced tech skills can take advantage of sample code provided on the site to use during exercises presented at the end of each chapter.

Part II: Current Awareness

Let's be honest. By the time you have finished perusing this chapter, there will probably have been a new breakthrough in the field of AI. Unfortunately, keeping up-to-date presents some challenges. There are so many blogs, news articles, newsletter services, academic articles, and books published on the topic that it is difficult to know where to begin. To help readers stay plugged-in to this ever-changing field, this section contains a selection of current awareness tools that have been evaluated for their relevance, audience, currency, reputation, breadth, and manageability.

Blogs[1]

Becoming Human. https://becominghuman.ai/.

This blog features a wide variety of articles written by contributors in various fields within AI. Articles range from beginner to intermediate in terms of technological background required to understand them, with the majority requiring some background knowledge to be most impactful.

Berkeley Artificial Intelligence Research (BAIR). https://bair.berkeley.edu/blog/.

The blog provides beginner-friendly summaries of more-complex research papers produced by or affiliated with BAIR. Posts include visual aids, nontechnical language, and broad appeal to persons even outside of the field. It is limited in that it doesn't venture beyond the research of BAIR, but its "elevator pitch" articles summarizing research make those complex projects easy to understand.

DeepMind. https://deepmind.com/blog/.

DeepMind, owned by the Alphabet Group (Google), is developing AI that learns independently with the goal of creating programs that can solve complex problems without supervision. DeepMind applies their research to games as well as real-world problems like clean energy and health care. Blog posts on DeepMind's research feature easy-to-understand language as well as multimedia visualizations.

Human Centered AI (HAI). https://hai.stanford.edu/news/.

A part of Stanford University, this center focuses on research, education, and policy to ensure that AI moves forward in the best interests of humanity. Most of its news and research is centered on projects conducted under the auspices of the center, which can be limiting, but is still worth reading.

Machine Intelligence Research Institute. https://intelligence.org/blog/.

The Machine Intelligence Research Institute (MIRI) is nonprofit researcher of mathematics that comprise the framework for intelligent behavior, in order to develop tools to make AI safe and reliable. Their blog contains a combination of news, analysis, articles promoting original research, conversations with leading minds in AI, and a regular post of their monthly newsletter, which readers can also subscribe to separately.

Machine Learnings. https://machinelearnings.co/.

Machine Learnings offers a wide range of coverage of AI-related topics, laid out in plain language and presented informally. The site, which is highly accessible to beginners, contains a newsletter as well as a blog.

OpenAI. https://blog.openai.com/.

Open AI is a nonprofit research company that employs 60 researchers and engineers dedicated to safe general AI. Articles featured on the site focus on breakthroughs in research. Research papers are accompanied by articles that walk the reader through the papers step by step with examples and the occasional interactive graphic. It then addresses the policy implications of the papers in relatively nontechnical language.

This Week in Machine Learning & AI. https://twimlai.com/.

This Week in Machine Learning & AI (TWiMLAI) offers a range of options for keeping up-to-date on the latest in AI. The blog features a regular round-up of the latest news in research and development, as well as posts promoting new content. TWiMLAI's original content comes in the form of interviews with leaders in the field, which are available via podcast or streaming on the site, with referenced materials hyperlinked for further reading. It is also unique in that it features a diverse group of interviewees, regularly highlighting researchers from underrepresented groups. Interviewees occasionally get a bit technical, but generally, they keep the jargon to a minimum to appeal to a wide audience.

Social Media

TIP: To ensure the highest ratio of quality content, follow reputable organizations rather than hashtags or topics. Those organizations publish their own content and often circulate quality third-party content as well.

Top 5: Organizations Worth Following on Social Media

AI Now. @AINowInstitute

AI Now is a research institute affiliated with New York University (NYU) that examines the social implications of AI. It conducts research around four themes: rights and liberties, labor and automation, bias and inclusion, and safety and critical infrastructure.

DeepMind. @DeepMindAI

Very active and widely connected, this company frequently publishes its own research and that of its collaborators, as well as coverage of that research.

MIT Computer Science & Artificial Intelligence Laboratory. @MIT_CSAIL

Despite being MIT's largest research laboratory, CSAIL doesn't take itself too seriously. Its Twitter feed consists of state-of-the-art research and amusing coding fails alike. The tweets are an excellent source of current news and informal applications of AI, as well as humor.

OpenAI. @OpenAI

This nonprofit research institute regularly updates its Twitter feed to include groundbreaking research, as well as news and updates on their affiliates.

O'Reilly Media. @OReillyMedia

O'Reilly covers a much wider range of areas than AI, but its Twitter feed is chock-full of AI goodies.

Newsletters

Blog subscriptions, RSS feeds, and news alerts all deliver content, but a good newsletter service will be curated and, in many cases, annotated for maximum efficiency. This selection of newsletters covers a broad range of topics, and each has distinctive features to help you make the most of your time.

The Algorithm. MIT Technology Review. https://go.technologyreview.com/newsletters/the-algorithm/

Featuring a combination of an original content article along with links to other news items broken down by topic area, this newsletter is a must read for those wanting a streamlined service that does more than provide a bare list of links.

AI Topics. https://aitopics.org/class/AI-Alerts

Use AI to get your AI news! The Association for the Advancement of Artificial Intelligence (AAAI) provides a weekly digest selected by AI techies.

AIWeekly. http://aiweekly.co/

This newsletter is broad in scope, but primarily includes articles that are aimed at laypersons or the general public and are not too technical. An excellent source of ongoing news for those with limited technical knowledge.

Import AI. https://us13.campaign-archive.com/home/?u=67bd06787e84d73db24fb0aa5&id=6c9d98ff2c

Written by Jack Clark, one of the minds behind OpenAI, this weekly newsletter offers summaries of breakthrough research. Each entry includes a handy "why this matters" section to explain the significance of the research findings, particularly useful for beginners who are new to the field.

Inside AI. Technically Sentient. https://inside.com/ai.

The only daily newsletter featured here, *Inside AI* contains a mix of the news of the day and is sponsored by corporate entities like IBM Watson. It provides brief summaries of each featured item for those who would rather get the big picture and skip the click-through.

The Wild Week in AI. https://www.getrevue.co/profile/wildml.

This weekly AI and machine learning (ML) newsletter highlights news and blog posts that are great for beginners, along with research papers, tutorials for programmers, code, and ongoing projects that are more suitable for advanced readers. The mix of materials and its frequency make it a good choice for those who want a broad overview of AI happenings, but don't want to get overwhelmed by frequency or volume.

News Sites

You don't have to sift through your regular news feed to find AI-related articles. A visit to these sites instantly offers you a curated list of news relating to AI.

AITrends from the Cambridge Innovation Institute. https://www.aitrends.com/category/features/.

AITrends focuses on the business side of AI. Its articles explore how businesses can integrate AI into workflows and what trends are currently at play in AI implementation. The site covers application more than theoretical research.

Artificial Lawyer. https://www.artificiallawyer.com/.

This blog is focused on how AI is impacting the legal sector, and frequently covers news and opinions related to automation of legal work, such as automated document review, e-discovery, legal bots, and emerging smart contracts. It also provides a directory of companies that offer legal tech solutions.

Big Data Made Simple. https://bigdata-madesimple.com/tech-and-tools/artificial-intelligence/.

Branding itself as a tech portal, *Big Data Made Simple* provides topical articles that simplify complex AI and big-data concepts. It also features posts aimed at sectors such as crime/law and banking/finance. These articles are aimed at industry decision makers, and are a mix of original content and news from other sources.

Future of Life Artificial Intelligence News. https://futureoflife.org/ai-news/.

The Future of Life Institute focuses on the security and safety of AI. Its posts promote its podcast episodes, but also feature interviews with industry experts on existential issues facing humanity at the prospect of widespread AI implementation. The articles are accessible for beginners and heavily focused on policy.

O'Reilly AI. https://www.oreilly.com/topics/ai.

While the O'Reilly Media group covers subjects far beyond the world of AI, it is one of their featured topics. Its topic site for AI contains links to a broad array of articles, each written in clear, beginner-friendly language, and many contain visual aids to enhance understanding.

Science Daily: Artificial Intelligence. https://www.sciencedaily.com/news/computers_math/artificial_intelligence/.

This site offers a wide range of articles outlining recent breakthroughs in scientific research on AI, robotics, ML, and other related topics. It is aimed at laypersons, is not too technical, and offers an RSS feed option in addition to its social media presence.

Top 5: Podcasts on AI

Concerning AI. https://concerning.ai/

For a thought-provoking, philosophical approach to AI, this podcast can't be beat. Hosts Ted Sarvata and Brandon Sanders explore existential concerns about AI and what can be done about them.

Future of Life Podcasts. https://soundcloud.com/futureoflife.

The *Future of Life's* podcasts tackle issues like climate change, nuclear and automated weapons, ethics, morality, bioethics, and law, which face us as AI develops and expands its reach. There are two regular series: *AI Alignment*, hosted by Lucas Perry, and *FLI Podcast*, hosted by Ariel Conn.

O'Reilly Data Show Podcast. https://www.oreilly.com/topics/oreilly-data-show-podcast.

Ben Lorica, the host of this podcast, interviews a variety of experts on their work to explore the many possibilities opened up by big data, AI, and data science.

Talking Machines. https://www.thetalkingmachines.com/.

Hosted by Katherine Gorman and Neil Lawrence, *Talking Machines* features interviews with experts in ML. These episodes cover complex topics in clear, easy-to-understand language.

This Week in Machine Learning & AI podcast. https://twimlai.com/

In each episode, host Sam Charrington interviews an expert in the field discussing their work, their stories, and their research in AI and ML. The podcast regularly features researchers from underrepresented groups, and interviewees generally keep the jargon to a minimum for broad appeal.

Part III: Further Discussion

The development of AI has given rise to a seemingly infinite number of questions across disciplines. Although this chapter could not possibly highlight all of them, you will find here many of the topics that impact professionals in the legal and information fields. Most resources featured below are written for a broad audience and are therefore appropriate for any reader from beginner to advanced. Any resources requiring additional technical knowledge are noted.

U.S. Government Policy and Recommendations

National Science and Technology Council Committee on Technology, Executive Office of the President. *Preparing for the Future of Artificial Intelligence.* (2016) https://permanent.access.gpo.gov/gpo75059/preparing_for_the_future_of_ai.pdf.

This October 2016 report made 23 recommendations for federal agencies relating to AI. Among these were recommendations for use of open data, recommendations that agencies examine how they could utilize AI for the benefit of society, and recommendations that agencies and industry work together to develop appropriate strategies for safety and security.

Executive Order No. 13859, 84 F.R. 3967 (Feb. 11, 2019) "Executive Order on Maintaining American Leadership in Artificial Intelligence." https://www.govinfo.gov/content/pkg/FR-2019-02-14/pdf/2019-02544.pdf.

Outlines new policy of the USA with the stated intent of "maintaining American leadership in artificial intelligence."

Agency, Accountability, Liability, and the Law

Who or what is legally responsible when AI makes a mistake? What rights (if any) can robots claim? What liability will attach when machines make decisions? How can we leverage AI in the legal industry? These are just some of the questions addressed in the following works.

Ashley, Kevin D. *Artificial Intelligence and Legal Analytics: New Tools for Law Practice in the Digital Age.* Cambridge: Cambridge University Press, 2017.

Technical in nature, *Artificial Intelligence and Legal Analytics* explores Computation Models for Legal Reasoning (CMLRs) and the various ways technology is being used to connect these models with actual legal texts. The book describes various models—including models of statutory reasoning and case-based reasoning, and also takes a deep look at models for legal text analytics. It is not recommended for beginners.

Chopra, Samir, and Laurence F. White. *A Legal Theory for Autonomous Artificial Agents.* Ann Arbor: University of Michigan Press, 2011.

The authors of this book operate on the premise that AI will give rise to a new kind of legal actor/agent. They examine our current schemes of tort liability, notions of personhood, theories of agency, contracts, and attribution of knowledge to grapple with how these new entities will be dealt with in our legal system.

Corrales, Marcelo, Mark Fenwick, Nikolaus Forgo, editors. *Robotics, AI, and the Future of Law.* Singapore: Springer, 2018.

This work places new technological advancements within current legal contexts to analyze the theory underlying our legal principles and determine whether they must be altered with the rise of the robot. Each chapter focuses on a different legal topic, including legal personhood, liability, regulatory responses to AI, automated decision-making/profiling, and privacy.

Gunkel, David J. *Robot Rights*. Cambridge, MA: The MIT Press, 2018.

Can robots have rights? If they can, *should* they? David Gunkel explores these questions through philosophical modalities, and outlines the costs and benefits of their potential answers. The author accepts the premise that the "robot invasion" promised by science fiction has already taken place, and flips the familiar script of examining moral and ethical questions raised by robots as agents, instead focusing on how we (people) should respond to those agents.

Turner, Jacob. *Robot Rules: Regulating Artificial Intelligence.* London: Palgrave MacMillan, 2019.

In this work, Jacob Turner sets out to comprehensively consider how AI will shape our future and how we should regulate it from the outset to better prepare ourselves for that future. Material is arranged around three main themes: responsibility, rights, and ethics. By examining these issues in advance, Turner hopes to elude known pitfalls, backlash against the technology, and other avoidable problems.

Walters, Ed, editor. *Data-Driven Law: Data Analytics and the New Legal Services.* Boca Raton, FL: CRC Press, 2019.

This edited work contains some pearls of wisdom for law firms large and small seeking to leverage AI and data analytics to improve legal services. Contributors focus on data mining, quantifying success and quality, and the use to which firms can put their data by examining specific contexts in which data science is being used today.

Bias in AI Decision-Making

Are the AI-driven systems we use truly fair?

Angwin, Julia, Jeff Larson, Lauren Kirchner and Surya Mattu. "Machine Bias: There's software used across the country to predict future criminals. And it's biased against blacks." *ProPublica*, May 23, 2016, https://www.propublica.org/article/machine-bias-risk-assessments-in-criminal-sentencing.

In their exposé of risk prediction software used at sentencing, the authors compare similarly positioned criminal defendants to demonstrate how race appears to have an extraordinarily high impact on assessment of risk. *ProPublica* also regularly publishes the results of its ongoing investigations into bias found in algorithms used daily by people and institutions across America, including social media and software used in criminal justice. https://www.propublica.org/series/machine-bias.

Eubanks, Virginia. *Automating Inequality: How High-Tech Tools Profile, Police, and Punish the Poor*. St. Martin's Press: New York, 2017.

Automating Inequality is a compelling read, as it uses individual stories to highlight the problems in automated decision-making systems, such as those used to flag fraud in public assistance programs or those used to predict risk in the criminal justice system. Eubanks draws a link between the poorhouses of the nineteenth century and the set of complex systems that she refers to as the "digital poorhouse" today.

Kroll, Joshua A., Joanna Huey, Solon Barocas, Edward W. Felten, Joel R. Reidenberg, David G. Robinson, and Harlan Yu. "Accountable Algorithms," *University of Pennsylvania Law Review* 165 (2017): 633-705. https://heinonline.org/HOL/P?h=hein.journals/pnlr165&i=648.

The authors here argue that the legal standards governing human decision-making have not evolved to accommodate increasingly technology-driven, decision-making processes. The article provides an in-depth look into the ways that machines now drive decision-making and proposes a broad-reaching agenda to address the problems.

O'Neil, Cathy, *Weapons of Math Destruction: How Big Data Increases Inequality and Threatens Democracy*. New York: Broadway Books, 2016.

Cathy O'Neil's bestseller focuses on the downsides of big data-driven systems that seek to maximize efficiency—what the author terms "weapons of *math* destructions." O'Neil explores what optimization means for real people, and how that process, driven by politics and profit, impacts our lives at various points in our lives. She highlights the impacts to access to higher education, loan approval, prison sentences, and even employment. The book might read like a novel, but it gives the reader serious food for thought.

Artificial Intelligence and Security

How will AI shape the future of warfare, security, and international diplomacy?

Cummings, M. L., Heather M. Roff, Kenneth Cukier, Jacob Parakilas and Hannah Bryce. International Security Department & US and the Americas Programme. *Artificial Intelligence and International Affairs: Disruption Anticipated.* Chatham House: The Royal Institute of International Affairs, June 14, 2018. https://reader.chathamhouse.org/artificial-intelligence-and-international-affairs#.

Containing four substantive chapters, this policy report provides conclusions and recommendations relating to the challenges that could arise from the proliferations of AI. The report addresses the ways that AI impacts international politics, the future of warfare and the economy, and how AI can be used to advance human security.

Hodley, Daniel S. "Artificial Intelligence and National Security" Congressional Research Service, report no. R45178. Last updated by Kelley M. Sayler, January 30, 2019. https://crsreports.congress.gov/product/details?prodcode=R45178.

Prepared for Congress, this report represents the latest information on uses of AI in security and defense. It outlines the issues Congress is debating and explores current known research on applications of AI in defense, its impact on combat, challenges to integration, and current intelligence on international competitors.

Scharre, Paul. *Army of None: Autonomous Weapons and the Future of War.* New York: W. W. Norton & Company, 2018.

For those interested in military applications of AI, Paul Scharre, a Pentagon defense expert and former U.S. Army Ranger, discusses the field of military robotics and automation thoroughly. Scharre starts by defining autonomous weapons, then discusses how these new weapons are built and approved, and ultimately explores the morality and safety of these systems.

Technology's Psychological and Sociological Impacts

How is AI rewiring us?

Alter, Adam. *Irresistible: The Rise of Addictive Technology and the Business of Keeping Us Hooked.* New York: Penguin Press, 2017.

Professor Adam Alter probes the history of addictive behaviors, their rise in recent decades, and the way technology is designed to exploit these behaviors. He offers insight into the psychological processes that make today's AI-driven tech so difficult to put down, and discusses how we can minimize addictive behaviors and harness the same psychological processes for the benefit of humanity.

Carr, Nicholas. *The Shallows: What the Internet Is Doing to Our Brains*. New York: W. W. Norton & Company, 2011.

Although Nicholas Carr focuses on the web as a whole, AI is so integrated with web searching that this book seems like a natural fit for this resource list. The author places the web in a long line of new information mediums to examine how it is impacting our lives and our brains, and what the cost of new conveniences might be.

Jackson, Maggie. *Distracted: Reclaiming Our Focus in a World of Lost Attention*, 2nd edition. Amherst, NY: Prometheus Books, 2018.

Journalist Maggie Jackson explores the ways that technology around us is impacting our ability to engage in deep focus, critical analysis, and creative thinking. This work, fully grounded in the historical narrative of technological advancement, delves into the darker side of modern technology. The author argues that we are losing the capacity to engage in deep, sustained attention necessary for cultural progress, the cultivation of intimate relationships, and the gaining of wisdom. Likening the lack of depth of today's culture to the decline of Rome, Jackson posits that we might be heading for a cultural dark age of an entirely new kind.

Panova, T. "Thoughts on AI from a Psychological Perspective: Defining Intelligence," *Becoming Human* (blog), November 2, 2017. https://becominghuman.ai/first-of-all-although-it-may-be-obvious-to-some-its-important-to-note-that-artificial-b2258be52e7a.

What is intelligence? A quick read, this article discusses that foundational question as we work to define and design AI.

Sparrow, Betsy, Jenny Liu, Daniel M. Wegner. "Google Effects on Memory: Cognitive Consequences of Having Information at Our Fingertips," *Science* 333 (August 5, 2011): 776–78.

This quick, three-page article summarizes research that shows how poorly our memories perform now that we have the world of information at our fingertips.

Turkle, Sherry. *Alone Together: Why We Expect More from Technology and Less from Each Other*. New York: Basic Books, 2017.

MIT professor Sherry Turkle provides a fascinating look at technology's impact on modern relationships. She argues that the increased use of technology is actively damaging our emotional lives and our ability to form intimate connections with the people around us. Through the lens of hundreds of interviews, she explores the significance of human connection, while examining the ways that we use technology to avoid the potential pain and discomfort of intimate relationships.

AI-Driven Automation and the Future of Work

How will AI and automation affect the future of employment?

Ford, Martin. *Rise of the Robots: Technology and the Threat of a Jobless Future*. New York: Basic Books, 2015.

Martin Ford paints a bleak picture of the future, industry by industry. He postulates that technology will lead—and in many cases is already leading—to increased automation and fewer jobs. He proposes a new economic paradigm, dismissing the idea that increasing or changing education and training will alleviate the problems to come.

Manyika, James, Michael Chui, Mehdi Miremadi, Jacques Bughin, Katy George, Paul Willmott, and Martin Dewhurst. *A Future That Works: Automation, Employment and Productivity*. McKinsey Global Institute, January 2017. https://www.mckinsey.com/~/media/McKinsey/Featured%20Insights/Digital%20Disruption/Harnessing%20automation%20for%20a%20future%20that%20works/MGI-A-future-that-works_Full-report.ashx.

The result of global research on automation and its potential impact on labor markets and work, this paper estimates the percentage of work that has the potential to be automated in the near future across industries and global markets, and demonstrates the possible implications of these changes on global labor markets.

Futurists

How will AI impact our cultures, society, and lives?

Callaghan, Victor, James Miller, Roman Yampolskiy, Stuart Armstrong, editors. *The Technological Singularity: Managing the Journey*. Germany: Springer-Verlag GmbH, 2017.

This edited volume is the second in a series exploring the possibility of a coming "technological singularity"—the point beyond which we cannot predict the future as AI exceeds human intelligence. Each contributing author addresses how to manage such an occurrence to achieve optimal outcomes for humanity.

Husain, Amir. *The Sentient Machine: The Coming Age of Artificial Intelligence*. New York: Scribner, 2017.

Humanity is on the verge of an era of unprecedented creativity, one in which we are capable of creating new life in the form of AI. Amir Husain's work explores many of the themes common to futurists using nontechnical language. His blend of computer science, theoretical physics, and philosophy make this optimistic work a worthwhile read.

Reese, Byron. *The Fourth Age: Smart Robots, Conscious Computers and the Future of Humanity*. New York: Atria Books, 2018.

To understand the future, Byron Reese looks backward to the whole of human history to explore what it is to be human, what artificial intelligence is, and how we can understand these new technologies in light of that knowledge. Rather than express his own views, Reese shows readers how to think about AI so that they can understand many popularly expressed opinions and form their own.

Tegmark, Max. *Life 3.0: Being Human in the Age of Artificial Intelligence*. New York: Vintage Books, 2017.

This book explores many of the ideas addressed by other books, such as the definition of intelligence and how AI will affect humans. However, this book also goes a step further. It zooms out from the 10,000-foot view to the 10,000-lightyear view, by examining future scenarios and discussing the impact of these new developments beyond our planet. An excellent read for anyone who likes thinking big.

NOTE

1. While all major technology companies (such as Google, Microsoft, Apple, and IBM) host their own blogs, these have been excluded from the list in favor of blogs with narrower focus.

Index

G

H

R

T

www.ingramcontent.com/pod-product-compliance
Lightning Source LLC
Chambersburg PA
CBHW070826150926
51501CB00043B/992
9780838946275